# PERSON-IN-ENVIRONMENT SYSTEM

# PERSON-IN-ENVIRONMENT SYSTEM

*The PIE Classification System for Social Functioning Problems*

**Editors**

James M. Karls
Karin E. Wandrei

NASW PRESS

**National Association of Social Workers**
Washington, DC

Ann A. Abbott, PhD, ACSW, *President*
Sheldon R. Goldstein, ACSW, LISW, *Executive Director*

First impression, September 1994
Second impression, January 1996
Third impression, October 1997
Fourth impression, September 1998
Fifth impression, December 1999
Sixth impression, May 2001


Linda Beebe, *Executive Editor*
Nancy Winchester, *Editorial Services Director*
Stephen Pazdan, *Production Editor*
Annette Hansen, *Copy Editor*
Maria Barry, Elizabeth Mitchell, Marina Rota, *Proofreaders*
Bernice Eisen, *Indexer*

**Library of Congress Cataloging-in-Publication Data**

Person-in-environment system : the PIE classification sys-
tem for social functioning problems / editors, James M.
Karls, Karin E. Wandrei.
    p.  cm.
    Includes bibliographical references and index.
    ISBN 0-87101-240-5 (pbk. : alk. paper) : $32.95.—
ISBN 0-87101-254-5 (manual)
    1. Person-in-environment system.   I. Karls, James
M., 1927–  II. Wandrei, Karin Evon.  III. National
Association of Social Workers.
HV43.5.P47  1994
361.1'014—dc20                    94–23170
                                     CIP

Printed in the United States of America

# Contents

# Foreword

On behalf of all social work professionals, I express my gratitude to Dr. James Karls and Dr. Karin Wandrei for their commitment to a revolutionary project that embodies important ramifications not only for social work but for the entire field of human services. The authors have used their organizational and clinical talents to produce the person-in-environment (PIE) classification system that is presented in this book. The challenge of initiating is rarely easy. However, through their continuing responsiveness to the many people who contributed to PIE, their diligence, and their advocacy, Drs. Karls and Wandrei have advanced the social work profession with this timely publication of their work.

At this moment in social work history, as we move toward heightened professional autonomy, long-deserved recognition, and strategic positioning within the field of human services, PIE emerges in support of our momentum. PIE's objectives and implications are far-reaching and instrumental in empowering social work as a profession. In addition to serving as an invaluable resource for social work practice, administration, research, and education, PIE extends to the related areas of employment in social work and human services, fees and third-party reimbursement, and social policy.

My friend and colleague, Jim Karls, introduced the concept of PIE to me while I served as president of the California chapter of the National Association of Social Workers (NASW) in the early 1980s. I recognized at the outset that PIE was a visionary idea that warranted serious attention. PIE's fundamental nature and broad implications led me to wonder how social work had functioned for so long without it. I welcomed the development of PIE and was pleased to see it receive an NASW Advancement Fund grant as a meritorious project. My confidence in PIE has spanned the years that followed, including those of my presidency at the national level of NASW (1987 to 1989). It is a personal and professional pleasure to be part of this important work.

As social workers we are cognizant of the values, ethics, tradition, knowledge, and diverse perspectives that our profession embodies. We convey the understanding of these principles through our practice, education, research, administration, and policy-making. PIE assists us in our efforts to communicate social work principles and provides a concrete resource to which our principles relate. PIE also provides us with an alternative to the classification systems of other professions. Instead of adjusting to the standards of other disciplines, social work can now relate its own standard of measurement and codification—one that is ours, unique to social work. This leverage undoubtedly strengthens our professional status in the community of human services providers.

Despite our commitment to common values and principles, the profession of social work has suffered from the lack of a unifying framework that might bring together the diverse areas of expertise within our profession. PIE helps to strengthen and unify social workers in our diversity. As a grounding piece PIE shapes the way social work views and understands the world. This system furnishes a new frame of reference for experts in all areas of social work and links the fields of practice, research, education, and administration into a unified whole. PIE also helps other disciplines, the political decision makers and policymakers, and the public better understand what we do.

In short, PIE helps those within and outside the profession acquire a clearer understanding of the field of social work. This system solidifies our professional identity by projecting a strengthened and unified image to other disciplines.

For practitioners PIE identifies social work's expertise in understanding and assisting the person who is having difficulties with social roles within the context of interacting with other individuals and the environment. PIE underlines the importance of conceptualizing a person in an interactive context rather than in a person-in-a-vacuum scenario. Pathological and physiological limitations are accounted for but are not accorded extraordinary attention by the PIE system. Instead, PIE addresses the roadblocks that complicate living in the here and now by helping clients master these hurdles on their way to self-actualization and capacity building. PIE operates on the notion that problematic conditions can be changed based on the individual's unique strengths, limitations, and environmental situation, rather than on external standards of normalcy. PIE facilitates the process of enhancing coping abilities, alleviating distress, connecting people with other people and community resources, and maximizing each individual's potential for optimal living. This system provides practitioners with a pragmatic tool for assessment and intervention in a systematic manner, thus reducing confusion and misperceptions. PIE can undoubtedly contribute to efficiency and consistency in third-party billing and reimbursement.

Administrators will embrace PIE as a tool that lends justification for social work programs in regard to cost-effectiveness, accountability, credibility, and quality. This resource can help practitioners identify which problems can be addressed effectively by social work and which should be addressed by other professionals. Such identification will facilitate assessment and intervention by clinical staff and enable administrators and program planners to concentrate on enhancing their existing social work programs as well as designing and implementing new ones. In short, PIE goes beyond the direct practice of social work.

Similarly, researchers will find PIE helpful. Research is commonly identified as a weak area in social work, partly because of the inherent difficulties in measuring human cognition, affect, and behavior. Much information is revealed through case studies, but documentation of the social work process in these studies is often lacking. PIE gives us a baseline for testing social work methods and facilitates research that might support social work practice. Further research and experimentation will enhance our theoretical knowledge, facilitate greater efficiency in social work programs and modalities, and contribute to the creation of alternative strategies to enhance service delivery, the last of which can affect public understanding and funding.

PIE can provide educators and students with an invaluable tool for studying social work. PIE can also support social work curricula by reinforcing the importance of understanding a person in his or her environment. Using PIE to educate students will help convey a clearer understanding of the identity of social work and its unique area of expertise in the human services field.

By using PIE, policymakers may have a clearer understanding of the social problems they wish to address. Needs assessments to discover collective social trends, individual and community problems, and the effect of social policy will help policymakers be more responsive to communities. Ease in collecting and organizing this information will likely assist policymakers in improving communities. I envision PIE as instrumental in inspiring new generations of decision makers to improve our communities.

Finally, as president of the International Federation of Social Workers, I can speak to the unprecedented impact PIE can have on unifying social work on an international level. The use of PIE in Japan, Italy, the Netherlands, Belgium, Australia, and Canada attests to the potential universality of the system. PIE can provide a universal language for classifying problems of social functioning. This universality may open doors to cross-cultural and multinational applications of social work and to an enlarged international exchange network that will inevitably further our knowledge of heterogeneous populations and their needs. PIE's global applicability also highlights our similarities as human beings, regardless of culture, ethnicity, religion, nationality, or gender.

PIE is an essential resource for every social work clinician, researcher, student, educator, administrator, policymaker, and community organizer. PIE provides a unique and efficient system for classifying life problems for all social work fields of practice, including mental health, children and families, and health care as well as occupational, international, administrative, planning, and legislative fields. The system's far-reaching influence includes uniting social workers as integral members of a very special and noble profession.

Most important, PIE will help us provide competent, effective, and efficient services to our clients.

Again, I congratulate Drs. Karls and Wandrei for their achievement. Their work reminds us of the importance of being open to new ways of meeting the needs of the people we serve. This innovative work inspires all of us to challenge the status quo for the betterment of our clients, our profession, and our society.

SUZANNE DWORAK-PECK

# Foreword

In 1981 the California chapter of the National Association of Social Workers (NASW) applied for and was awarded funding from the NASW Program Advancement Fund to develop a classification system for the social functioning problems experienced by clients of social workers. This was one more step by the social work profession in its ongoing effort to classify and codify the problems presented by social workers' clients to more accurately determine appropriate intervention strategies and to more adequately develop agency and community programs.

The need to diagnose psychosocial problems and develop a classification system was first articulated in Richmond's *Social Diagnosis* in 1917:

> Social diagnosis, then, may be described as the attempt to make as exact a definition as possible of the situation and personality of a human being in some social need—of his situation and personality, that is, in relation to the other human beings upon whom he in any way depends or who depend upon him, and in relation also to the social institutions in his community. (p. 357)

Without some way of classifying problems (emotional, mental, or social), social workers must rely on descriptive statements that may or may not convey essential components and that may vary in format, focus, and language from worker to worker and from agency to agency.

This need for common descriptors is not unique to social work. Psychiatry has struggled for more than a century to find a way to classify mental illness. Its *Diagnostic and Statistical Manual of Mental Disorders, Fourth Edition* (DSM-IV) (American Psychiatric Association, 1994) is the fourth attempt to classify mental and emotional disorders since the original *Diagnostic and Statistical Manual of Mental Disorders (DSM)* was published in 1952.

Because mental health providers and third-party payers have accepted DSM so widely, many social workers also use it and it is now their most frequently consulted reference book (Kirk, Siporin, & Kutchins, 1989). DSM-IV does not, however, address Richmond's and social work's need to integrate and understand the interrelationship of the person and his or her situation or environment.

The potential danger of any classification system is in labeling people, and thus incurring the possibility of bias, discrimination, or dehumanization. This is one of the possible pitfalls in developing any nosology, but this should not inhibit the profession from moving ahead; it should only raise flags of caution in how we do so.

Thus, in 1981 when the California chapter of NASW indicated it was interested in developing a classification scheme for social problems as a complement to the existing manual that describes mental illnesses, the association supported this effort through the Program Advancement Fund, a fund for chapter projects. Additional funds were provided in 1983 and 1984 to do field testing of the newly developed system.

The first draft of the *PIE Manual* for coding the problems of social functioning was received positively by selected reviewers and by attendees at professional meetings where it was presented. The next step was to apply for funding from the National Institute of Mental Health to undertake a national reliability study. Repeated attempts for such national funding were met with positive evaluations of the proposal, but unfortunately only one small grant was awarded to develop data to sharpen the grant proposal. The project still has not received any major funding.

Although unsuccessful in securing federal government support, Dr. James Karls and Dr. Karin Wandrei, who have worked on the project from its inception, have tirelessly promoted and refined the system, and practitioners and teachers find it useful. Drs. Karls and Wandrei give unstintingly of their time and effort on a voluntary basis and as a result PIE is becoming well-known within the profession. In some schools of social work, PIE is used as an educational tool. Some agencies also use PIE. PIE has become so much a part of social work that the 19th edition of the *Encyclopedia of Social Work* will include an entry on PIE (Karls & Wandrei, in press).

No classification system is "finished," and just as psychiatry's DSM has gone through a number of iterations and refinements, so too will PIE. Because the process of developing a classification scheme is evolutionary, we must seek ways to strengthen this process. The profession owes a debt of gratitude to Jim Karls and Karin Wandrei for keeping PIE alive, helping it grow and develop, implementing changes, and constantly seeking ways to make it more effective.

As Richmond (1917) wrote nearly 80 years ago, careful assessments at the beginning of treatment "are steps in what we hope will be a helpful course of action. They lead up through social diagnosis to a plan to treatment. The relation of diagnosis to this practical end cannot be too much insisted upon" (p. 51).

This book brings us a few steps closer to the practical end of being more effective in our attempts to help our clients.

LEILA WHITING

## References

American Psychiatric Association. (1952). *Diagnostic and statistical manual of mental disorders*. Washington, DC: American Psychiatric Press.

American Psychiatric Association. (1994). *Diagnostic and statistical manual of mental disorders* (4th ed.). Washington, DC: American Psychiatric Press.

Karls, J., & Wandrei, K. (in press). Person-in-environment. In R. Edwards (Ed.-in-Chief), *Encyclopedia of social work* (19th ed.). Washington, DC: NASW Press.

Kirk, S. A., Siporin, M., & Kutchins, H. (1989). The prognosis for social work diagnosis. *Social Casework, 70,* 295–304.

Richmond, M. (1917). *Social diagnosis.* New York: Russell Sage Foundation.

# Preface

The person-in-environment (PIE) system is a work in progress. The careful reader of this book will learn that the PIE system is not yet a finished or thoroughly tested instrument for classifying the problems of social functioning. And it may never be! For it is in the nature of any classification system to be in evolution and in an ongoing state of refinement as it is applied in practice. There are those of our colleagues who would have had us wait to publish the PIE system until it had been thoroughly tested and demonstrated to be totally accurate and reliable (Karls & Wandrei, 1993a, 1993b; Kutchins & Kirk, 1993a, 1993b; Wandrei, 1992–1993). To them we say that if one had to wait to meet those standards, there would never be any classification system—for medicine, psychiatry, social work, or any field of practice. Other colleagues have advised us to proceed with publication so that the social work community will have a chance to learn about this system and take this important step in the development of the profession. It is with some trepidation that we put out a work we know is incomplete, and yet we have chosen to take this stance and let the social work community know about, study, and try the PIE system. We hope that this will be the first of many steps needed to produce a universal classification system for our profession.

We have two other reasons for producing this book. First, we are unabashedly ambitious for our profession. We want consumers and other professions alike to recognize social work as *the* profession that can best help with the social functioning problems that befall us all. We are convinced that, for this to happen, social work must acquire and use its own language to communicate the work it does and the role it plays in eliminating or alleviating problems in the human condition. We are clearly advocating that PIE be that language. Thus, we have devoted a considerable amount of time and energy to producing a book that can help social workers learn this new language and learn how to use it in work with their clients.

Our second motive is a little less selfish. As social workers we want our clients to receive the help they need as quickly and efficiently as possible. Since the PIE project began, both case management and managed health care have come into increasing prominence. We are convinced that for social work to meet the demands that these approaches to service delivery will require, there must be a uniform yet comprehensive assessment of the client's problems. Along with this assessment there must be clearer intervention planning and implementation than generally occurs in human services programs. We are certain that PIE can be the tool that leads to better, quicker, more cost-effective assessment and intervention planning.

We are also convinced, or perhaps just hopeful, that the social work profession has reached a degree of maturity at which its educators, practitioners, administrators, and researchers, can see the importance of establishing a common language for communicating with each other and move into an era of closer collaboration. We hope PIE will help social work address the societal and individual social functioning problems it was created to solve.

## References

Karls, J., & Wandrei, K. (1993a, April). PIE Project. *NASW California News*, p. 4.

Karls, J., & Wandrei, K. (1993b, September). Another slice of PIE. *NASW California News*, p. 11.

Kutchins, H., & Kirk, S. (1993a, February). Response: *Selling of the DSM*. *NASW California News*, p. 8.

Kutchins, H., & Kirk, S. (1993b, May). Response to a response. *NASW California News*, p. 3.

Wandrei, K. (1992–1993, December–January). Review of *The Selling of DSM*. *NASW California News*, p. 5.

# Acknowledgments

It should be clear to the reader that the person-in-environment (PIE) system was not created or produced by only the two of us but is the work of many. Major credit for producing PIE goes to the task force members who labored for two years debating what kind of information the practitioner needed to understand the client's problems and how to communicate this information so it would be usable by the practitioner and the client.

Task force members and their affiliations at the time the task force was meeting were Paul Chikahisa, MSW, ACSW, Asian American Community Mental Health Services, Los Angeles; Tessie Cleveland, DSW, ACSW, Martin Luther King Medical Center, Los Angeles; Jerome Cohen, PhD, ACSW, University of California, Los Angeles, School of Social Welfare; Manuel Fimbres, MSW, ACSW, San Jose State University, Division of Social Work; Rosalie Kane, DSW, ACSW, Rand Corporation, Santa Monica, California; Bok-Lok Kim, San Diego State University, Division of Social Work; Shelomo Osman, MSW, ACSW, Center for Behavioral Sciences, Lake Forest, California, and University of Southern California Medical School, Los Angeles, Department of Psychiatry; Steven Segal, DSW, ACSW, University of California, Berkeley, School Of Social Welfare; Lola Selby, MA, ACSW, University of Southern California, Los Angeles, School of Social Work; Harry Wasserman, DSW, ACSW, University of California at Los Angeles, School of Social Welfare; Jo Gumbiner, MSW, ACSW, Family Service Agency of Los Angeles; and Jean Selden, MSW, ACSW, private practice, Los Angeles.

Two of the original task force members have since died: Marquis Wallace, PhD, ACSW, University of Southern California, Los Angeles, School of Social Work, the task force's expert on family systems; and Jack Stumpf, PhD, ACSW, San Diego State University, Division of Social Work, who gave us much of what became Factor II in the PIE system.

Staff and consultants to the task force included Glenn Allison, MA, ACSW, Episcopal Social Services, San Diego; Elizabeth Allison, San Diego; and Karin Wandrei, DSW, LCSW, private practice, Oakland, California.

The task force was chaired by Jim Karls, then assistant director at the Mental Health Training Center, Los Angeles, and at UCLA

School of Social Welfare. The project could not have gotten the moral and financial support it received from NASW without the work of Suzanne Dworak-Peck, who as NASW president carried the project to the national board of directors and obtained NASW funding for development and testing. The support of other NASW presidents—Bob Stewart, Dorothy Harris, Dick Edwards, and Barbara White—helped us continue the effort. On the national NASW staff Leila Whiting has shepherded the project over the years, seeing that it and we did not get lost during changes of administration and shifts in NASW priorities.

During the testing phases of PIE, many social workers around the country made significant contributions to the refinement of the system. Janet Williams of the New York State Psychiatric Institute and Columbia University spent innumerable hours developing grant proposals that sharpened and focused the PIE system. Through Williams's work with psychiatry's DSM-III-R and DSM-IV task forces, she was able to nudge the profession of psychiatry into incorporating some of PIE's ideas on environmental influences and social functioning into DSM-IV. Her colleague Cheryl Cohen helped develop the Mini-PIE, which has turned out to be highly useful in practice, research, and teaching. In Massachusetts, Elizabeth Irvin of the Massachusetts Mental Health Department and her colleague Walter Penk helped to cultivate interest in PIE and subsequently used it in a number of research and demonstration projects. Irvin also produced the current version of Mini-PIE presented in the *PIE Manual*.

There is a long list of PIE supporters who have made contributions to the development of the system along the way. Among them are the first review panel: Carel Germain, Barbara Silverstone, Janet Williams, Stan Taubman, Federico Souflee, Scott Briar, William Reid, Max Siporin, Abraham Lurie, Patricia Ewalt, David Fanshel, Eda Goldstein, Alfred Kadushin, David Miller, Corrine Wolf, and Ruth Knee. As the project developed, many from the PIE advisory committee gave valued input and support. Among these are Allyson Ashley, David Austin, Gerald Beallor, Patricia Ewalt, Ann Hartman, John Lemmon, David Neal, Helen Northen, Howard Parad, Carl Leukefeld, Robert Stewart, Susan Sung, and Stan Weinstein.

The publication of three articles (Karls & Wandrei, 1992a, 1992b; Williams, Karls, & Wandrei, 1989) on our work brought dozens of inquiries and reports of attempts to implement the system in other countries. Katie Hoekstra's experience in the Netherlands, Dick Ramsay's independent conceptualization of PIE in Canada, and Jim Mandiberg and Kyoko Miyaoka's efforts in Japan are reported in this book. We acknowledge the interest of colleagues in several other countries: Catherine James in Australia; M. Demarsin in Belgium, who translated PIE into Flemish and tested it in his agency; Antonino Mastroeni in Italy, who used parts of PIE in a psychiatric clinic in Milan; Mikko Salo in Finland; and Humberto Ortega and Raisa Dominguez in Cuba.

I, Jim Karls, wish to acknowledge the dedication and hard work of my colleague in this venture, Karin Wandrei. What I had thought might be a brief project-oriented period in our careers has turned into a 10-year working relationship in which we have had many ups and downs. Up, when we received compliments from eminent colleagues and thanks from social work practitioners and teachers to whom we introduced PIE; down, when our grant applications were approved but not funded or when we were discounted by some of our academic colleagues. Through this we have been able to work together quite amiably and productively.

I, Karin Wandrei, wish to thank my colleague Jim Karls for his original conception of the PIE system. I never would have guessed that what started out as a relatively small, time-limited, part-time position to staff the PIE task force in 1984 would develop into a major part of my career. I am thankful to Jim for allowing me to become codirector of the project and for helping to keep my spirit going during those many times when it seemed like PIE was going nowhere. Through the PIE project I have met thousands of social workers; and through their excitement about PIE, I have learned to value anew what is unique about this profession.

## References

Karls, J., & Wandrei, K. (1992a). The person-in-environment system for classifying client problems: A new tool for more effective case management. *Journal of Case Management, 1*, 90–95.

Karls, J., & Wandrei, K. (1992b). PIE: A new language for social work. *Social Work, 37*, 80–85.

Williams, J. B. W., Karls, J., & Wandrei, K. (1989). The person-in-environment (PIE) system for describing problems of social functioning. *Hospital and Community Psychiatry 40*, 125–127.

# Introduction

This book has been produced by practitioners and teachers for practitioners, teachers, and students in social work and other human services professions. Practitioners will find it a useful tool for clarifying the problems presented by their clients; teachers will find it an instrument to instruct students in how the long-held construct of person-in-environment can be put into practice. The types of students likely to use this book are advanced undergraduates and graduate students beginning their study of interpersonal helping processes. The practitioners and teachers likely to use it are those who are open to new ideas and who may be looking ahead toward ways of enhancing the social work profession.

We have organized the book into four sections. Section I has two chapters: one presents the history of the person-in-environment (PIE) perspective and the concepts and constructs used in creating it; the second chapter is the "how-to" section, which together with the *PIE Manual* should allow the studious reader to use the system with actual cases.

Section II illustrates the use of PIE in various practice settings. Of the seven most common fields in which social workers currently practice (family and children's services, physical health, mental health, occupational social work, aging, education, and corrections), we have had the good fortune to find practitioners in most of them using PIE. Several practitioners who had been using PIE in various practice settings were willing to write about their experience. Joanne Turnbull and Helen Cahalane explore PIE's use in outpatient mental health settings. Joe Kestnbaum and Maureen Wahl describe PIE's use in family services agencies. Elizabeth Adkins, who worked with Jim Piazzola and Olga Sarabia in testing PIE at Los Angeles County–University of Southern California Medical Center, tells us how PIE can be used in a physical health care setting by medical social workers. Paul Saxton addresses the use of PIE in employee assistance and managed care programs. Mehl Simmons applies PIE in a public welfare setting. Elizabeth Irvin and Walter Penk use PIE with mentally ill persons in recovery from addictions. The authors of the chapters in this section were asked to include brief histories of practice in their settings along with their experience in using PIE. For this reason, there is a certain amount of repetition and redundancy for the reader who studies all the practice settings. We believe most readers will focus on the chapter that pertains to their practice and so may not experience the redundancy.

We added Section III after receiving a number of reports from social workers in countries outside the United States on how they were using PIE. James Mandiberg and Kyoko Miyaoka discuss how PIE is used to teach social work skills in Japan. Karen Walsh and Richard Ramsay present a Canadian field test of PIE in a multidisciplinary mental health setting. And Kathleen O'C. Hoekstra describes her experiences introducing the ecological perspective in the Netherlands. These chapters should give the reader some perspective about how PIE translates into other cultures and political systems.

Section IV covers other matters of importance in the development and use of PIE. We have written a chapter on how PIE can be used in case management. Cathie Hanes Delewski relates her use of PIE in teaching social work students. For the reader willing to look even beyond systems and ecological models, we include an essay by Richard Ramsay on a synergistic model for conceptualizing the practice of social work. Janet Williams discusses the testing of PIE and its use in research. We also have included a chapter on how a computerized version of PIE may make the task of capturing and reporting assessment findings less tedious.

The *PIE Manual*, which is a separate companion piece, includes the Mini-PIE (an invaluable tool for both teaching PIE and completing client assessments), several data collection and reporting tools used in the course of PIE's development, a listing of current interventions in social work practice that can be used to complement a PIE listing, and a section on training others to use PIE.

# Section I

# The PIE Perspective:
# Its Development and Structure

*This section is intended to inform the reader about the conceptualization and development of the PIE system (chapter 1) and to guide the practitioner in the mechanics of the system (chapter 2). By using the instructions in chapter 2 with the accompanying* PIE Manual, *the social worker should be able to use the PIE system in direct practice.*

# 1.

# PIE: A System for Describing and Classifying Problems of Social Functioning

James M. Karls and Karin E. Wandrei

*This chapter provides a brief description of the PIE system; the rationale for developing a classification system for social work; a brief history of the development of PIE; a review of the theories, constructs, and concepts considered in its formulation; a discussion of reliability and validity issues; and a commentary on the future of PIE.*

**D**eveloped under a grant from the National Association of Social Workers (NASW), the person-in-environment (PIE) system describes, classifies, and codes the social functioning problems of adult clients of social workers. Using the organizing construct of person-in-environment, PIE creates uniform statements of social role; environmental, mental, and physical health problems; and client strengths. The system seeks to balance problems and strengths; it delineates problems pertinent to both the person and the environment and qualifies them according to their duration, severity, and the client's ability to solve or cope with them. PIE is intended for use in all current fields of social work practice and by practitioners of varying theoretical positions. It is not a diagnostic system because it does not offer a cause-and-effect relationship for the problems identified. Instead, it is a tool for collecting and ordering relevant information that can produce a comprehensive assessment of a client's problems in social functioning, which in turn allows for the application of interventions from varying theoretical positions that might relieve or solve the problems presented.

## Why a Classification System for Social Work?

From the time of the ancient Greeks, and indeed even before, humans have tried to make sense of the seeming chaos in the world surrounding them. Aristotle posited the four elements of nature that for centuries served as the basis for the development of physical science. In the 18th century the Swedish botanist Carolus Linnaeus devised classification systems for two kingdoms of living

things: vegetable and animal. He also classified the mineral kingdom and started a classification system of diseases. Chemistry has
developed the table of elements. In the social sciences, cultural an-
thropologists and sociologists have classified types of humans and a
range of their characteristics. Medicine has classified the diseases it
treats. Such activity suggests that it is an inherent human trait to
make order out of chaos. One way to do that is to classify the phenomena one encounters. As social work becomes a more clearly defined profession, it is natural for it to define itself more clearly by
developing a system for classifying the problems of the clients it has
been established to serve.

The social work profession has long struggled to establish its
identity and to assert its independence and uniqueness among the
human services professions. For lack of a common system of communication, social work has had to rely on the systems of other professions to describe its clientele. For example, it uses the language
of psychiatry in working with persons who are mentally ill or emotionally troubled, the language of general medicine when working
with persons who are physically ill, and the language of law when
dealing with penal and civil code violators and their families. Social
work must acquire its own language and its own nomenclature to
describe its unique area of service. In so doing, social work will establish a clearer definition of its areas of expertise and will also
establish itself as a major profession.

Some people in social work and other human services fields ob-
ject to classification systems. Classification labels can and have become vehicles for social control and stigmatization, as with those
practitioners who identify individuals as mentally ill, delinquent,
mentally retarded, handicapped, terminally ill, and so forth. Classification can deny the uniqueness of the individual and thus be in
conflict with one of social work's basic values. Despite this danger
there are prevailing arguments for establishing some form of categorization.

Lewis (1982) proposed that typologies are necessary to serve the
client more effectively. He stated that "[a] sound assessment scheme
should free the worker to consider more carefully the unique aspects of individual requests and to tailor the process of intervention
to fit the peculiarities of each instance of a class of cases" (p. 197).
He noted that classification systems are important aids to effective
case planning. Lourie (1978), writing about case management in social work, stated the following:

> First, we need uniform definitions of the problems families and individ-
> uals have which are universally understandable and acceptable for use
> and which all concerned would be willing to apply. Perhaps, as with
> concepts of dependency and neglect, we need to mandate these if they
> are to work. We need to recognize that present diagnostic, legal, and so-
> cial labels do not describe how people function. They are labels more
> comforting to the professionals than useful for client's care and treat-
> ment. Without a consistent vocabulary we can never get to a reason-
> able application of the case management objective. So long as the
> definitions of problems are made unilaterally by each helping agent

there can be no clarity of boundaries of rational and workable assignment of responsibilities. (p. 161)

In this vein Meyer (1987) wrote that

it is important [for social work] to find a unifying perspective that will provide greater cohesiveness to social work practice. Such a perspective would have to reflect the person-in-environment focus that has become central to the purpose of social work practice. Furthermore, to capture the multiple strands of practice, it should not espouse any particular approach or theory; ideally, it should allow for an eclectic approach to case phenomena. Finally such a perspective would have to address the complexity that characterizes the case situations dealt with in social work practice. The purpose of a perspective on practice is to bind together social workers who are all doing different things to carry out the same purposes. (p. 161)

The concern in social work about classifying is not because of the classification systems themselves but more because of their misuse or potential for misuse. Any tool can be misused, but that is not a sufficient reason to deny social work clients and practitioners the great benefits that can come from clear thinking about the problems brought to social workers. To minimize the problems that can accompany misuse of classification, we must heed Northen's (1982) advice:

1. The problem should be based on facts, not inferences, and it should be defined in operational terms.

2. Classifications are merely tools that alert a practitioner to major combinations of relevant factors. They are thus useful in communicating the central tendency of the condition to colleagues.

3. The classification influences what is perceived and how the perceptions are organized for action. Formulating a useful psychosocial assessment requires knowledge beyond that in the classification. The evaluation is of patterns of behavior, not of a person or family.

4. Classification is a means of ascertaining what characteristics a person or family has in common with other individuals or groups in a population. It emphasizes also what is unique in the person or family, that is, how an individual or group differs from others of its type. This is the well-known principle of individualization.

5. Problems are viewed not as existing in the person only, but as a characteristic of the person–situation interaction. Interpersonal processes are all taken into account in defining the problem.

6. In undertaking service with a client identified as having a particular type of problem, the social worker does not permit the label to obscure the client's strengths or the value of intervening in a variety of systems to meet the client's needs.

7. The search for understanding is reciprocal between a practitioner and a client. In line with social work values, clients have a right and a responsibility to participate actively in the process. (p. 175)

This is an era in which case management and managed care, each with its requirement for clear treatment objectives and accountability for effectiveness, are in ascendancy. It is important not only to have classification systems but to have systems that lead to intervention decisions that produce the results requested by both the client and those providing funding for service.

## Classification Systems and Professional Status

A classification system does not a profession make, nor does it make a science out of an art form. However, the development and adoption of a classification system is an important and necessary step in the evolution of an occupation to a major profession. By virtue of not having its own classification system applicable in all practice settings, social work fails a major test by which society judges professionalism. A system of classification communicates to society what a profession does. This system is a consolidation of a profession's body of knowledge, as in medicine's *International Classification of Diseases* (U.S. Department of Health and Human Services, 1991) and the various codifications of laws used by the legal profession. A classification system also clarifies a profession's domain, the aspect of work in which it has greater knowledge and skill than others practicing in the same field.

Some brief comments about professionalism might be useful here. From the work of Etzioni and others (1969), we have learned that a profession, in contrast with an occupation, is generally construed as work to which an individual is committed for life. It encompasses dedication to service in an area in which one has or claims to have special knowledge and the status of an expert. In addition to being able to fulfill a personal commitment of service to humanity, a professional, as opposed to one engaged in an occupation, is offered a degree of prestige and power by society. The major professions of law, medicine, and the ministry illustrate this idea.

To be accepted by society as a profession, an occupational group must develop certain characteristics. It must have a body of abstract knowledge and a mechanism for transmitting this knowledge to its members. Social work meets this requirement with a recognized, agreed-upon curriculum monitored by the Council on Social Work Education and with a network of professional schools in the United States and many industrialized nations.

A profession must also have a professional association through which it socializes its members, communicates new knowledge, advocates for the interests of its members, and ensures their ethical behavior. Social work has NASW and the Society for Clinical Social Work, membership in which provides access to professional meetings, professional journals, information about developments in the profession, and most importantly, an enforceable code of ethics, an essential for a profession.

A profession must also have sanction by society, that is, permission by the society to do things not permitted to others. Societal sanction is affirmed by licensure. In the United States regulation of social workers exists in all political jurisdictions. Most states in the United States and many other countries license social workers who are bound by state laws regulating professional behavior as well as the ethical code of their professional association.

Most relevant to developing a classification system, a profession must have a recognized area of expertise or specialization in relationship to others working in the same field. That is, there must be a means for showing that social work's expertise is different from that of the psychiatrist, the psychologist, the clergy, and others in the human services field. By providing uniform descriptions of the common problems of social work's clientele, PIE helps clarify to the consumer public and other human services professionals the kinds of human problems social work uniquely addresses.

PIE produces descriptions of social functioning problems in terms that most clients, other social work practitioners, and other human services professionals can easily understand. PIE serves as a mechanism for collecting and ordering data, drawing conclusions about the interrelated factors contributing to the problem, and selecting interventions that might relieve or solve the problem. As a classification system PIE provides

- common language for all social work practitioners in all settings to describe their clients' problems in social functioning
- a common capsulated description of social phenomena that could facilitate treatment or amelioration of the problems presented by clients
- a basis for gathering data required to measure the need for services and to design human services programs and evaluate effectiveness
- a mechanism for clearer communication among social work practitioners and between practitioners and administrators and researchers
- a basis for clarifying the domain of social work in the human services field.

## History of Classification Systems in the Human Services Field

The PIE system is not the first attempt among the human services to classify and codify the problems of its clientele. Earlier efforts include the attempt of the Committee on Psychosocial Diagnosis and Classification, sponsored by the American Orthopsychiatric Association in 1964 to develop a classification system for "psychosocial functioning" (personal communication from Committee on Psychosocial Diagnosis and Classification, American Orthopsychiatric Association, 1982). In its final report, the committee reaffirmed the

need for a standard classification system but acknowledged its lack
of success in developing such a system. It cautioned the professional community about apparently insurmountable hurdles in the
development of such a system, including the lack of an acceptable
conceptual framework, the disparate backgrounds and skills of practitioners, and the lack of normative data.

The *International Classification of Diseases–Ninth Revision–Clinical
Modification* (ICD-9-CM) (U.S. Department of Health and Human
Services, 1991) has a supplementary classification listing of psychosocial problems under "Factors Influencing Health Status and
Contact with Health Services." These problems are grouped into
three large categories: (1) housing, household, and economic circumstances; (2) other family circumstances; and (3) other psychosocial
circumstances. Within each of these large categories, there are a
number of more-specific problem areas, most with examples. Unfortunately, this classification is too limited in its coverage and degree
of specificity to address the range of social problems that most social workers deal with in this country.

The *International Classification of Health Problems in Primary Care*,
also called the ICHPPC (World Organization of National Colleges,
Academies, and Academic Associations of General Practitioners/
Family Physicians, 1979), includes a limited supplementary classification of social, marital, and family problems and maladjustments
likely to be encountered by primary health care practitioners. This
classification is merely a simplification of the ICD categories into 37
items; hence the limitations noted about ICD apply here as well.

*A Reason for Visit Classification for Ambulatory Care* (RVC) was developed by the National Center for Health Statistics as an effort to classify reasons for seeking primary health care from the patients' point
of view (Schneider, Appleton, & McLemore, 1979). This document
contains a classification of "social problem counseling" that includes nine specific categories, each with a list of specific problems.
For example, the problems listed under occupational problems include unemployment, job dissatisfaction, and problem with boss or
coworkers. The RVC is far too simplistic and limited to be useful for
comprehensive treatment planning.

The General Practice Research Unit Classification (Fitzgerald,
1978) developed in the United Kingdom includes a classification of
social problems for which clients are referred to social workers. The
list of problems included was derived from a national survey of
case recording systems in the United Kingdom and was developed
primarily for researchers. Despite the detailed listing of three main
problem areas (social factors, personal and social relations, and
health), 14 subcategories, and many specific problems, this classification and some of it subcategories lack sufficient detail to be useful for classifying the varied and complex types of problems with
which most social workers deal.

The Social Maladjustment Schedule (SMS) (Clare & Cairns, 1978)
provides for ratings of material conditions, social management, and

degree of satisfaction of an individual in each of six areas of social functioning: housing, occupation/role, economic situation, leisure/ social activities, family and domestic relationships, and marital relationship. The SMS was developed as an assessment tool but does not provide a comprehensive listing of psychosocial problems. In addition SMS does not provide for the recording of parameters of problems other than degree of difficulty and satisfaction.

*Developing Codes and Classifications for Social Workers in Health Care* (Henk, 1985) lists psychosocial codes that are relevant to general social work practice but were designed to identify problems unique to the primary health care setting. Thus, these codes do not cover the full range of settings in which social work is practiced.

*Classification and Codes for Children and Youth,* by Minnesota Systems Research (1977), classifies common social functioning problems of children, therefore limiting itself to that population.

The most significant classification system currently used by many social workers is the *Diagnostic and Statistical Manual of Mental Disorders,* known as DSM-III (American Psychiatric Association [APA], 1980) and in more recent revisions as DSM-III-R (APA, 1987) and DSM-IV (APA, 1994). This diagnostic and classification system provides in its Axis I and Axis II listings of the mental disorders that are the focus of psychiatric interventions. It is based in the medical disease model, which locates the problem primarily in the individual. The DSM system has, however, recognized in Axis IV that social stressors may contribute to mental disease and has allowed for noting this in the psychiatric diagnosis. However, there was no mechanism in DSM-III to systematically identify and record the psychosocial functioning factors that the social workers are primarily trained to deal with.

In 1987, DSM-III-R, a revision of DSM-III, expanded the scope of Axis IV, permitting a statement about psychosocial stressors with an indication of their severity and whether they were acute or enduring. The client's coping ability was also indirectly addressed on Axis V, which called for an estimate of global functioning (a person's psychological, social, and occupational functioning as measured by the global assessment of functioning [GAF] scale). DSM-IV has moved the social functioning descriptor (Axis IV) a step closer to reflecting the social work approach to assessing human problems. Influenced by PIE and other social work concepts, the title of Axis IV has been changed to "Psychosocial and Environmental Problems," and the axis provides a list of nine factors that may be used "for reporting psychosocial and environmental problems that may affect the diagnosis, treatment, and prognosis of mental disorders" (APA, 1993, p. D:4).

Because a DSM diagnosis is required by most insurance companies for reimbursement for services, it is widely used by social workers and in social work agencies. However, its major emphasis on treatment of mental disease is essentially antithetical to social work theories about the human condition. The changes in DSM-IV's

Axis IV have to some extent introduced social work thinking into
the psychiatric diagnosis. DSM-IV, however, still does not provide
the specificity regarding social functioning that most social work
practitioners find necessary to develop an effective intervention
plan. By placing the locus of the problem in the individual and by
emphasizing treatment of a specific disease or disorder, DSM-IV
fails to meet the need of social work for a system that gives primacy to the enhancement of social functioning and recognizes the
great importance of interpersonal and environmental problems.
There is some question in the mental health field as to whether
there is a relationship between the psychiatric diagnosis and the prescribed treatment. We observe that treatment by most mental health
professionals is often social treatment that consists of modifying behaviors by psychotherapy or environmental manipulation. Improvement or recovery of the patient is more often measured in terms of
social functioning rather than resolution of intrapsychic conflict.

## Other Social Work Classification Approaches

In addition to these classification systems, several classifications of
client's needs and problems have been developed by eminent social
work teachers and theorists. These have generally reflected the social work practice goal of enhancing social functioning and have
tended to be based on the observation that clients of social workers
usually define their problems in terms of social relationships, social
role functioning, and external difficulties. In her work on social diagnosis, Richmond (1917) discussed an approach to classification that
might be compared to a current ecomap (Hartman, 1978).

Perlman (1968) developed three classifications of human problems: (1) deficiencies or deficits in tangible material means,
deficiencies in personal capacity that restrict or thwart role performance, and deficiencies of knowledge and preparation; (2) personality disturbances or mental disorders; and (3) discrepancies
found in roles, including discrepancies between several valued
roles, between expectations of self and others, or between personality needs and role requirements, or discrepancies that result from
ambiguous and contradictory definitions of roles. Perlman's classification ideas are still used and have influenced the development of
the PIE system.

Coulton, Paschall, Foster, Bohnengel, and Slivinske (1979) developed a listing of needs and problems of social work clients in
health settings. Germain and Gitterman (1980) classified people's
needs, problems, or predicaments into three categories: (1) life transitions involving developmental changes, status role changes, and
crisis events; (2) unresponsiveness of social and physical environments, and (3) communication and relationship difficulties in families and other primary groups. Reid and Epstein (1978) developed a

classification of problems for task-centered casework positing several categories of interpersonal conflict: dissatisfaction in social relationships, problems with formal organizations, difficulties in role performance, decision problems, reactive emotional distress, inadequate resources, and psychological and behavioral problems. Northen (1982) built on Reid and Epstein's classifications, adding loss of relationships and cultural conflicts. Monkman (1976) developed a framework called Transaction Between Individuals and Environment to clarify the phenomena in which social workers intervene. All of these classification systems are essentially compatible and have served in the conceptualization and development of the PIE system.

## History of the Development of PIE

PIE originated as a response to the same need apparently felt by those engaged in these earlier classification efforts—the need to clarify the often complex problem array presented by clients. As reflected in these earlier efforts, the field of social work has made great strides since the 1960s in establishing a more scientific base for its theories and practice approaches. However, the major event precipitating the development of PIE was the publication in 1980 of psychiatry's DSM-III. This manual's multiaxial descriptive schema and inclusion of psychosocial stressors was seen as a creative approach to providing a more comprehensive description of the human condition. However, the publication of DSM-III heightened the awareness that if social work could not establish its own classification system, it would have to use the language of another discipline (psychiatry) to describe its clientele.

In this climate PIE was conceived, in part a reaction to DSM-III and in part a reflection of the trends and new developments in social work practice and theory. In 1981 NASW funded a two-year project for its California chapter to develop a system for classifying the problems of social functioning experienced by the clients of social workers. A task force of prominent social workers, practitioners, and academicians took the major responsibility for formulating the issues and content of the system. The task force members' diversity of theoretical orientation, practice setting, culture, and ethnicity helped ensure that as many aspects as possible of social work practice and dimensions of social functioning would be considered.

The task force's goal was to develop a way of giving as clear and concise a picture as possible of what was going on in the life of a client seeking social work help. The task force's expectation was that such a descriptive system would provide a common language for communicating the broad range of problems experienced by social work clientele, that is, a problem classification system. Members anticipated that, to be usable by busy practitioners, such a system must be succinct and yet must provide sufficient depth of description to be useful in planning and conducting interventions that would help relieve the clients' problems. The task force was aware of the imprecision that exists in establishing classes or categories in any of the sciences, but especially in the social sciences. Members were also aware of the limits of such a system in describing the dynamic interaction among the factors that might be described. Recognition of these difficulties did not change the imperative that social work must develop at least a rudimentary classification system that all practitioners in all fields of practice could use regardless of their theoretical orientation to practice.

What kind of communication system or language should social work have? What should this system's characteristics be and what principles should guide its development? These were among the first questions addressed by the task force that developed the PIE system. The task force members noted that there had been a reawakened interest in the long-held construct in social work of person-in-environment. Also influencing the conceptualization of the PIE system was the application of systems, ecological, and holistic theories of human behavior to social work practice models and theory. Social work has historically advocated a holistic approach in its concern for both person and environment but for lack of a bridging mechanism has focused at different times on psychological issues or environmental matters. By isolating and describing the person and environment factors, the task force visualized that PIE might serve as that bridging tool, allowing the practitioner to analyze the problem complex (biological, psychological, social, environmental) in a more efficient manner and to plan, execute, and test interventions in an orderly way.

Over a two-year period the task force reviewed a large array of relevant concepts and theories from the behavioral and social sciences before formulating the design and content for the PIE system. The debate about what might constitute a social work classification system ranged from using a life cycle model such as that of Erikson's (1950) to adapting some of the existing social work classification systems noted earlier. Because of the prominence of the DSM model, there was considerable discussion of whether it might serve as a social work classification vehicle. The conclusion was that because DSM-III, DSM-III-R, and now DSM-IV described human behavior problems primarily in terms of mental disease (as befits the medical profession from which it originates), it was inappropriate as a social work classification system. Except for some social work practitioners who identify very strongly with psychiatry, social work as a profession has diligently resisted a medical disease-oriented model to describe and classify client problems. Recently, there has been a general disdain for narrowing the focus on human problems to the individual's psychopathology and minimizing social or environmental conditions or the client's strengths. If social work were to adopt the DSM classification scheme, it would be documenting individual and societal disequilibrium in the language of psychiatry, which has little relevance to the work for which social workers have been trained. To use the DSM classification schema for social work would confirm social work's ancillary role to psychiatry and its inability to adopt and promulgate its own classification system.

## Adoption of Person-in-Environment as Organizing Construct

The person-in-environment construct, also referred to in social work literature as "person in situation" and "person:environment," has been espoused by many social work theorists. It is generally considered a foundation piece for social work practice and is key to the development of the PIE system. Several theorists influenced the task force debate that led to the adoption of person-in-environment as its foundation construct. Incorporated into the task force's thinking was Richmond's (1917) idea that

> in social diagnosis there is an attempt to arrive at as exact a definition as possible of the social situation and personality of a given client. Investigation or the gathering of evidence begins the process, the critical examination and comparison of evidence follow, and last come its interpretation and definition of the social difficulty. A worker's skill comes into play with the weeding out of those matters of lesser importance and the arrival at an effective and cooperatively implemented action plan. (p. 97)

Richmond's diagnostic system included consideration of the availability and effectiveness of the social institutions of the day and with some modifications could be used in conducting a social diagnosis today. Reid and Epstein's (1978) task-centered approach, Perlman's (1968) problem-solving model, and Germain and Gitterman's (1980) ecological model advocated the person-in-environment construct. Gordon (1981) proposed that the professional objective of social work was to bring about person-in-environment transactions and improve environments for those who function within them to facilitate their growth, health, and social functioning.

To avoid the difficulties encountered by the American Orthopsychiatric Association—the impossibility of finding one theory of behavior acceptable to all practitioners and a lack of consensus on the variables to be included in a classification system—the task force decided to develop a system that would not advocate any current theory of human behavior but be as atheoretical and simple as possible without compromising depth of problem description. In this vein the task force also opted for a system that was primarily descriptive of the major features of the client's problem, leaving to the practitioners the task of deciding a cause and effect relationship and allowing them to use their own particular theoretical orientations.

## Social Functioning

In addition to the person-in-environment construct, the task force adopted the concept of social functioning as another foundation piece for the PIE system. What is social functioning and how can it be described and categorized? The task force noted that most social casework models used the term "social functioning" and considered enhancement of social functioning the primary goal of social work intervention. To develop a schema for describing and categorizing social functioning, the task force looked to sociology and social psychology and adapted some of the ideas of Sarbin (1954), Thomas and Feldman (1967), and Turner (1954). Their writings on role theory provided the list of social roles people occupy and allowed the task force to consider how clients' problems related to these roles. The task force diligently avoided incorporating role theory as such into the PIE schema but chose to borrow some of its ideas and terminology. The task force used the idea that each person occupies at least one social role at any given time. Furthermore, the difficulties a client presents to the social worker can be identified as performance problems in that social role.

It is easy enough to observe that a client is having a problem in a social role as a parent, spouse, worker, or patient. To answer the question as to what kind of social role problem a person has is more difficult, particularly if one is to avoid advocating any single theory of human behavior. In light of the absence of any generally accepted system, the task force approached the need to provide a more in-depth description of the social role functioning problem by surveying its practitioner members to learn the kinds of problems they observed in their practice. Thus, the descriptors for social role functioning problems were derived from the direct experience of practitioner members of the task force. These descriptors reflected various social work models and behavior theories, notably those of Hollis (1981), Perlman (1968), Reid and Epstein (1978), and psychodynamic and ego psychology concepts that members of the task force had incorporated into their social work practice.

## Recognizing Client Strengths

The task force made a concerted effort to incorporate into the PIE system a clear recognition of a client's strength to cope with the problems brought to the social worker. The awareness and usefulness of clients' strengths is another foundation piece in social work practice theory and is a recurring theme in the literature. The idea is a simple one: Every person has the potential to adapt to stress and solve the problems of living that occur. Indeed, most of social work intervention is aimed at mobilizing and enhancing personal strengths and resources to solve both interpersonal and environmental problems. Client strength, also referred to as coping ability, is generally interpreted as the client's use of knowledge, experience, and psychological and physical strength to master stressful situations. The task force chose to use the strengths concept by incorporating a coping-ability assessment for each interpersonal or social functioning problem presented. In the absence of any tested

or agreed upon measures of coping ability, the task force chose to
have the social worker record in the PIE statement an individual
clinical judgment about the clients' abilities. Thus a client with a severe spousal role problem, for example, could be judged by the social worker as having good coping ability for this problem and the
intervention would be planned accordingly.

## Definition of Environment

After considerable debate about what the term "environment," so
commonly used in social work, really meant, the task force chose to
use it to refer to the community in which the social work client re-
sided. The concept of environment was used in a model of community developed by Warren (1963). As Warren stated, "[I]ts focus is
less on a particular geographic area as the focus of analysis than on
the types of systemic relationships into which people and social organizations come by virtue of their clustering together in the same
location" (p. vii). Adaptation of the Warren model resulted in the
formulation in PIE of a six-element descriptor covering the social institutions and organizations generally found in most communities
to facilitate the social well-being and social functioning of individuals. The category of environment in PIE was further construed to be
descriptive of the interaction problems between the individual and
a community's social institutions, that is, the interaction between
the client and the public assistance, health, safety, and protective services, as well as economic support services, religious institutions,
and so on. The problems in the environment are the barriers or
other factors that prevent the person's access to the needed institution. As with the problems in social interaction or social functioning, each of the six elements served as categories and were further
expanded to provide descriptions of the problems that occur
in each.

## Mental and Physical Health

Following the principles of a holistic approach, the task force concluded that a comprehensive picture of the client's problem must include the intrapsychic difficulties as well as physical health
problems he or she might be experiencing. In the absence of any
universally acceptable theory about psychopathology, the task force
decided to use Axes I and II of DSM-III-R to describe mental health
problems and the ICD-9-CM to report physical health problems.

## Holistic Perspective

PIE is perhaps best described as an integrated practice model (Parsons, Hernandez, & Jorgensen, 1988). In this model, the whole problem complex is presented and provides a comprehensive range of
targets for intervention. The system that was adopted also reflects

systems theory concepts and the ecological model of Germain and Gitterman (1980). The system also uses concepts of prevention in mental health proposed by Parad (1965) and Bloom (1979), emphasizing concern for precipitating factors and the linking of interventions with stressful life events. From this adaptation of the public health prevention model comes the notion that effective treatment of a problem is achieved as much by control of the problem in the environment as by control of the individual's interactional difficulty.

The system that was finally developed is influenced by concepts and constructs from sociology, psychology, psychiatry, and social work. Guiding the development was the "Working Statement on the Purpose of Social Work" (NASW, 1981): "The purpose of social work is to promote or restore a mutually beneficial interaction between individuals and society in order to improve the quality of life for everyone" (p.6). Among the objectives in this purpose statement was that

> Social workers focus on person-and-environment *in interaction*. To carry out their purpose they work with people to achieve the following objectives:
>
> • Facilitate interaction between individuals and others in their environment.
> • Help people enlarge their competence and increase their problem solving and coping abilities.
> • Influence social and environmental policy. (p. 6)

## Focus on Adults Only

PIE is a system that describes the problems of adult clients of social workers. The PIE task force had originally hoped to develop a classification system that included children and adolescents. However, such an endeavor was beyond the scope and resources of the task force. In focusing on adults, the task force did not overlook the need to eventually establish such systems as PIE for children and families. The PIE system can be used with families and children by describing the individual adult's problems in the case situation. PIE assessments of the parents are highly useful in clarifying the child's problems and in developing intervention plans that affect the child.

## Reliability and Validity Issues

Important steps in establishing the usefulness of a classification system include the systematic assessment of its reliability and validity as well as consideration of its acceptability, feasibility, and coverage. The reliability of a system indicates how well practitioners using the system can agree with each other on the identification of the categories. The validity of a system is a measure of its usefulness and reflects how well it measures what it is supposed to measure. Acceptability is whether users agree that the categories and their definitions have face validity, that they encompass the language and ideas of the profession. Feasibility indicates whether the system is understandable and easily applied. Coverage is achieved to the extent that there is a goodness of fit of the system in practice, that it is a useful tool for helping the client.

Thus far the PIE system has undergone a variety of test procedures. The first (Wandrei, 1984) was a review by a panel of highly respected and nationally recognized social work practitioners and teachers. Sixteen eminent social workers throughout the country were asked to study and review the PIE system. Of these 16 experts, 14 responded favorably to the system. Additional feedback was obtained in the course of many workshops in various parts of the country. Responses from participants at these workshops have been overwhelmingly positive, with many expressing their belief that the PIE project is an important and timely one.

In 1984 a nationwide pilot test of PIE was conducted (Wandrei, 1985). Two chapters from nine of NASW's 13 regions were selected, and five members from each chapter, representing differing theoretical orientations, direct practice settings, and length of time in practice, were asked to use the system with two clients and then complete a questionnaire about their experience. Feedback on the use of the system was generally positive. Most of the 62 social workers who responded to the questionnaire indicated that they were able to use the system to describe their clients with a minimum of difficulty. Forty-seven of the respondents stated they thought the manual was clear and that it described the client's situation clearly and concisely. A total of 51 of the respondents agreed that PIE helped identify when social work interventions were needed. Another 40 said PIE would help them communicate with other practitioners and that it provided a basis for gathering data useful in measuring the need for services.

A pilot reliability study (Williams, 1989) funded by NASW was conducted at four sites: United Charities of Chicago, the Los Angeles County–University of Southern California General Hospital, the Social Work Department of the New York State Psychiatric Institute, and the Massachusetts Department of Mental Health. Using videotaped case material in these tests, 197 ratings were made across 16 videotapes, with from four to 30 raters per tape. Although the size of this study did not give enough ratings across the range of PIE categories to make definitive statements about their reliabilities, the findings were generally positive. (There was a high degree of agreement among the social workers using the system on the identification of the PIE categories in the types of problems tested.) An application is in process for a National Institute of Mental Health grant to conduct a systematic test of the PIE system's reliability in a large multisite national field test with a variety of cases that represent the range of social work practice. With publication of an earlier version of the *PIE Manual* (Karls & Wandrei, 1989) and several journal articles on PIE (Karls & Wandrei, 1992a, 1992b; Williams, Karls, & Wandrei, 1989), an international interest has developed. Informal tests of PIE have occurred in Italy, the Netherlands, Japan, Canada, and Australia with positive responses from users in those countries. Further evidence of the impact of the PIE system is found in the inclusion of some of its features in DSM-IV's Axis IV, which focuses on social supports and environmental resources.

This preliminary testing has suggested that the PIE system has face validity and likely reliability and feasibility in practice. As with any work in progress, further testing for interrater reliability and validity is anticipated and expected to be an ongoing process.

## Future of PIE

If social work is ever to gain parity with the other major "person" professions (medicine, psychiatry, law, and ministry), it will need to adopt and use a nomenclature system for describing its area of expertise. The future of PIE is linked to the readiness and willingness of social work practitioners, administrators, and educators to take the difficult step of learning and implementing a new or unfamiliar way of identifying client problems. There are not many occupational groups that are willing to pay the costs of transforming themselves, even though the benefits in power, prestige, and money of higher professional status are inviting. Medicine's efforts to raise educational standards in the early 1900s required great expenditures of money and energy; the effort changed the image of medicine dramatically in one generation. The creation of DSM and psychiatry's promotion of it as a universal classification system required millions of dollars and a great expenditure of energy by psychiatry, with accompanying defections by various practitioners. However, as a result of that effort, almost all mental health workers use the system and the status of psychiatry was greatly enhanced.

Inherent in the development of a new system is the risk of intraprofessional conflicts between those who are content with the state of things or at least are not open to radical change and those who seek to upgrade the field. And there is a risk in the promulgation of PIE that splits in the profession could occur, as in the old functional versus diagnostic issue. Making a change is a calculated risk that could both increase the professional status of social work and meet the ideals and values of social work by improving the quality of care provided to its clientele.

Like Henry Ford's Model T, the current version of PIE is an early model of a vehicle for describing the problems of social functioning of social work clients. It works. It helps unravel the problem complex brought to the social worker and leads to better intervention planning. It provides the bridge between person and environment that allows for a truly holistic approach in social work practice. As it is now being used in practice, it allows the social worker to clearly and succinctly describe the client's problem complex. It serves as a tool for developing interventions that can be used by client and social worker to reduce or resolve the client's distress.

As a developing system PIE will need continued testing and refinement. The language for describing some problems is still awkward and categories need refinement and perhaps expansion. But, like the first step in a journey of a thousand miles, the continued development of the PIE system can lead social work to a new clarity and understanding of its domain. By unraveling the problem complex, it can help social work fulfill its mission of reducing to the minimum the common problems clients bring to social workers.

With the increasing importance in the United States of case management and managed care and the advent of a national health policy that will demand more accountability, PIE, with its uniform, succinct descriptors of social problems, could provide useful information to those wanting harder data on what services social workers provide. Should such a time come when the third-party reimbursement system might be less oriented to the disease model, it is possible that social work practitioners could be reimbursed for services provided to ameliorate problems in social functioning and to reduce environmental problems. A computerized version of PIE, now in development, could make it possible to expedite the assessment process and to produce uniform data about the human condition that could benefit consumers of social work services, practitioners, administrators, program planners, and researchers alike.

Now is the time for social work to take the giant step toward adoption of its own classification system!

## References

American Psychiatric Association. (1980). *Diagnostic and statistical manual of mental disorders* (3rd ed.). Washington, DC: American Psychiatric Press.

American Psychiatric Association. (1987). *Diagnostic and statistical manual of mental disorders* (3rd ed., rev.). Washington, DC: American Psychiatric Press.

American Psychiatric Association. (1993). *DSM–IV draft criteria*. Washington, DC: American Psychiatric Press.

American Psychiatric Association. (1994). *Diagnostic and statistical manual of mental disorders* (4th ed.). Washington, DC: American Psychiatric Press.

Bloom, B. (1979). Prevention of mental disorders: Recent advances in theory and practice. *Community Mental Health Journal, 15*, 179–191.

Clare, A. W., & Cairns, V. (1978). Design, development and use of a standardized interview to assess social maladjustment and dysfunction in community studies. *Psychological Medicine, 8*, 589–604.

Coulton, C. J., Paschall, N. C., Foster, D. L., Bohnengel, A., & Slivinske, L. (1979). *Nationwide survey of hospital social work practice*. Cleveland: School of Applied Social Sciences, Case Western Reserve University.

Erikson, E. (1950). *Childhood and society*. New York: Basic Books.

Etzioni, A. (Ed.). (1969). *The semi-professions and their organizations*. New York: Free Press.

Fitzgerald, R. (1978). Classification and recording of social problems. *Social Science and Medicine, 12*, 225–268.

Germain, C., & Gitterman, A. (1980). *Life model of social work practice*. New York: Columbia University Press.

Gordon, W. E. (1981). A natural classification system for social work literature and knowledge. *Social Work, 26*, 134–136.

Hartman, A. (1978). Diagrammatic assessment of family relationships. *Social Casework, 59*, 465–476.

Henk, M. (1985). *Developing codes and classifications for social workers in health care*. (Available from Public Health Service, 601 East 12th St., Kansas City, MO 64106.)

Hollis, F. M. (1981). *Social casework: A psychosocial therapy* (3rd ed.). New York: Random House.

Karls, J., & Wandrei, K. (1989). *PIE manual: Person in environment (PIE)* (9th rev.). Silver Spring, MD: National Association of Social Workers.

Karls, J., & Wandrei, K. (1992a). The person-in-environment system for classifying client problems. *Journal of Case Management, 1*, 90–95.

Karls, J., & Wandrei, K. (1992b). PIE: A new language for social work. *Social Work, 37*, 80–85.

Lewis, H. (1982). *The intellectual base of social work practice: Tools for thought in a helping profession*. New York: Haworth Press.

Lourie, N. (1978). Case management. In J. Talbott (Ed.), *The chronic mental patient: Problems, solutions and recommendations for a public policy* (pp. 159–164). Washington, DC: American Psychiatric Press.

Meyer, C. H. (1987). Direct practice in social work: Overview. In A. Minahan (Ed.-in-Chief), *Encyclopedia of social work* (18th ed., Vol. 1, pp. 409–422). Silver Spring, MD: National Association of Social Workers.

Minnesota Systems Research. (1977). *Classification and codes for children and youth (social work)*. Minneapolis: Author.

Monkman, M. M. (1976). A broader more comprehensive view of school social work. *School Social Work Journal, 1*, 7–16.

National Association of Social Workers. (1981). Conceptual frameworks II: Special issue. *Social Work, 26*.

Northen, H. (1982). *Clinical social work*. New York: Columbia University Press.

Parad, H. (1965). *Crisis intervention*. New York: Family Service Association of America.

Parsons, R. J., Hernandez, S. H., & Jorgensen, J. D. (1988). Integrated practice: A framework for problem solving. *Social Work, 5*, 417–421.

Perlman, H. H. (1968). *Social casework: A problem solving process*. Chicago: University of Chicago Press.

Reid, W. J., & Epstein, L. (1978). *Task centered casework*. New York: Columbia University Press.

Richmond, M. E. (1917). *Social diagnosis*. New York: Russell Sage Foundation.

Sarbin, T. (1954). Role: I: Psychological aspects. In G. Lindzay (Ed.), *Handbook of social psychology* (pp. 546–552). Cambridge, MA: Addison-Wesley.

Schneider, D., Appleton, L., & McLemore, T. (1979). *A reason for visit classification for ambulatory care* (Vital and Health Statistics, Series 2, No. 78, DHEW Publication No. PHS 79–1352). Hyattsville, MD: U.S. National Center for Health Statistics.

Thomas, E., & Feldman, R. (1967). *Behavioral science for social workers*. New York: Free Press.

Turner, R. (1954). Role: II: Sociological aspects. In G. Lindzay (Ed.), *Handbook of social psychology* (pp. 552–557). Cambridge, MA: Addison-Wesley.

U.S. Department of Health and Human Services. (1991). *International classification of diseases–9th revision–clinical modification* (4th ed.). Washington, DC: U.S. Government Printing Office.

Wandrei, K. (1984). *Expert review of PIE*. Unpublished report, National Association of Social Workers.

Wandrei, K. (1985). *The person-in-environment (PIE): A coding system for the problems of social functioning* (Final Report, project year 1984). Unpublished report, California chapter, NASW.

Warren, R. (1963). *The community in America*. Chicago: Rand McNally.

Williams, J. (1989). *Pilot reliability test of PIE*. Unpublished report, New York State Psychiatric Institute.

Williams, J.B.W., Karls, J., & Wandrei, K. (1989). The person-in-environment (PIE) system for describing problems of social functioning. *Hospital and Community Psychiatry, 40*, 1125–1126.

World Organization of National Colleges, Academies, and Academic Associations of General Practitioners/Family Physicians. (1979). *International classification of health problems in primary care* (2nd ed.). Ann Arbor, MI: Author.

# 2.

# Structure of the PIE System

Karin E. Wandrei and James M. Karls

*This chapter provides a description of how the PIE system is structured. It also describes how to use the* PIE Manual *and how to record written descriptions and numerical codes. After a careful study of this chapter and the* PIE Manual, *the reader should be able to apply PIE to actual cases.*

The person-in-environment (PIE) system arose out of the need of social workers in a variety of settings to describe the problems presented by their clients and to use the unique focus of the social work profession on person-in-environment. Chapter 1 described some of the debate that transpired during the development of the PIE system about which specific categories of information needed to be included in the system. The task force finally agreed that four classes of information would be important for social workers to use in describing their clients: social functioning problems, environmental problems, mental health problems, and physical health problems.

Similar to the *Diagnostic and Statistical Manual of Mental Disorders, Fourth Edition* (DSM-IV) (American Psychiatric Association, 1994), a multiaxial system that involves a diagnostic notation on each of five axes, the PIE system consists of four factors and calls for a description of the client on each of them. An overview of the PIE system is presented in Exhibit 1.

Information on each of the four factors of the PIE system is discrete, that is, it stands as a description of one facet of the client's problem complex, although obviously problems on one factor can influence problems on the other factors. Because PIE is a system organized around the concept of person-in-environment, Factors I and II in the PIE system are those which we believe to be unique to social work practice.

Factor III merely borrows what we believe is most useful for social work practice from the DSM-IV system: Axes I and II. These two axes denote the existence of mental and developmental disorders. Factor IV is a listing of physical health problems, using the *International Classification of Diseases–Ninth Revision–Clinical Modification* (ICD-9-CM) (U.S. Department of Health and Human Services, 1991).

Exhibit I
**Basic Structure of PIE**

**Factor I:  Social Functioning Problems**

A.  Social role in which each problem is identified (four categories)
B.  Type of problem in social role (nine types)
C.  Severity of problem (6-point indicator)
D.  Duration of problem (6-point indicator)
E.  Ability of client to cope with problem

**Factor II:  Environmental Problems**

A.  Social system where each problem is identified (six systems)
B.  Specific type of problem within each social system (number varies for each social system)
C.  Severity of problem (6-point indicator)
D.  Duration of problem

**Factor III:  Mental Health Problems**

A.  Clinical syndromes (Axis I of DSM-IV)
B.  Personality and developmental disorders (Axis II of DSM-IV)

**Factor IV:  Physical Health Problems**

A.  Diseases diagnosed by a physician (Axis III of DSM-IV, ICD-9)
B.  Other health problems reported by client and others

Whereas the first two factors constitute social work's primary focus, all four factors are necessary to provide an adequate picture of a client's problems. Thus, by identifying primacy of social work in social intervention and environmental areas, PIE clearly helps differentiate the role of the social worker from that of other mental health and health professionals.

## Factor I: Social Functioning Problems

Most clients of social workers present themselves or are referred for help because they are having difficulties in their social functioning. "Social functioning" in PIE refers to a person's performance in his or her social roles (for example, the client is having trouble with a spouse, an employer, or a child).

A person's social role can be defined in terms of fulfilling a recognized and regulated position in society, for example, as a parent, student, or employee. Tradition, law, and societal and family values define the content of roles. Although the major functions of these roles remain generally the same across cultures, the way the functions are accomplished may vary from culture to culture and from unit to unit within a specific culture.

PIE attempts to avoid defining social roles in a culture-specific context. It is imperative that the social worker using the system take into account the specific cultural and societal role definitions influencing the client. For example, in the African American community, physical punishment of children may be viewed as a more socially acceptable method of disciplining a child than in some other communities. To determine whether or not an African American parent has a parent role problem, the social worker must take into account whether the parent's discipline of the child would be considered excessive within the norms of the client's reference group and, of course, whether the discipline meets the legal conditions of physical child abuse.

One of the additional strengths of the Factor I listings is in recognizing the diversity in the lives of clients. For example, this is the PIE definition of the role entitled Worker Role–Home under the Occupational Roles subcategory in the *PIE Manual*.

> The Worker Role–Home includes all responsibilities and expectations associated with the activities a person performs to maintain a home— such as shopping, cooking, cleaning, and sewing—but does not include parenting. The role involves unpaid work performed in the home by a person of either sex. (A person who is paid for such work would fit into the Worker Role–Paid Economy category.) (p. 12)

Traditionally this role would be known as the "housewife" role, but in PIE it is a role that can be performed by either men or women.

Similarly, the *PIE Manual* definition of Spouse Role is that it "encompasses the responsibilities and expectations assigned to each of two persons who have formed a legal, religious, or private union for the purposes of basic physical and economic security, emotional and sexual gratification, social recognition, companionship, and in some instances, procreation" (p. 17). Note that this definition may be used for any two people who have formed a union, regardless of their sex or legal marital status.

The social role problem areas on Factor I are grouped into four major categories: (1) Family Roles, (2) Other Interpersonal Roles, (3) Occupational Roles, and (4) Special Life Situation Roles. Each of these categories contains subcategories giving more specificity to the category.

*Family Roles* are social roles that are played out in the context of a family setting in which people are linked by blood, the law, or formal or informal arrangements. There are six roles within the family role subcategory: (1) Parent Role, (2) Spouse Role, (3) Child Role, (4) Sibling Role, (5) Other Family Role, and (6) Significant Other Role.

*Other Interpersonal Roles* are social roles that are also played out in interpersonal relationships between individuals, but these persons are not members of the same family. They interact with each other because of physical proximity or common interests. There are five roles within the other interpersonal roles subcategory: (1) Lover Role, (2) Friend Role, (3) Neighbor Role, (4) Member Role, and (5) Other Interpersonal Role.

*Occupational Roles* are those social roles that are performed in the paid or unpaid economy or in academic settings. There are five roles within the occupational roles subcategory: (1) Worker Role–

Paid Economy, (2) Worker Role–Home, (3) Worker Role–Volunteer, (4) Student Role, and (5) Other Occupational Role.

*Special Life Situation Roles* are roles people may voluntarily or involuntarily assume throughout the course of their lives. They are time-limited, situation-specific roles people assume in addition to or in place of their usual roles. Most frequently, strict societal, legal, institutional, and professional expectations govern the responsibilities and expectations of these roles. There are nine roles within the special life situations subcategory: (1) Consumer Role, (2) Inpatient/Client Role, (3) Outpatient/Client Role, (4) Probationer/Parolee Role, (5) Prisoner Role, (6) Immigrant Role–Legal, (7) Immigrant Role–Undocumented, (8) Immigrant Role–Refugee, (9) Other Special Life Situation Role.

Each of the social roles is defined in the *PIE Manual* and several examples are given of situations that the social worker might encounter. For example, here is the definition of Friend Role taken from the manual:

> *Friend Role.* In the Friend Role a person maintains a relationship with another person of the same or the opposite sex for the purpose of mutual emotional and spiritual support and companionship. The role usually does not include a sexual relationship as that would be included in the Lover Role.
>
> The following are examples of Friend Role Problems:
>
> • A woman who is upset that her best friend is ignoring her since she got involved with a lover
> • A man who is wondering how to be supportive of his friend who is undergoing a difficult custody battle
> • A woman who is having a fight with a friend who has not returned money lent to her. (p. 11)

The four categories of social roles, each with a number of subcategories, encompass most social functioning problems that are likely to be encountered in current social work practice. To allow for the possibility that the social worker may encounter a client with a social role problem that truly does not fit into one of the predefined social role categories, a residual category within each of the four subcategories is included. If this category must be used, the social worker should specify the social role he or she is describing.

## Types of Social Functioning Problems in Factor I

The social role problem categories just described allow the social worker to identify the social roles with which the client is experiencing difficulty. It is important for intervention planning to know not only the problem area but also the kind of problem being experienced. There is a need to describe the kind of interactional difficulty that is occurring or has occurred between the client and another person. To address this need for more specificity, the PIE system includes a mechanism for describing the types of social role problems identified.

The nine types of interactional difficulties in the PIE system are

1. power type
2. ambivalence type
3. responsibility type
4. dependency type
5. loss type
6. isolation type
7. victimization type
8. mixed type
9. other type.

These types of interactional difficulties are believed to be descriptive of most interactional difficulties that are likely to be encountered in social work practice. Because the types are not mutually exclusive, it is possible that a client's interactional difficulty may include more than one descriptor. If this occurs, the practitioner should identify the dominant type. If more than one type is prominent, the practitioner should use the mixed-type category. Definitions and descriptions of the types can be found in the manual.

It is assumed that a relationship is now strained, disrupted, or broken. It is the social worker's task to describe the nature of the strain, disruption, or break, both to provide a clearer picture of the problem and to facilitate remedial interventions. For example, a Spousal Role Problem in which the client is complaining of loneliness and confusion related to the death of a spouse is described as loss type. This is significantly different from a Spousal Role Problem in which the client is complaining about a spouse's physical and psychological abuse, which would be described as power type.

The listing of types of problems in social role functioning attempts to provide standardized terminology to describe the most commonly observed types of interactional difficulties. Both the social role functioning problem and the type are descriptive of the client's difficulty, not of the other person in the relationship. Because in most interactional difficulties forces from both persons are involved, it is important when classifying the type of problem that the focus is on the client presenting the problem. For example, an abused spouse's problem might be typed as victimization; the abusing spouse's problem might be typed as power.

After having identified the social role area in which the client's problem exists, the social worker chooses the particular type that is most descriptive of the interactional dynamics presented by the client. The listing in the manual of the types of problems includes illustrative case examples to clarify the concepts. Here, for example, is the *PIE Manual's* definition of the loss type:

> Separation is the breaking apart from a person or thing to which an individual has attached emotional significance. Loss is a permanent separation and a grieving process that usually accompanies such an event. The loss or threatened loss of a significant person by separation, death,

or physical distance can create anxiety, resentment, anger, hopeless-
ness, and lack of energy, will, or ability to deal with the change. Social
role performance under these circumstances becomes difficult.

For many people the loss of a role is in itself a highly significant life
event. A change in status is also frequently experienced as a loss and is
included under this type. Status is a person's condition or position
with regard to the law, a relationship, a group, the community, or society as a whole. (p. 19)

---

## Case Study

Gail, a young working mother of two small children, is having intense anxiety attacks that are interfering with her work performance to the extent that
her job is in jeopardy. Six months previously her husband committed suicide.
Gail had been emotionally dependent on her husband and his family, but
now his family has turned on Gail and told her that her husband's death was
her fault. Gail's relationships with her own family of origin are strained because of their strong opposition to her marriage.

---

Although this woman is having difficulties in several social roles,
the primary problem seems to be in the loss of her spousal role.
This woman's situation would be coded as Spousal Role Problem,
loss type.

Other examples of loss problems include a man whose wife dies
in an accident, a man who loses his job, and a client whose therapist moves away.

### Factor II: Environmental Problems

The environment is both the physical context and the social context
in which a person lives. It is the sum total of the natural setting and
the human-made circumstances outside of the person. The environment provides both resources and opportunities, and it activates
needs as well as barriers to their fulfillment.

In social work, a person and his or her environment are regarded
as interacting, each using and shaping the other. In the social role
descriptions listed, attention has been given to interpersonal factors
that impinge on social functioning. The environmental descriptions
listed on Factor II focus on the external factors outside of the client
that affect the client's social functioning and social well-being. For
example, if a client has a substance abuse problem that interferes
with his ability to find a job and the job market for his field is good
in his community, this client would be described as having a
Worker Role–Paid Economy Problem. However, if a client complains that she can't find a job and no jobs in her field exist in the
community, this would be an environmental problem described as
Economic/Basic Needs System, unemployment.

In developing the environmental problems listed in the PIE system, the task force was strongly influenced by Warren's *The Community in America* (1963). Warren identified five dominant social systems in society that, in their optimal manifestation, create a sense of social well-being. That is, if these five social systems operate well, society will have reached an utopian state. Neither the United States nor any political state has yet reached a level at which its social institutions are capable of meeting the needs of all its citizens efficiently or effectively; it is important, therefore, to identify the problems in the institutions and social systems that impinge on the social functioning problems presented by clients.

By clearly identifying a problem in the social system or environment, the social worker can make a considered decision about whether to intervene in a client's interpersonal problem or environmental problem, or both. Each social work client is likely to report some degree of difficulty in both the social functioning and the environmental areas; the clear delineation of each should facilitate the social worker's choice of intervention and the resolution or relief of the client's problems.

## Environmental Problem Areas

The PIE system includes six environmental problem areas. The first five were drawn from Warren's (1963) conceptualization. The sixth, the Affectional Support System, was added at the suggestion of social workers participating in the pilot testing of the system. The six environmental problem areas are as follows:

1. Economic/Basic Needs System
2. Educational/Training System
3. Judicial/Legal System
4. Health, Safety, and Social Services System
5. Voluntary Association System
6. Affectional Support System.

Within each of the six social systems on Factor II, there are subcategories of problems and within each subcategory there are a varying number of specific problems. For example, the specific problem of inaccessibility of mental health services is located within the broader Health, Safety, and Social Services System (subcategory Health/Mental Health). The example given to describe inaccessibility of mental health services is that the community mental health clinic is located 100 miles from the client's residence. The specific example of documented malnutrition with threat to health is located within the broader Economic/Basic Needs System (subcategory Food/Nutrition). The example given to describe documented malnutrition with threat to health is that only powdered infant formula is available with poor water system.

To address social work's special mission to enhance social justice, each social system includes a problem statement on discrimination on the basis of the following:

- age
- ethnicity, color, or language
- religion
- sex
- sexual orientation
- lifestyle
- noncitizenship status
- veteran status
- dependency status
- disability
- marital status
- other discrimination.

The first social system on Factor II is the Economic/Basic Needs System. Problems in this category refer to the production, distribution, and consumption functions of the economic system, that is, the capability of a community to meet the basic needs of its citizens for food, shelter, employment, and so on. Problems that can be identified here are the means of acquiring economic goods and services as well as the adequacy of the goods themselves. Economic/Basic Needs System problems include the community's problems in providing food/nutrition, shelter, employment, economic resources, and transportation.

The Educational/Training System is the second social system in Factor II. This problem area refers to the ability of the community to meet the goals of the educational system to nurture intellect, to develop social skills, and to foster individual potential to its optimal level. The barriers to these goals include access to education, discrimination in providing educational services, and cultural influence on the quantity and quality of educational programming. Education is construed as either formal or informal and under either secular or religious auspices. Two examples of educational/training system problems are regulatory barriers to existing educational and training services, such as residency requirements, and the community's lack of educational or training facilities, such as the absence of vocational training facilities.

The third system in Factor II is the Judicial/Legal System. Problems in this system are related to the criminal justice system's primary function of social control. Enforcement measures by a police or sheriff's department can create closed environments and increase the danger of crime in a community. Lack of enforcement can result in anarchy. Some examples of Judicial/Legal System problems are lack of adequate prosecution, inadequate defense, or insufficient police services.

The fourth system is the Health, Safety, and Social Services System that encompasses a community's health, mental health, and social services delivery systems. Problems in this category are not the problems of the individual but rather of the community as a whole and the social and health services that exist in most developed societies. Examples of problems in this system are the absence of support services needed to use mental health services, absence of adequate social services, or a natural disaster.

The fifth category in Factor II is the Voluntary Association System. This system consists of the common ways that people satisfy needs for social support and interaction outside of the family and the workplace: joining and participating in organized or informal religious and community groups. Religious groups are formal organizations with belief systems pertaining to a philosophy, an ultimate reality, or a deity and that have a commitment to a religious faith or observance. Community groups are composed of people with common interests or characteristics and generally function to help their own members. Examples of Voluntary Association System problems are the lack of a client's religious group of choice in the community or the lack of community acceptance of a client's community group of choice, such as Alcoholics Anonymous.

When the PIE system was first field-tested, several social workers strongly expressed a need to record the situation of clients who had either underinvolved or overinvolved personal environments. Thus, the Affectional Support System was added as a sixth category to identify this problem in the client's community. The Affectional Support System is the network of social relationships that can be found in most individual's personal social support system. This system consists of marital family, extended family, family of origin, friends, acquaintances, coworkers, paid or volunteer helpers, and service providers. The Affectional Support System includes everyone who is part of a client's personal social system and who has an affectional tie with the client. Problems in this category are limited to those in the support system of the community, not in the client's ability to access the system (which would be listed on Factor I instead). Examples in this category are the absence of an Affectional Support System in the community (there is no one in the community who really cares for the client) or the existence of an excessively involved support system.

Further descriptions of these categories with examples can be found in the *PIE Manual*.

## Severity, Duration, and Coping Indexes

During the early testing of PIE, many social workers thought there was a need to amplify the assessment to decide whether social work intervention was needed and, if needed, how quickly. Although many possible indicators were suggested, the task force decided to limit the indexes to three: (1) severity of the problem, (2) duration of the problem, and (3) coping skills of the client. In the PIE assessment the social worker uses the three indexes to complete the description of the client's social functioning and environmental problems and to provide an indication of what degree of social work intervention is required.

## Severity Index

The Severity Index is used on both Factors I and II. Change and transitions are factors of everyday life, and thus changes in roles, relationships, and events characterize most cases that come to the attention of social workers. The practitioner should use the Severity Index to differentiate instances when change is extensive, rapid, and problem-producing from instances when change is less problematic for the client. When change is pervasive and highly disruptive, the need for social work intervention is probably high. Conversely, when there is little disruption social work services may be brief or not needed.

There are six levels on the Severity Index:

1. no problem—the problem is perceived as nondisruptive by both the client and the practitioner. No intervention is needed.

2. low severity—the problem may include some change but is perceived as nondisruptive by the client, although disruption may be noted by the practitioner. Intervention may be desirable but not necessary.

3. moderate severity—the problem is disruptive to the client's functioning but the distress is not judged as impairing general functioning. Intervention would be helpful.

4. high severity—the problem involves fewer or less dramatic changes but the client is in a clear state of distress. Early intervention is indicated.

5. very high severity—the problem is characterized by changes in key or multiple areas of social role functioning or in the environment. Immediate intervention is probably necessary.

6. catastrophic—the problem is characterized by sudden, negative changes out of the individual's control, with devastating implications for adjustment. Immediate direct intervention is indicated.

## Duration Index

The Duration Index is used on both Factors I and II. The Duration Index indicates the length or recency of the problem. Along with the Severity Index, the Duration Index alerts the practitioner to the degree of urgency for intervention. Coupled with the Coping Index for Factor I problems, the Duration Index is a measure of the prognosis for problem resolution. For example, a client with good coping skills and a recently developed problem has a higher probability for problem resolution than a client with a chronic problem and poor coping skills.

The Duration Index has six levels: (1) more than five years, (2) one to five years, (3) six months to one year, (4) one to six months, (5) two to four weeks, and (6) two weeks or less.

## Coping Index

The Coping Index is used only on Factor I because external problems recorded on Factor II are generally beyond the coping ability of a single client. This indicator identifies the degree of the client's ability to manage social role functioning problems with his or her own internal resources. The Coping Index records the social worker's judgment of the client's ability to solve problems, capacity to act independently, and his or her ego strength, insight, and intellectual capacity. The practitioner should also assess the client's positive social role functioning. Social work intervention is most needed in situations in which the client lacks adequate coping skills.

The Coping Index has six levels:

1. outstanding coping skills—the client's ability to solve problems; act independently; and to use ego strength, insight, and intellectual ability to cope with difficult situations is exceptional.
2. above-average coping skills—the client's ability to solve problems; act independently; and to use ego strength, insight, and intellectual ability to cope with difficult situations is more than would be expected in the average person.
3. adequate coping skills—the client is able to solve problems; can act independently; and has adequate ego strength, insight, and intellectual ability.
4. somewhat inadequate coping skills—the client has fair problem-solving ability but has major difficulties in solving the presenting problems; acting independently; and using ego strength, insight, or intellectual ability.
5. inadequate coping skills—the client has some ability to solve problems but it is insufficient to solve the presenting problems; the client shows poor ability to act independently; and the client has minimal ego strength, insight, and intellectual ability.
6. no coping skills—the client shows little or no ability to solve problems; lacks the capacity to act independently; and has insufficient ego strength, insight, and intellectual ability.

## General Guidelines in Using Factors I and II

- The statement of a problem should be in terms of the social worker's assessment, not the client's. That is, the social worker should record what he or she perceives as a problem, even if the client would not necessarily agree with that assessment.
- There need not be a problem on each factor.
- It is possible to defer a problem listing.
- If a problem is stated, it should be possible to document it.

- The problem description can be done at various points in the social worker–client interaction (intake, beginning, midpoint, or termination), and the description may change over time.

- The social worker may record as many problems as have been identified on each factor, but because one of the goals of this system is to clarify the focus for social work intervention, emphasis should be on problems that have a significant impact on a client's social functioning. Rarely will a practitioner need to record more than four problems.

- In its present form, this system is to be used only for coding the social functioning problems of adults. An adult is a person age 18 or older or a legally emancipated minor.

- If there is more than one problem on a factor, each one should be noted in order of seriousness according to the worker's judgment.

- The social worker should list only the Factor II problems that affect Factor I problems. The notation of a problem on Factor II does not necessarily point to any maladaptive or socially unacceptable behavior on the part of the client; it could point to a problem in that social system.

- If the social worker is working with more than one person (for example, with a family or a group), a PIE statement should be done on each adult.

## Factor III: Mental Health Problems

After a long debate the developers of PIE decided to include a way of noting the existence of mental disorders, and they determined that the best way to do this would be to use Axis I and Axis II of DSM-IV.

DSM-IV, a five-axis system for recording the mental disorders of clients, was developed by the American Psychiatric Association, and is widely used throughout the world by mental health practitioners of all kinds. There are five axes, or categories of information, recorded in DSM-IV:

Axis I       Clinical Syndromes and Other Conditions that May be a Focus of Clinical Attention
Axis II      Personality Disorders
Axis III     General Medical Conditions
Axis IV      Psychosocial and Environmental Problems
Axis V       Global Assessment of Functioning

Factor III in the PIE system, therefore, is the client's Axis I and Axis II listing from DSM-IV. If the social worker practices in a jurisdiction in which social workers are not legally allowed to make diagnoses using DSM-IV, the social worker should note the source of the DSM-IV diagnosis that he or she has listed. For example, "Adjustment Disorder with Depressed Mood, diagnosed by Dr. X" or

"Post-Traumatic Stress Disorder, from client's records at Y Veterans Hospital."

## Factor IV: Physical Health Problems

Factor IV is equivalent to Axis III on DSM-IV. This factor permits the practitioner to indicate any current physical disorder or condition that is potentially relevant to the understanding or management of the social role or environmental problems of the individual. These are the conditions exclusive of the Mental Disorders Section of the ICD-9-CM (U.S. Department of Health and Human Services, 1991).

Social workers should routinely inquire about any significant physical health problems and record the results of this inquiry on Factor IV, but as professionals who are not licensed to make physical health diagnoses, practitioners should note the source of the information. For example, one might record the results of an intake evaluation noting on Factor IV "diabetes, by report of the client," "asthma, diagnosed by Dr. X," or "client reports no physical problems."

In some instances, the physical condition may be an important source of the client's social role or environmental problems, such as a client who has acquired immune deficiency syndrome (AIDS) and a Lover Role Problem, loss type. In other instances the physical disorder may not be the source of the client's problems but may be important in planning an overall intervention strategy, such as genital herpes in a person with a Spouse Role Problem, ambivalence type. In yet other instances, the practitioner may wish to note significant associated physical findings, such as history of heart attacks in a client with a Worker Role Problem, loss type. The practitioner should refer to ICD-9-CM for further information pertaining to coding on this factor. If ICD-9-CM is unavailable, the practitioner may describe the physical disorder in lay language.

## Sample PIE Statement

When the PIE system is used with a client, the result will be a description of a client based on his or her social functioning problems, environmental problems, mental health problems, and physical health problems.

---

## Case Study

Jean is a 23-year-old single mother of two preschool-age children who visits her local family services agency at the suggestion of a friend who had received help there. She tells the intake social worker that for the past two years she has been worried about her ability to be a good enough parent for her children. In the past Jean has had some problems acting independently as a parent, but she has been able to solve most parenting problems. She loves her children and wants them to have a better life than she had growing up. She does well at her low-paying job in a factory, the only kind of work available in her community for the past three years. When she returns home from work each evening after picking up her children from a friend's house, she is afraid that she "tunes out" her children and becomes inattentive to their needs. Until three weeks ago she was barely able to make ends meet, but now, with an increase in rent, she can't see how she can provide for herself and her children. Rents in her community have escalated dramatically within the past 10 months.

A secondary concern is her relationship with her boyfriend, Mike, who is very much in love with her. For the past three months she has wondered whether or not she wants to continue seeing him. He's nice enough, and she enjoys seeing him, but he's not the "love of her life." She doesn't want to hurt his feelings so she continues to see him.

Jean reports that all of these concerns have made her feel very confused and depressed. She keeps breaking into tears, can't sleep, and barely has enough energy to get through the day. She's thought about taking her own life. She has also noticed that her asthma, which hadn't bothered her for several years, has been getting worse lately.

---

At the end of the intake interview, the social worker describes Jean's situation using PIE.

| | |
|---|---|
| Factor I | Parent Role Problem, responsibility type, moderate severity, one to five years' duration, somewhat inadequate coping skills (presenting problem) |
| | Lover Role Problem, ambivalence type, low severity, one to six months' duration, somewhat inadequate coping skills |
| Factor II | Economic/Basic Needs Problem, insufficient economic resources in community to provide for client and dependents, high severity, one to five years' duration |
| | Economic/Basic Needs Problems, shelter, other shelter problem (unavailability of affordable housing), moderate severity, six months' to one year's duration |

| Factor III | | |
|---|---|---|
| Axis I | 296.22 | Major Depression, single episode, moderate severity |
| Axis II | V71.09 | No diagnosis |

| | |
|---|---|
| Factor IV | Asthma, reported by client |

## Numerical Coding System

The PIE listing, such as the one just developed for Jean, can constitute a complete listing for a client. However, a numerical coding system has been developed for the practitioner who needs to have a
shorthand method of recording the results of the PIE assessment.
There is no need to memorize numerical codes or the structure of
the numerical coding system because each listing in PIE includes a
numerical code.

### Coding Factor I

On Factor I each social role is designated by a four-digit number,
and each type of social role problem has a two-digit code, which is
incorporated into this four-digit number. The first two digits always
designate the social role in which problems are identified. For example, a Parent Role Problem is 11XX.XXX and a Spouse Role Problem is 12XX.XXX. The second two digits always designate the type
of social role problem. For example, a power type problem is
XX10.XXX and an ambivalence type is XX20.XXX.

Each of the levels on the three indexes is designated with a one-
digit code, from 1 to 6. The first digit to the right of the decimal
point (____ .X __) denotes the severity of the problem, the second
digit to the right of the decimal point (____ . _ X _) denotes the duration of the problem, and the third digit to the right of the decimal
point (____ . __ X) denotes the coping ability of the client.

Thus, a social role problem can be written and numerically coded
by combining the social role code and the type of role problem code
with the severity, duration, and coping indexes coding. Exhibit 2 is
an example of this numerical coding.

The code for a deferred problem listing on Factor I is 9999.999
and the code for no problem on Factor I is 0000.000.

### Coding Factor II

In Factor II each environmental problem or condition is designated by a four- or five-digit number. The first digit (X ___ . __),

*Exhibit 2*

**Numerical Coding of a Social Role Problem**

|  | Social Role Problem | Type of Problem | Severity | Duration | Coping |
|---|---|---|---|---|---|
|  | Parent role problem | Power type | High severity | Six months to one year | Inadequate coping skills |
| Numerical code | 1  1 | 1  0 | 4 | 3 | 5 |

or pair of digits for the Affectional Support System problems (XX ___ . __), designate the general social system in which the problem occurs. For example, the designation of an Economic/Basic Needs System Problem is 5XXX.XX and the third digit to the left of the decimal point (_ X __ . __) indicates the subcategory of the social system in which the problem occurs. Thus, 54XX.XX is the designation for an Economic/Basic Needs System, economic resources problem. The first and second digits to the left of the decimal point (__ XX. __) indicate the specific problem within the subcategory. For example, 5401.XX is an Economic/Basic Needs System Problem, economic resources, insufficient economic resources in community to provide for client and dependents. The first digit to the right of the decimal point is for the severity indicator (____ .X _) and the second digit to the right of the decimal point is for the duration indicator (____ . _X). There is no coping ability indicator on Factor II.

Thus, an environmental problem can be written and numerically coded by combining the social system code, subcategory code, and specific problem code with the severity and duration indexes coding (Exhibit 3).

The code for a deferred problem listing on Factor II is 9999.99 and the code for no problem on Factor II is 0000.00.

### Sample PIE Listing Using Numerical Codes

---

## Case Study

A social worker in a psychiatric inpatient unit is assigned to work with June, a 57-year-old woman who has been in and out of the mental health system many times over the past 40 years. June has never been able to survive outside an institutional setting for very long but because of the laws and service cutbacks, it has not been possible to keep her in the hospital for an extended stay. June constantly engages in behavior (in this case, wandering in and out of traffic) that causes her to be rehospitalized. June's problem seems to be very serious, has been going on for 40 years, and she has no coping skills to deal with this problem.

---

This client is having a Special Life Situation Problem (4XXX.XXX) in the Inpatient/Client role (4200.XXX) which appears to be a dependency type (4240.XXX). The client's problem is very severe (4240.5XX), has been going on for more than five years (4240.51X), and the client has no coping skills to deal with this problem (4240.516). Therefore, this client's Factor I problem is written as follows:

Factor I      4240.516      Inpatient/Client Role Problem, dependency type, very high severity, more than five years' duration, no coping skills

*Exhibit 3*

**Numerical Coding of an Environmental Problem**

|  | Social System | Subcategory | Specific Problem | Severity | Duration |
|---|---|---|---|---|---|
|  | Education/ training system | Education and training | Lack of culturally relevant educational or training opportunities | Very high severity | More than five years |
| Numerical code | 6 | 1 | 0   3 | 5 | 1 |

June's problem is increased by the lack of adequate mental health services available in her community outside of an institutional setting. This lack of services is severe and has been going on for 50 years. This client is having a Factor II problem in the Health Safety, and Social Services System (8000.XX), health/mental health subcategory (8100.XX), and the specific problem is absence of adequate mental health services (8105.XX). This problem is of high severity (8105.4X) and has been going on for more than five years (8105.41). This client's Factor II problem is listed as follows:

Factor II      8105.41      Health, Safety, and Social Services System, absence of adequate mental health services, high severity, more than five years' duration

As the result of a mental status examination, it is determined that this client is suffering from chronic paranoid schizophrenia. She does not have a personality or developmental disorder. Therefore, her Factor III would be listed as follows (code numbers for DSM-IV are from the DSM-IV manual):

Factor III
  Axis I      295.32      Schizophrenia, paranoid type, chronic
  Axis II      V71.09      No diagnosis on Axis II

A physical examination reveals that this client has scabies and diabetes. Therefore, this client's Factor IV would appear as follows:

Factor IV                  Diabetes (by Dr. Z)
                           Scabies (by Dr. Z)

A complete multifactorial report on this client follows.

Factor I      4240.516      Inpatient/Client Role Problem, dependency type, very high severity, more than five years' duration, no coping skills

| Factor II | 8105.41 | Health, Safety, and Social Services System, absence of adequate mental health services, high severity, more than five years' duration |

Factor III
| Axis I | 295.32 | Schizophrenia, paranoid type, chronic |
| Axis II | V71.09 | No diagnosis on Axis II |

| Factor IV | | Diabetes (by Dr. Z) |
| | | Scabies (by Dr. Z) |

Now that this client's problems have been described using the PIE system, it is relatively easy to take the optional next step of listing possible interventions for each of her problems.

| **Problem** | **Possible interventions** |
| --- | --- |
| Inpatient role, dependency | Case management, possible hospitalization |
| Absence of adequate services | Advocacy with state legislature |
| Schizophrenia | Case management, medication |
| Diabetes and scabies | Referral to health clinic |

Using this chapter and the *PIE Manual* as guides, the reader is now encouraged to choose a case from his or her own social work practice and attempt to use the system. With each case the social worker will discover that the process of using PIE will become easier, and its use will assist the social worker in clarifying the focus of intervention.

## References

American Psychiatric Association. (1994). *Diagnostic and statistical manual of mental disorders* (4th ed.). Washington, DC: American Psychiatric Press.

U.S. Department of Health and Human Services. (1991). *International classification of diseases–9th revision–clinical modification* (4th ed.). Washington, DC: U.S. Government Printing Office.

Warren, R. (1963). *The community in America*. Chicago: Rand McNally.

# Section II

# Application of PIE in Practice Settings

*This section is intended to help readers gain a perspective on how PIE might be used in a variety of practice settings. The social work profession covers a broad range of human concerns. Since the development of professional social work more than 100 years ago, fields of service have developed in response to social needs or societal problems. Social work specializations developed as knowledge demands became too much for any one person to acquire. For example, the special knowledge and skill needed to work with neglected or abandoned children (child welfare) became considerably different from that needed to work with physically ill people (medical social work), mentally ill people (psychiatric or clinical social work), people with learning problems (school social work), the provision of money and material resources (public welfare), or family problems (family services). Specialization led to the recognition of seven common fields of practice: (1) family and children's services, (2) physical health, (3) mental health, (4) occupational social work, (5) aging, (6) education, and (7) corrections. Although each field has its own body of knowledge, each has in common social work's central concern of social functioning. The authors in this section provide some history of the evolution of their specific field; they describe the special problems they deal with in their settings*

*and comment on the use of PIE in addressing
the social functioning problems of their clients
or patients. Although we would have liked to
demonstrate PIE's use in all practice settings,
the sampling presented will give the reader a
sense of how PIE can be used in fields of practice
other than those reported here.*

*Turnbull and Cahalane focus on outpatient
mental health settings. Kestnbaum and Wahl discuss the use of PIE in family services agencies.
Adkins applies PIE to medical social work practice. Saxton addresses the use of PIE with employee assistance and managed care programs.
Simmons shows how PIE might be used in public welfare agencies. And Irvin and Penk address
PIE's use with dual diagnosis clients in inpatient psychiatric settings.*

# 3.

# Use of PIE in Outpatient Mental Health Settings

Joanne E. Turnbull and Helen Cahalane

*This chapter presents a brief history of outpatient psychiatric social work treatment. We explore some of the problems in outpatient psychiatric social work's reliance on other diagnostic systems and the use of other assessment tools. We also explore the benefits of PIE to outpatient mental health settings and present a case example.*

Today social workers constitute the largest group of mental health care providers in the United States (Fishman, 1991; Goleman, 1985). In some areas of the country, particularly rural areas, social workers are not only the primary providers, they are the only providers of mental health services (National Center for Social Policy and Practice, 1988). Since the mid-1980s, the number of social workers offering psychotherapy has increased dramatically. Ten years ago an equal number of psychiatrists and social workers offered psychotherapeutic services; today, social workers outnumber psychiatrists two to one (Goleman, 1985). Although social workers are the major providers of therapy in institutional settings, an increasing number of clinical social workers are moving into private practice, working with clients who are more affluent and less severely ill.

## Brief History of Outpatient Psychiatric Treatment in the United States

Social work in outpatient mental health settings is usually synonymous with clinical social work, that is, direct psychosocial practice with clients. The terms *psychiatric social worker* and *clinical social worker* are both used to designate the social worker in outpatient mental health. Both are used interchangeably throughout this chapter. Social work in outpatient mental health settings has strong historical ties with psychiatry and often is practiced in a setting where psychiatry is the host profession.

What we know today as clinical social work began in the public hospitals of the early 20th century. Hospital or medical social work had begun with a distinctive social orientation, with social workers carrying the responsibility for bringing the social viewpoint into the hospital. The marked contrast between the physician's organic, pathology-based focus and the social worker's concern with social factors allowed for significant and distinctive social work roles (Bartlett, 1957).

In 1906, social workers were hired to work with patients with mental problems at three different hospitals and the first aftercare program was established (Bracht, 1978; Cannon, 1952; French, 1940). In 1913, psychiatric social workers were employed at the Johns Hopkins School of Medicine and social workers were routinely employed in mental hospitals in the eastern United States.

Psychiatric social work emerged as a separate professional entity in 1914 with the establishment of the Social Service Department of the Boston Psychopathic Hospital, under the direction of Mary Jarrett. The title of psychiatric social worker was used for the first time and the first training program in psychiatric social work was initiated there (French, 1940). Thus, as it emerged from medical social work, psychiatric social work arose as a new aspect of social work, rather than a new function (French, 1940).

Social work was accepted quickly by psychiatry, in large part because a complementary relationship had developed between the two in the early 20th century. Psychiatry relied on social work for understanding of the personality in the context of environmental situations; social work increasingly relied on psychiatry to provide theory and method about human attitudes and behavior (French, 1940).

Between 1910 and 1920 the social work profession shifted its focus from social to psychological and from environmental to individual. Interest in the inner world of individual experience was stimulated by the influence of psychoanalysis and the establishment of family agencies. The child guidance movement changed the role of clinical social work further (Germain, 1970). For example, in the child guidance movement, direct treatment of the child was provided by the psychiatrist; the clinical social worker took on the role of direct work with parents, teachers, and other family members, albeit under the psychiatrist's direction.

## Shift from Psychosocial to Psychodynamic

In response to the publication of Richmond's (1917) *Social Diagnosis*, Southard and Jarrett argued that the social worker's role should be limited to that of healer or therapist and the individual should replace the family as the unit of social inquiry (Southard & Jarrett, 1922). Southard and Jarrett's departure from the emphasis on environmental issues by rebuttal to Richmond reflects their position in founding the Smith School for Social Work, where the profession's first training course in psychiatric social work was established in 1918.

At this time psychiatric social workers began to leave state hospitals and adult psychiatric clinics to assume direct treatment relationships with individual clients as the influence of psychoanalysis and the child guidance movement grew. In the period following World War II (1945 to 1960), psychiatric social work became the practice of individual psychodynamic psychotherapy, rather than the practice of social casework. With the publication of *Theory and Practice of Social Casework* (Hamilton, 1940), which stressed the "therapy" or "individual" emphasis and reinforced the individual as the unit of attention, the individual emerged as the profession's unit of concern.

This reinforcement of the individual as the unit of concern had a profound influence on professional social work development because both in education and practice psychological issues were emphasized with little attention paid to the social aspects of a client's problem. Clinical social workers began to practice psychotherapy rather than social casework, and social work's unique role faded.

Although now more than 50 years old, some of the themes in these early historical developments are eerily reminiscent of current issues. The profession's awareness of its social change roots was reawakened by the civil rights movement and the discontent of the Vietnam era. The infusion of systems theory into social work practice created a holistic focus. Nonetheless, an individualistic, psychological bias has persisted in social work practice in mental health settings for the past 40 years.

Individual psychological causes are posited for the problems that have been caused by the drastic and sudden reduction of social resources and the concomitant multiplication of social needs in recent years. The long-term focus on individual psychodynamics to the exclusion of the social aspects of practice has left the profession in a difficult position. It places social work in the center of a highly competitive situation, struggling with allied occupations for position in a field that once was social work's alone (Bartlett, 1957; Sussman, 1965). In mental health, advances in medical technology have placed psychiatrists into a more technical, scientific role with a biological emphasis, whereas clinical social workers have tried to maintain preeminence in the psychosocial domain. Because our social roots were buried, clinical social workers today are faced with territorial battles with other professions. Social work cannot afford an outmoded, arbitrary separation of psychological and social issues. It is a profession that thrives on integrating the two. In mental health care, an exclusive psychological bias is obsolete and too narrow in focus for comprehensive care. As the largest group of mental health services providers in the country, clinical social workers are in a unique position to address the social context of clients' problems and to recapture the psychosocial domain of social work practice. To do so, clinical social workers in outpatient mental health settings need an assessment tool that is uniquely theirs and that captures both the social and psychological domains of their practice.

## Problems in Reliance on Other Diagnostic Systems

Clinical social workers in outpatient mental health settings can be distinguished from social workers in other settings by their knowledge and use of instruments that screen for psychiatric problems; rating scales; and diagnostic assessment tools. Without a problem classification system, social workers in outpatient mental health settings are left to address their clients' mental health and physical health problems using other disciplines' diagnostic criteria. For example, most social workers who practice in outpatient mental health settings must rely on the *Diagnostic and Statistical Manual of Mental Disorders, Fourth Edition* (DSM-IV) (American Psychiatric Association, 1994), which provides a psychiatric framework for classifying mental health problems and is required for use in most mental health facilities.

*The Diagnostic and Statistical Manual of Mental Disorders, Third Edition* (DSM-III) (American Psychiatric Association, 1980) provided a multiaxial system for codifying and recording different domains of information for assessment (Williams, 1981). The system included five separate axes, two for recording mental disorders (Axes I and II), one for physical disorders (Axis III), one for severity of psychosocial stressors (Axis IV), and one for overall level of adaptive functioning (Axis V). Although the inclusion of separate axes for psychosocial stressors and functioning in the multiaxial system of DSM-III and its revision DSM-III-R (American Psychiatric Association, 1987) marked the first time information was recorded on separate "social" axes for individuals with psychiatric problems (Axes IV and V), the assessment is limited to two summary ratings. Thus, the system is too narrow to be considered an adequate instrument for assessing environmental problems and problems in psychosocial functioning. DSM-III and DSM-III-R do not identify specific social problems, but rate only the severity of psychosocial stressors. There is no systematic information about the types of problems that exist, the social roles that are affected, the duration of the problem, nor any explicit appraisal of the person's capacity to cope with the problem. These factors are important to consider when planning for social work intervention. In addition, the DSM-III-R multiaxial system does not provide any information about environmental conditions that impinge on a person's functioning.

Because of these shortcomings, DSM-III, DSM-III-R, and the newly published DSM-IV have little to offer practitioners whose primary unit of attention and area of expertise is the adaptive and dysfunctional aspects of social systems. A survey of the American Family Therapy Association revealed that family therapists viewed DSM-III as "overfocusing or even misdirecting attention almost exclusively on the individual-system level" and that DSM-III "inadequately addresses the issue of . . . the relational context of individual disorders and persons" (Wynne, 1987, p. 477). This exclusive focus on the individual-system level may impede the use of intervention approaches that may be more effective because they focus on the functioning of the individual within his or her social roles, and on the relationship of the individual and his or her environment. DSM-III provides no mechanism to report impaired functioning of a person in his or her role as a family member, even if it is the principal reason for visiting a mental health professional (Wynne, 1987).

## Other Assessment Tools in Outpatient Mental Health Settings

In addition to DSM-III, many diagnostic instruments and screening scales are used to assess the severity of mental health problems in outpatient mental health settings, but these tend to focus on symptoms and ignore the dimensions that indicate the dynamic influences of specific mental illnesses. Some general outpatient clinics will use screening instruments such as the Symptom Checklist–90 (SCL–90) (Derogatis, 1977) and the Brief Psychiatric Rating Scale (BPRS) (Overall, 1974) to screen for symptoms of a variety of psychiatric problems. Clinics, that specialize in problems such as depression will use scales such as the Center for Epidemiologic Studies Depression Scale (CES-D) (Radloff, 1977) or the Beck Depression Inventory (BDI) (Beck, Ward, Mendelson, Mock, & Erbaugh, 1961). Other outpatient clinics forego screening tools and use full-blown assessment instruments such as the Diagnostic Interview Schedule (DIS) (Robbins, Helzer, Croughan, & Ratlife, 1981) or the Schedule for Affective Disorders and Schizophrenia (Spitzer & Endicott, 1977). Some clinics use both a screen and a full diagnostic assessment, with clients who score above a predetermined threshold of symptoms on the screen receiving the full assessment.

The reader is referred to chapter 1 for an overview of assessment instruments that have attempted to classify psychosocial problems. These, like DSM-III, fall short of meeting the needs of social workers in outpatient mental health settings. Some instruments have attempted to capture the dimensions that indicate the dynamic influences of specific mental illnesses. For example, researchers have linked social inequality with higher rates of depression in women (Belle, 1982; McGrath, Keita, Strickland, & Russo, 1990), and some rating scales such as the BDI (Beck et al., 1961) attempt to include the influence of the environment. No existing rating scale, however, captures the specific aspects of the interaction between manifest psychopathology or symptoms, and environmental influences, such as seems to exist between gender inequality and depression. None of the existing symptom scales or assessment instruments classify social problems systematically and none are geared toward the type and range of problems in which social workers assess and intervene.

## Limited Scope

Unlike DSM-III these instruments are "setting-specific," which means that the specific scale used in an outpatient mental health setting most often depends on the orientation of the clinic practitioners or is a function of the problem that the clinic or program specializes in, such as depression. Psychologists, for example, often use the Minnesota Multiphasic Personality Inventory (Hathaway & McKinley, 1943). None of the foregoing classifications are used universally by social workers in outpatient mental health settings. Like DSM-III, all are too limited in their coverage of problems and their degree of specificity to address the range and complexity of social problems that are dealt with by social workers. None of them provide for the recording of problem parameters such as chronicity or the client's ability to cope with the problem.

The use of these scales poses several problems for the practice of clinical social work in outpatient settings. One problem is that the measures contained in these assessment scales do not adequately capture the types of problems presented by clinical social work clients in outpatient mental health settings. For example, the CES-D is the most widely used screen for depression in community and primary care settings. Research has shown that community subjects who score in the mid–20s on the CES-D have a 60 percent chance of meeting criteria for major depression according to the DIS (Schulberg et al., 1985), and that the CES-D has an acceptable level of agreement with DSM-III diagnoses of major depressive episode based on the DIS (Zich, Attkisson, & Greenfield, 1990). What is uncertain, however, is how well these screening instruments perform with different ethnic or age groups. It may be that other instruments, such as the BDI, perform comparably to the CES-D as a screen and have superior performance in ethnic populations (Golding & Aneshensel, 1989; Guarnaccia, Angel, & Worobey, 1989; Manson, Ackerson, Dick, & Baron, 1990; Roberts, Rhoades, & Vernon, 1990; Roberts, Vernon, & Rhoades, 1989) and in younger populations (Roberts, Lewinsohn, & Seeley, 1991). Because so little is known about the validity of diagnostic instruments in ethnic and disadvantaged populations, social work practitioners cannot be certain that these symptom scales are valid for their clients. Moreover, social workers in outpatient mental health settings who rely solely on symptom-based instruments for assessment will not be assessing the full range of client needs, and therefore will not be in the best position to provide quality services to their clients.

## Benefits of PIE to Outpatient Mental Health Settings

From a social work perspective, existing scales are constrained by their focus on symptoms or personality and do not capture those aspects of client assessment that are the distinctive domain of social work. Social work's unique contribution to the assessment of clients with mental health problems in outpatient mental health settings is the assessment of environmental needs and person-in-environment functioning. This critical aspect of the clinical social worker's role in outpatient mental health settings, coupled with the presence of clinical social workers as primary providers of mental health services, mandates the classification of the social and environmental problems that address the primary focus of the social work profession. The person-in-environment (PIE) system has been developed to systematically identify the problems that are the focus of social work interventions.

For example, it is well recognized that problems related to housing, finances, leisure time, employment, health, transportation, family integration and support, and securing needed services are stressors that can eventually manifest in psychiatric crises, especially in people who are severely mentally ill, and are obstacles to smooth reintegration into the community (Clare & Corney, 1982; Goldstein, 1987; Syme, 1992; Westermeyer, 1988). Furthermore, social role and environmental problems are especially significant in people who are severely mentally ill. These problems require effective interventions and case management techniques to improve the quality of the individual's life and to reduce the costs of long-term care to society (National Institute of Mental Health, 1991). To develop these interventions, there must be reliable and valid definitions of the problems these interventions are trying to address.

## Lack of Standardization

Because standardized social work assessments are not in place in outpatient mental health settings, most social workers report the results of assessment or intake evaluations in lengthy narratives. These inefficient forms of reporting vary from agency to agency and worker to worker in format, focus, and language. Such inefficiency results in a lack of comparability across settings and creates problems in data analysis for researchers and administrators. More significantly, because of the lack of a standardized reporting format, some social work evaluations are less focused than they should be. A less-focused evaluation may result in a less-focused and therefore less-effective intervention strategy.

## Lack of Balance in Assessment Tools

Interventions that are based solely on assessment of symptoms and deficits in functioning tend to result in treatment interventions that emphasize medication, particularly in outpatient mental health settings in which medication is usually administered by psychiatrists. Although medications are often needed to ameliorate symptoms of mental disorders, these interventions often diminish the importance

of psychosocial issues. The fact is that environment profoundly influences the expression of many psychiatric disorders, even those
with a physical basis.

By virtue of their training in the psychosocial perspective, clinical
social workers are particularly well equipped to help individuals
deal with the psychosocial aspects of psychiatric disorders and mental health problems. Social workers can educate clients about the
social factors related to their disorders, present options and alternatives for treatment, and offer guidance regarding adaptive strategies
for optimal social functioning.

## PIE as a Logical Next Step for
## Outpatient Psychiatric Clinics

Given social work's long-standing understanding of the importance
of psychosocial factors, an opportunity exists to develop a clearly
defined role for clinical social workers in outpatient mental health
settings by using the PIE system. PIE can help clinical social workers in mental health settings develop skills in assessing the environmental issues and social role problems experienced by people
with psychiatric disorders. It offers clinical social workers in outpatient mental health settings an opportunity to claim a unique
position among the helping professions in ameliorating mental
disorders.

The PIE system uses the common core of concepts that consti-
tutes the social work profession's focus on the linkages and interactions between people and resource systems, between individuals
and society (Pincus & Minahan, 1973). The focus of social work, particularly in psychiatric settings, is the person-in-environment perspective. In addition to the traditional psychiatric evaluation, PIE
identifies a client's social functioning and environmental problems
and strengths and provides credibility for the social work profession. PIE emphasizes strengths and capabilities in a medical system
in which disease and dysfunction have been focal points. With PIE
as a tool, social workers can take a lead in the outpatient mental
health field by pointing out that it is not just symptoms that matter,
but role functioning and environment as well.

Recent managed care initiatives heighten the need for a comprehensive description, classification, and codification system. In a
health care environment fraught with increased restrictions, limitations, and monitoring of services, social workers will be faced with
tough choices in resource allocation. In times of scarce resources, difficult and painful decisions will be made about who receives services and who does not. It is crucial to develop measures to use in
making these determinations. Outcome and functioning appraisals
will be paramount as the health care system struggles with upcom-
ing changes. The PIE system provides social work with a multipur-
pose assessment tool that captures the dimensions of the client's

problems that can be used in making decisions about resource allocation.

Perhaps it is time to challenge clinical social work behavior in outpatient mental health settings. As clinicians, social workers in outpatient mental health settings have tended to focus on pathology, often to the exclusion of the social realities that complicate clients' lives. Social workers often give up their identity as they move into the outpatient arena, preferring to call themselves clinicians or therapists instead of social workers. Because of this tendency to identify themselves as therapists, other social workers accuse clinical social workers in outpatient mental health settings of selling out their social work identity.

The reality is that social workers do not have to make a choice between psychiatry and social work. PIE blends the two disciplines of social work and psychiatry in a way that not only mental disorders but problems in social functioning and in the client's environment can be addressed.

The following example shows how PIE can be used by clinical social workers in outpatient mental health settings.

## Case Study

Joyce, a 30-year-old single mother of three children, has been employed for three years as a secretary in a large urban bank. She was referred to her local community mental health center by the employee assistance counselor at the bank after her supervisor complained of Joyce's absenteeism, mistakes on the job, and irritability with customers and coworkers. In addition, Joyce appeared to be preoccupied, was frequently tearful, and often interrupted her work with personal phone calls. These behaviors had been noticeable for four months.

A psychiatric evaluation revealed that Joyce had experienced an episode of depression during her early twenties and that she had sporadic thoughts of suicide. Her mother had struggled with bouts of depression throughout Joyce's childhood. Relevant social information indicated that Joyce had no ongoing relationship with the father of her two oldest children, and an on-again, off-again involvement with the married father of her youngest child. She lived in an area of the city where crime and violence had increased in recent years and where gang activity seemed to be on the rise. Joyce had few friends and avoided involvement with her neighbors.

Joyce lacked affordable and stable child care and she frequently relied upon her mother to care for her children. This caused conflict between Joyce and her mother, especially regarding which of them maintained better control of the children. Joyce's oldest son, age 14, was beginning to skip school and travel with a rough crowd. At work, Joyce was becoming increasingly uneasy around her boss who criticized her performance and made vague comments regarding her single parenthood.

## Conventional Assessment

Joyce's case can be analyzed in two different ways, each affecting
the strategy for assessment and treatment. In the first method, a
traditional psychiatric approach would focus on the presence of a recurrent depressive episode with suicidal features. An astute diagnos-
tician would note the presence of a family history of affective illness
and might question Joyce about her mother's symptoms and past
treatment. If Joyce's mother had responded to a particular antidepressant, it is possible that a trial of the same medication might be
initiated with Joyce. A social worker who was sophisticated in the
biological aspects of psychiatric illness might explore the possibility
of psychopathology in Joyce's children. Adjunctive supportive psychotherapy might focus on Joyce's relationship with her mother and
children, with the expectation that Joyce's work-related problems
would improve as her depression lifted. A cognitive approach
would emphasize Joyce's self-perceptions and her possible distor-
tion of interactions on the job. Exhibit 1 presents Joyce's case using
DSM-III-R.

## PIE Assessment

Use of the PIE system expands the assessment and intervention options for Joyce. In the social role domain, Joyce is experiencing problems with parenting, as well as problems in other interpersonal
relationships (mother, employer, neighbor, lover). As a parent, Joyce
is struggling with the responsibilities of being a full-time single
mother to children who range in age from a toddler to early adolescence. As a lover, Joyce is distressed by her conflictual feelings toward her married boyfriend and is ambivalent about staying in a
no-win relationship. She is having difficulties with her mother regarding child care. In her community, Joyce is fearful of her neighbors and avoids participation in local activities. At work, Joyce is
experiencing harassment by her boss. She feels powerless to confront the hostile working atmosphere because she cannot afford to
lose her job.

*Exhibit 1*

**DSM-III-R Analysis of Joyce**

| Assessment Findings | | Recommended Interventions |
|---|---|---|
| Axis I | | |
| 2196.32 | Major Depression, moderate | Medication, individual psychotherapy |
| Axis II | | |
| V71.09 | No diagnosis | |

Environmental factors identified by using the PIE system point to barriers in resources, which compound Joyce's current stress. There are no services, formal or informal, that address the violence and crime in Joyce's neighborhood. The increase in gang-related activity raises significant safety issues for Joyce and her family, and her son is a prime candidate for gang affiliation. The absence of adequate and reliable child care presents another problem for Joyce, placing her in a position of having to rely on her mother and necessitating frequent calls during work hours to confirm arrangements for her children. At work, Joyce's potential for emotional support is hindered by prejudicial attitudes regarding her lifestyle.

Exhibit 2 presents Joyce's case using PIE. The PIE assessment, which enhances rather than competes with a traditional psychiatric evaluation, provides a broad view of Joyce's problems and strengths and a comprehensive analysis of the biological, social, and environmental factors that affect Joyce at the present time. This comprehensive list suggests to the worker points of entry at which interventions can begin. Clearly a major precipitant in Joyce's depression is her sense of helplessness, and a clear delineation of problems is the first step to empowerment. In addition, this list of community problems, overwhelming to any one person or agency, by virtue of being compiled with others, gives a clearer picture of problems that need addressing in the community and documented ammunition for those in the front lines of social change.

## Discussion

PIE represents an important tool for identifying and classifying the problems presented by clients of clinical social workers in outpatient mental health settings. Social workers have generally used other classification systems that have inhibited critical thinking about problems that are the specific domain of social work. The need for a standard classification of psychosocial variables was acknowledged as early as 1964 (Bahn, 1964), but development of such a system was unsuccessful until PIE. PIE is a comprehensive system for classifying social functioning problems that when fully developed will match the increasingly sophisticated nomenclatures in medicine and psychiatry.

The PIE system of classifying social functioning problems accomplishes at least three purposes in the outpatient mental health setting. First, it provides a common nomenclature for social work practitioners for describing the problems of their clients. Second, it provides a coding system, which will facilitate research on the effectiveness of social work practice and might eventually be useful for third-party reimbursement. Third, PIE will provide a system for gathering prevalence data that can be used by researchers and administrators in needs assessment studies.

*Exhibit 2*
## PIE Analysis of Joyce

| Assessment Findings | | Recommended Interventions |
| --- | --- | --- |
| **Factor I** | | |
| 1130.344 | Parent Role Problem, responsibility type, moderate severity, one to six months' duration, somewhat inadequate coping capacity | Parent management skill training<br>Single parents group therapy<br>Parent support group<br>Psychoeducation<br>Referral to youth program for son |
| 1310.324 | Child Role Problem, power type, moderate severity, one to five years' duration, somewhat inadequate coping capacity | Conjoint counseling |
| 2120.344 | Lover Role Problem, ambivalence type, moderate severity, one to six months' duration, somewhat inadequate coping capacity | Individual therapy |
| 2360.344 | Neighbor Role Problem, isolation type, moderate severity, one to six months' duration, somewhat inadequate coping capacity | Individual therapy |
| 3170.444 | Worker–Paid Economy Problem, victimization type, high severity, one to six months' duration, somewhat inadequate coping capacity | Assertiveness training<br>Referral to employee assistance program |
| **Factor II** | | |
| 8201.42 | Health, Safety, and Social Services System, violence or crime in neighborhood, high severity, one to five years' duration | Referral to agencies in the area that develop neighborhood block and community action groups |
| 8301.32 | Health, Safety and Social Services System, absence of adequate social services (child care), moderate severity, one to five years' duration | Referral to child care developers in the community |
| 10206.32 | Affectional Support System, lifestyle discrimination, moderate severity, one to five years' duration | Locate or develop women's self-help support group |
| **Factor III** | | |
| Axis I | | |
| 296.32 | Major Depression, recurrent, moderate | Individual psychotherapy<br>Medication |
| Axis II | | |
| V71.09 | No diagnosis | |
| **Factor IV** | | |
| | No problem (by client report) | |

## Conclusion

The need for a classification of problems for clients of social workers in outpatient mental health settings is compelling. With the increasing influence and demands of managed care, all health professionals are being challenged to document the problems they treat and the specific treatments or approaches they use (Eddy, 1990) to contain health care costs and to ensure that treatment is both necessary and appropriate (McIntyre & Talbott, 1990). These challenges will be especially pertinent to outpatient mental health settings as costly inpatient hospitalizations decrease and more care is rendered in outpatient settings, such as partial hospitalization programs and ambulatory clinics. Practice guidelines have already been published in medicine, government, and other agencies (McIntyre & Talbott, 1990). PIE offers the criteria that are essential for defining and classifying the problems social workers deal with and are essential for the development of social work practice guidelines.

Although social workers provide the bulk of the services in outpatient mental health settings and they have a unique perspective on the environment, they have often borrowed and modified their approach and outlook from leaders in psychiatry rather than social work. Psychiatric social workers have been followers, not leaders, despite the breadth of their experience and the depth of their convictions. We must bring prominence to what we do and credibility to the profession. PIE brings us back into focus and clarifies the areas of intervention germane to social work: social role and the environment.

## References

American Psychiatric Association. (1980). *Diagnostic and statistical manual of mental disorders* (3rd. ed.). Washington, DC: American Psychiatric Press.

American Psychiatric Association. (1987). *Diagnostic and statistical manual of mental disorders* (3rd ed., rev.). Washington, DC: American Psychiatric Press.

American Psychiatric Association (1994). *Diagnostic and statistical manual of mental disorders* (4th ed.). Washington, DC: American Psychiatric Press.

Bahn, A. K. (1964). *Guidelines for classification of the psychosocial disorders.* Paper presented at the American Orthopsychiatric Association meeting, Chicago.

Bartlett, H. M. (1957). *Fifty years of social work in the medical setting: Past significance/future outlook.* New York: National Association of Social Workers.

Beck, A. T., Ward, C. H., Mendelson, M., Mock, J., & Erbaugh, J. (1961). An inventory for measuring depression. *Archives of General Psychiatry, 4,* 561–571.

Belle, D. (1982). *Lives in stress: Women and depression.* Beverly Hills, CA: Sage Publications.

Bracht, N. F. (1978). *Social work in health care: A guide to professional practice.* New York: Haworth Press.

Cannon, I. M. (1952). *On the social frontier of medicine: Pioneering in medical social service*. Cambridge, MA: Harvard University Press.

Clare, A. W., & Corney, R. H. (Eds.). (1982). *Social work and primary health care*. London: Academic Press.

Derogatis, L. R. (1977). *The SCL–90 manual I: Scoring, administration, and procedures for the SCL–90*. Baltimore: Johns Hopkins University School of Medicine, Clinical Psychometrics Unit.

Eddy, D. M. (1990). Practice policies: Where do they come from? *Journal of the American Medical Association, 263,* 1265–1275.

Fishman, K. D. (1991). Therapy for children. *Atlantic Monthly, 267*(6), 47–81.

French, L. M. (1940). *Psychiatric social work*. New York: Commonwealth Fund.

Germain, C. (1970). Casework and science: A historical encounter. In R. W. Roberts & R. H. Nee (Eds.), *Theories of social casework*. Chicago: University of Chicago Press.

Golding, J. M., & Aneshensel, C. S. (1989). Factor structure of the Center for Epidemiologic Studies Depression Scale among Mexican Americans and non-Hispanic whites. *Psychological Assessment, 1,* 163–168.

Goldstein, M. J. (1987). Psychosocial issues. *Schizophrenia Bulletin, 13,* 157–171.

Goleman, D. (1985, April 30). Social workers vault into a leading role in psychotherapy. *New York Times,* p. C–1.

Guarnaccia, P. J., Angel, R., & Worobey, J. L. (1989). The factor structure of the CES-D in the Hispanic health and nutrition examination survey: The influences of ethnicity, gender and language. *Social Science and Medicine, 29,* 85–94.

Hamilton, G. (1940). *Theory and practice of social casework*. New York: Columbia University Press.

Hathaway, S. R., & McKinley, J. C. (1943). *Manual for the MMPI*. New York: Psychological Corporation.

Manson, S. M., Ackerson, L. M., Dick, R. W., & Baron, A. E. (1990). Depressive symptoms among American Indian adolescents: Psychometric characteristics of the Center for Epidemiologic Studies Depression Scale. *Psychological Assessment, 2,* 231–237.

McGrath, E., Keita, G. P., Strickland, B. R., & Russo, N. F. (1990). *Women and depression: Risk factors and treatment issues*. Washington, DC: American Psychological Association.

McIntyre, J. S., & Talbott, J. A. (1990). Developing practice parameters. *Hospital and Community Psychiatry, 41,* 1103–1105.

National Center for Social Policy and Practice. (1988, July). *Preliminary report of the geographic distribution of mental health providers (a pilot study)*. Washington, DC: Author.

National Institute of Mental Health. (1991). *Caring for people with severe mental disorders: A national plan of research to improve services*. Washington, DC: U.S. Government Printing Office.

Overall, J. E. (1974). The Brief Psychiatric Rating Scale in psychopharmacology research. In P. Pichot & R. Oliver-Martin (Eds.), *Psychological measurements in psychopharmocology: Modern problems in pharmocopsychiatry* (pp. 67–78). New York: Karger.

Pincus, A., & Minahan, A. (1973). *Social work practice: Model and method*. Itasca, IL: F. E. Peacock.

Radloff, L. (1977). The CES-D Scale: A self-report depression scale for research in the general population. *Applied Psychological Measurement, 1,* 385–401.

Richmond, M. (1917). *Social diagnosis*. New York: Russell Sage Foundation.

Robbins, L. N., Helzer, J. E., Croughan, J., & Ratlife, K. F. (1981). National Institute of Mental Health Diagnostic Interview Schedule: Its history, characteristics, and validity. *Archives of General Psychiatry, 38*, 381–389.

Roberts, R. E., Lewinsohn, P. M., & Seeley, J. R. (1991). Screening for adolescent depression: A comparison of depression scales. *Journal of the American Academy of Child and Adolescent Psychiatry, 30*, 58–66.

Roberts, R. E., Rhoades, H. M., & Vernon, S. W. (1990). Using the CES-D Scale to screen for depression and anxiety: Effects of language and ethnic status. *Psychiatry Research, 31*, 69–83.

Roberts, R. E., Vernon, S. W., & Rhoades, H. M. (1989). Effects of language and ethnic status on reliability and validity of the Center for Epidemiologic Studies Depression Scale with psychiatric patients. *Journal of Nervous and Mental Disease, 177*, 581–592.

Schulberg, H. C., Saul, M., McClelland, M., Ganguli, M., Christy, W., & Frank, R. (1985). Assessment of depression in primary medical and psychiatric practices. *Archives of General Psychiatry, 42*, 1164–1170.

Southard, E. E., & Jarrett, M. C. (1922). *The kingdom of evils*. New York: Macmillan.

Spitzer, R. L., & Endicott, J. (1977). *Schedule for affective disorders and schizophrenia: Life-time version (SADS-L)* (3rd ed.). New York: New York State Psychiatric Association.

Sussman, M. B. (1965). *Sociology and rehabilitation*. Washington, DC: American Sociological Association.

Syme, S. L. (1992). Social determinants of disease. In J. M. Last & R. B. Wallace (Eds.), *Public health and preventive medicine* (13th ed., pp. 687–700). Norwalk, CT: Appleton & Lang.

Westermeyer, J. (1988). Resuming social approaches to psychiatric disorder: A critical contemporary need. *Journal of Nervous and Mental Disease, 176*, 703–706.

Williams, J.B.W. (1981). DSM-III: A comprehensive approach to diagnosis. *Social Work, 26*, 101–106.

Wynne, L. C. (1987). A preliminary proposal for strengthening the multiaxial approach of DSM-III. In G. Tischler (Ed.), *Diagnosis and classification in psychiatry: A critical appraisal of DSM-III* (pp. 477–488). New Rochelle, NY: Cambridge University Press.

Zich, J. M., Attkisson, C. C., & Greenfield, T. K. (1990). Screening for depression in primary care clinics: The CES-D and the BDI. *International Journal of Psychiatry in Medicine, 20*, 259–277.

# 4.

# Applications of the PIE System in Family Services Agencies

Joseph D. Kestnbaum and Maureen K. Wahl

*A brief history of family services agencies in the United States is presented. Problems in relying on DSM in family services agencies are discussed, and the benefits of using PIE are illustrated using a case vignette.*

O ver the years, family services agencies have shifted in form and function from charitable organizations, to providers of psychoanalytically oriented psychotherapy, and more recently to case management, client advocacy, and family and systems work.

The family services movement originated with the charity organization societies of the late 19th century and the relief and aid societies of the early 20th century. These agencies offered relief in the form of food, shelter, clothing, and counseling to individuals and families through home visits by affluent volunteers. The role of government in providing aid was limited at that time. The charity organizations were staffed by workers called friendly visitors who made recommendations to case committees about relief needed by families. Salaried staff replaced the visitors and formal training for family services staff began in the late 19th century. Illustrating the scope of their activities during the 19th century and early 20th century, family services agencies provided disaster relief for the Cincinnati flood, the Chicago fire, and the San Francisco earthquake.

In the 1930s family services agencies took a rather dramatic turn. "With the passage of the Social Security Act in 1935, which placed responsibility for relief upon the federal government, family agencies made a major shift in program emphasis from relief work to family casework, which was oriented to supporting the well-being of families" (Rice, 1990, p. 26).

Because public agencies funded by the government appeared to expand toward meeting needs that family services agencies had previously met, family services agencies began to shift their focus to direct services, psychotherapy, and counseling. It appeared that the government would now meet needs for food, shelter, and clothing. The family services agencies searched for a new role in the human services field.

Family services became what Specht (1990) called the "Church of Individual Reform." Emphasis was placed on personal change. But psychotherapy did not reform society in any noticeable ways. Social problems persisted. Many voices cried out that family services agencies had failed to fulfill their mission.

During the 1960s further changes in perspective and practice took place. Some observers asked why family services agencies were primarily providing individual psychotherapy. A renewed interest in families and family therapy developed. Individuals were viewed in a family context and families were viewed in a community context. New approaches in psychotherapy developed from the work of Minuchin (1974), Haley (1976), and Bowen (1978). The focus and context of family services practice gradually broadened from individuals to families to systems and then to ecosystems.

An important milestone in the development of systematic and well-conceptualized diagnosis was the publication of Richmond's *Social Diagnosis* in 1917. Although it has been accepted since the time of Richmond that the foundation of professional casework is the diagnostic process, this acceptance does not solve the issue of treatment planning. For example, one of the best diagnostic frameworks ever developed, Anna Freud's (1965) metapsychological profile for children, is formulated specifically for children, but it does not provide a family or environmental context on which to plan interventions.

Although there are diagnostic frameworks for working with families, none is universally accepted. Kirk, Siporin, and Kutchins (1989) discussed attempts to classify problems:

> The Family Service Association of America classified casework problems by dividing them into general categories of economic, employment, family relationship, health, social, and environmental problems. Several attempts were made to classify problems in terms of social role dysfunctions of children to help in child welfare placement decisions, for use in casework research, and for family and other life situations. However, these efforts to develop a diagnostic typology failed to provide a comprehensive scheme for practitioners or to facilitate the development of treatment approaches consistent with social work objectives. (p. 298)

Another recent development affecting the mission of family services agencies is the reemergence of case management, in which it is the social worker's job to ensure that the client receives and uses effectively the services necessary to resolve his or her problems. The typical case manager does not necessarily provide these services directly, but rather is knowledgeable about and able to link the client with them. If assessment is the key to a professional helping process and if the goal is to link one's client with needed services, it would be helpful to identify such needed services in a rigorous and organized manner.

## Assessment Problems in Family Services

Many family services agencies today use psychiatry's DSM as an assessment tool. Williams (1981) maintained that "DSM-III-R can serve as a comprehensive educational tool for learning and teaching about psychopathology in general and about mental disorders in particular" (p. 101). Although it seems clear that the *Diagnostic and Statistical Manual of Mental Disorders, Third Edition–Revised* (DSM-III-R) (American Psychiatric Association, 1987) has the potential for being a valuable clinical tool, that potential has not been fulfilled.

Data collected from more than 200 directors of psychiatric residency programs revealed a negative side to DSM-III-R. A majority of respondents indicated that DSM-III-R focused on signs and symptoms so much that it detracted from fully understanding the client's problem. It promoted a cookbook approach to assessment and gave the false impression that our understanding of mental disorders is greater than it is (Williams, Spitzer, & Skodol, 1986). According to a study by Kutchins and Kirk (1988), the four major reasons that DSM-III-R is used are for purposes of insurance reimbursement, agency requirements, Medicaid payment, and legal regulations. These reasons serve mainly nonclinical and nontherapeutic purposes.

It may be that DSM-III-R has considerable potential that has not been fully realized. However, this system was developed and based primarily on a medical model, emphasizing pathology and an intrapsychic focus. It does not, nor was it intended to, reflect family services philosophy and objectives.

A diagnostic approach that focuses on what is inside the individual may well be useful as far as it goes, but this approach also limits the intervention options. The more areas that are identified for potential intervention the more flexibility one has in deciding how, when, and where to intervene.

## PIE as a Logical Next Step for Family Services

Family services need an assessment tool that is oriented toward the social, the environmental, and toward health and wellness. It needs a tool that addresses coping skills and strengths. Family services need a tool that is sensitive to the interaction between the individual and his or her community and its institutions. PIE has the potential for being that tool. PIE provides a framework for identifying service needs and is consistent with social work principles and objectives. PIE is based on a broad ecosystemic context and also incorporates a focus on intrapsychic conflicts.

Family services agencies have a rich tradition that includes a concern and interest in the environmental pressures, deficits, and problems that affect its clients. A case management approach now widely used emphasizes obtaining necessary services from a broad spectrum of services and resources. But we are attempting to use this approach with inadequate tools. We need a closer fit between assessment and treatment planning. The ideal assessment tool should flow logically and easily into the treatment planning process. PIE is designed to be used in this manner (Karls & Wandrei, 1992).

The heritage and values of family services emphasize focusing on the environment, on systems approaches, and on social functioning. PIE provides an important tool that enables family services practitioners to fulfill this heritage in their daily work. Williams, Karls, and Wandrei (1989) described what PIE offers to social workers.

> A classification of problems in social functioning can provide social work practitioners with a common language for communicating about the problems of their clients, with descriptions of these problems that can facilitate identification and intervention, and with a system for gathering prevalence data that can be used in needs assessment studies. (p. 1125)

As many social agencies turn their energies to broader systems issues, PIE offers the potential for developing a systematic gathering of data regarding needs and problems, based upon the experiences of their own clients. Family services agencies are heavily focused on the integration of services, on the provision of case management services based upon a case management philosophy, and in collaborative efforts with other agencies. The PIE system provides a broad range of client data that can be used for providing integrated and comprehensive services.

## Benefits of PIE to Family Services Agencies

Family services agencies in the United States use a wide variety of diagnostic and classification systems, from DSM-III-R, used in programs containing a mental health component, to a self-designed boutique system of assessment. These various approaches work, more or less. So, why should agencies add or incorporate a new system? What can PIE do that is different?

One goal of DSM-III-R is to help clinicians think through how to best help their clients. However, it is not often used in this way. Unfortunately, it is more often perceived as a line on a form that a busy social worker must complete. PIE, on the other hand, because of its focus on problems and strengths, can help clinicians identify areas where change is needed. And these areas of change are in the arena that family services agencies uniquely target: the way people function in relation to others in their community. PIE is a tool that supports and guides clinical analysis and planning. By using PIE, the social worker finds that additional options and avenues for intervention become clear; thinking is expanded, not contracted.

In developing the PIE assessment, the social worker's thinking is channeled toward identifying the problems that are causing difficulties for the client. These identified problems are potential targets for intervention. The system also supports identifying client strengths and capacities, which will be supported and used in working on goals.

The PIE assessment, when conducted with an individual client, yields data that describes the systems and environmental issues confronting the client and gaps in community services that affect that client. When these data are collected for an aggregate of clients, PIE provides a systems view of which services are lacking in a given community. The data generated through PIE provide an overview of community needs and gaps in service and can be used to plan service programs and establish agency and community priorities. This potential is particularly relevant as family services agencies look to agency, government, and private sector collaboration to address difficult problems.

PIE's usefulness in family services agencies can best be illustrated with a case example.

---

## Case Study

Martha applied to the Happydale Family Services Agency after the counselor at her son's school urged her to seek help. Anthony, age 10, recently had yelled and cursed at his teacher when she asked him to stop talking in class. Although this was the first time that Anthony had been in serious trouble, his teacher had observed that his temper often seemed to flare. Martha was eager to get help and said she had considered doing so for some time. She felt that she and her daughter, age 13, also needed help.

Martha had been divorced three years ago. Her ex-husband had recently remarried. Martha was working as a receptionist and barely managing financially. She had recently been placed on probation for poor performance at work. She was under severe stress because of money, her job, the children, housing, and health care.

---

Exploration early in the work with this family revealed other issues and concerns. One major problem was the lack of affordable and accessible child care. This created extra stress and tension for all family members and contributed significantly to their problems. Also, Martha's social isolation was a major issue. Because she was extremely dependent on her children for gratification, Martha was unable to set realistic, age-appropriate expectations for them.

How would one assess Anthony and his family? A diagnostic approach that focused on Anthony would yield certain information. One would note that Anthony has certain ego deficits, that he is angry, that his symptoms involved both emotions and conduct. The social worker could label and code all these things, then do the same for Martha and her problems. The social worker could also describe this family in terms of family structure, boundaries, and so on. All of these efforts would yield potentially useful information.

However, the range of interventions to be considered with this family expands when using PIE. In the assessment process, the social worker attempts to obtain a broad spectrum of information, and he or she inevitably gains richer and fuller appreciation for the myriad issues and pressures confronting the client. The use of the PIE system opens up a wide range of matters for attention, and these are at the nexus of family services skill and genius.

The PIE analysis of Martha (Exhibit 1) indicates the results of a PIE assessment and the possible interventions derived from the assessment of Martha.

*Exhibit 1*

### PIE Analysis of Martha

| Assessment Findings | | Recommended Interventions |
|---|---|---|
| **Factor I** | | |
| 1180.354 | Parent Role Problem, mixed type (power, ambivalence), moderate severity, two to four weeks' duration, somewhat inadequate coping ability | Family therapy<br>Group therapy<br>Individual therapy for child<br>Psychoeducation about adolescent development |
| 1250.324 | Spouse Role Problem, loss type, moderate severity, one to five years' duration, somewhat inadequate coping ability | Individual therapy<br>Divorce group therapy<br>Psychoeducation about separation and life cycle issues |
| 3130.323 | Worker–Paid Economy Problem, responsibility type, moderate severity, one to five years' duration, adequate coping ability | Vocational training<br>Job placement assistance |
| **Factor II** | | |
| 8301.32 | Health, Safety, and Social Services System, social services, absence of adequate social services, moderate severity, one to five years' duration | Assistance locating child care |
| 10102.42 | Affectional Support System, support system inadequate to meet affectional needs of client, high severity, one to five years' duration | Women's group<br>Referral to church |
| **Factor III** | | |
| Axis I<br>  V71.09 | No diagnosis | |
| Axis II<br>  01.60 | Dependent Personality Disorder | Individual psychotherapy<br>Medication |
| **Factor IV** | | |
| | Benign mole (by client report) | Referral to physician |

## Conclusion

PIE is a valuable assessment and classification tool for family services agencies. Currently, these agencies do not have a universally accepted or commonly agreed-upon way to assess persons seeking their help. The history, tradition, and current practice needs of family services agencies mesh extremely well with the PIE system. PIE offers the potential to strengthen practice, both at a client level and a program and systems level.

PIE is a good fit for family services agencies. It offers a rigorous and systematic approach to understanding and providing help to families and is consistent philosophically with the family services approach. PIE meshes well with the integrated ecosystemic approach to treatment generally used in family services agencies. It yields data that can be used in planning interventions for clients as well as for developing and refining programs.

The genius of the social work profession has been its concern for the individual in his or her social context. The struggle for the profession has been how to apply this concern. PIE offers a unique and valuable tool and an opportunity for family service agencies to help people function at their optimal level.

## References

American Psychiatric Association. (1987). *Diagnostic and statistical manual of mental disorders* (3rd ed., rev.). Washington, DC: American Psychiatric Press.

Bowen, M. (1978). *Family therapy in clinical practice.* New York: Jason Aronson.

Freud, A. (1965). *Normality and pathology in childhood.* New York: International University Press.

Haley, J. (1976). *Problem-soving therapy.* San Francisco: Jossey-Bass.

Karls, J., & Wandrei, K. (1992). The person-in-environment system for describing problems of social functioning. *Journal of Case Management, 1,* 90–95.

Kirk, S., Siporin, M., & Kutchins, H. (1989). The prognosis for social work diagnosis. *Social Casework, 70,* 295–304.

Kutchins, H., & Kirk, S. (1988). The business of diagnosis: DSM-III and clinical social work. *Social Work, 33,* 215–220.

Minuchin, S. (1974). *Families and family therapy.* Boston: Harvard University Press.

Rice, R. (1990). Change and continuity in family service. *Families in Society, 71,* 24–31.

Richmond, M. (1917). *Social diagnosis.* New York: Russell Sage Foundation.

Specht, H. (1990). Social work and the popular psychotherapies. *Social Service Review, 64,* 345–357.

Williams, J. (1981). DSM-III: A comprehensive approach to diagnosis. *Social Work, 26,* 101–106.

Williams, J., Karls, J., & Wandrei, K. (1989). The person-in-environment (PIE) system for describing problems of social functioning. *Hospital and Community Psychiatry, 40,* 1125–1127.

Williams, J., Spitzer, R., & Skodol, A. (1986). DSM-III in the training of psychiatric residents and medical students: A national survey. *Journal of
Psychiatric Education, 10*, 75–86.

# 5.

# Use of PIE in a Medical Social Work Setting

Elizabeth A. Adkins

*This chapter presents a brief history of medical social work in the United States. The author describes how social work services are currently provided in medical settings and some current trends in medical social work. PIE's use in medical social work is illustrated with three case vignettes. The author examines how PIE answers Flexner's concern about social work's lack of distinctive knowledge and transmissible technique.*

The medical setting was one of the first places the newly developing profession of social work flourished. In 1905, Richard Cabot, MD, of Massachusetts General Hospital in Boston, asked Ida M. Cannon to form a social work department to help patients make a smooth transition from the hospital to the community. Cabot recognized that gains made in the acute care medical setting are maintained by maximizing independent functioning in the home and community. Cabot also saw that an individual's psychosocial health must be evaluated and, when indicated, improved to ensure his or her continued physical health.

In 1966, the legislation introducing Medicare required that it be a social worker with a master's degree in social work who could organize and direct a hospital social work department. As the number of patients covered by Medicare increased, so did the need for hospital social work departments. Because most people over the age of 65 have at least one chronic medical condition, the need for trained professional social workers to evaluate and assist in developing lifestyle changes increased as well.

At the same time, the American Hospital Association established the Society for Hospital Social Work Directors, a national organization that gave hospital social workers visibility in the health care industry and contributed to the credibility of social work as an integral hospital function. In 1973, through a collaborative effort with the National Association of Social Workers (NASW), the Hospital Accreditation Program of the Joint Commission on the Accreditation of Hospitals (JCAH) added a section on social work services to its accreditation manual (Joint Committee for the Accreditation of Hospitals, 1993).

In 1972, Congress passed the Social Security Amendments (P.L. 92-603), which created the professional standards review organizations (PSROs). This legislation included provisions mandating the establishment of peer review mechanisms and participation in the quality assurance programs of hospitals. Social work's acceptance of these provisions and its active participation in hospitals' efforts to establish professional accountability programs strengthened the profession's credibility and acceptance within the health care community.

In 1978, Congress amended the Social Security Act (Titles II and XVIII, P.L. 95-292) to provide expanded benefits for patients with end-stage renal disease. To qualify for funding under this program, hospitals were required to employ master's-level social workers to treat these patients. This was the first federally sponsored health program to require master's-level social workers.

Beginning in the late 1960s, social work licensing and certification legislation was enacted in states; 20 years later, all jurisdictions in the United States have legislation regulating the practice of social workers, and most states have licensing laws.

In 1984, the Deficit Reduction Act (P.L. 98-369) established a prospective pricing system for Medicare, the diagnosis related group (DRG), which determined the amount Medicare would pay for hospitalization for a particular diagnosis regardless of the actual cost or length of stay. Because the DRG system emphasizes outcome, hospital social workers have become particularly valuable in helping health care organizations achieve their goals of shorter stays and improved continuity of care.

## Settings for Medical Social Work Practice

Medical social work is practiced in a variety of settings:

- general and specialized acute-care hospitals and medical centers
- psychiatric hospitals
- rehabilitation centers
- long-term care facilities, such as skilled-nursing facilities, hospices, and adult day care programs
- primary care settings, such as health maintenance organizations (HMOs), urgent care centers, and physicians' offices
- home health care programs.

Medical settings are different from other social work settings in a number of ways. For instance, acute care facilities are open 24 hours a day, seven days a week. Social workers in these facilities may be present or on call at all times.

Health care institutions often set schedules, plan activities, and provide services with their own needs taking precedence over their patients' needs. Thus, there is a need for social work services to provide a broader framework for evaluation and planning, a need to help the institution be aware of the community it serves.

Medical settings are "host" settings, that is, individuals do not go to a medical setting because they believe they need social work services. However, many people seeking attention for a medical condition are often suffering from a psychosocial problem such as stress, unemployment, or a family problem, which manifests itself as a somatic symptom. As a result, social workers in medical settings constantly have to "interpret" to both clients and staff the importance of looking beyond the physical problem.

Because of the large number of disciplines employed in a medical setting, "role blurring" or confusion of functions is a common problem. For social workers, this role blurring happens most often with nurses, psychologists, psychiatrists, clergy, financial aid workers, and counselors such as substance abuse and discharge counselors. Thus, social workers must develop congenial working relationships with these other disciplines and at the same time maintain a clear sense of their professional identity and function.

## Description of Social Work in a Medical Setting

Clinical social work in a medical setting is based on established social work principles, and clients' problems viewed as similar, in fundamental ways, to those of clients in other settings. Some of the special considerations that face medical social workers are the need for interdisciplinary collaboration, the use of short-term counseling (in most situations), and familiarity with all aspects of illness and physical disability. As a result of illness or disability, the patient is sometimes unable to identify problems and make plans with a social worker. The patient's primary attachment may be to the physician or nurse. As a result, the social worker may find the client to be the patient's family or significant others. Social workers in medical settings are often associated with discharge planning. The American Hospital Association (1985) defined discharge planning as

> any activity or set of activities which facilitates the transition of the patient from one environment to another. The complexity of discharge plans varies and may be described by four levels of outcome. These are (1) patient and family understanding of the diagnosis, anticipated level of functioning, discharge medications, and anticipated medical follow-up, (2) specialized instruction or training so that the patient or family can provide post-hospital care, (3) coordination of community support systems which enable the patient to return home, and (4) relocation of the patient and coordination of support systems or transfer to another health care facility. (p. 3)

In its broadest sense, discharge planning involves an in-depth assessment of the individual, significant others, personal and environmental resources, physical and mental health status, and other relevant circumstances. Social workers in a medical setting often assist clients who are victims of domestic violence, rape, child abuse, spousal abuse, or elder abuse. They also assist clients who have attempted suicide and clients who have had sudden losses of physical or mental functioning. With these kinds of problems, discharge planning takes on an entirely different dimension than locating a placement facility.

In the medical setting, the social worker must be proficient in

- crisis intervention
- understanding the implications of a wide variety of physical and mental disabilities
- negotiating with other disciplines to devise the most appropriate plan for the patient
- knowledge of community resources
- advocacy skills
- defining the medical social worker's role.

In addition, medical social workers participate in hospital committees, such as biomedical ethics, use review, DRG coordination, quality assurance, and risk management, and in the education of other health care practitioners. They are also involved in the development of new social health programs, such as employee assistance, self-help groups, pain control, and stress reduction.

## Trends in Social Work in Medical Settings

A number of issues will affect the future of social work in medical settings. Advances in medical technology allow medicine to save the lives of individuals who previously would have died, such as those with spinal cord injuries, premature infants, and elderly people with acute or chronic conditions.

Consumerism has become an important factor in the provision of health care. People see themselves as entitled consumers of health care services rather than passive patients receiving those services deemed appropriate by a variety of health care providers.

Health care organizations have become increasingly competitive and cost conscious. With the emphasis on shortened length of hospitalization, hospitals have concentrated on both established and innovative practices from the business community, such as expanding the markets for products and services (substance abuse units, eating disorder clinics, and health promotion activities), vertical diversification (home care, nursing homes, and rehabilitation facilities), and cost containment efforts (centralized control and volume purchasing for lower unit prices).

All of these forces have resulted in a health care system that satisfies no one—consumers believe care is often unavailable or impersonal, physicians believe it is intrusive, and policymakers believe it is too expensive. It is therefore inevitable that consumers, providers, and policymakers will be discussing fundamental changes in the provision of health care services. Although enactment of health care reform legislation remains questionable, it is clear that the 1990s will move in a very different direction in providing health care. As a result, social workers will again have to build a base for themselves within the context of the health care establishment. It is possible that those social workers who have been based in an acute care setting may gradually be relocated within ambulatory care settings where they will concentrate on prevention of illness and injury rather than on intervention after the fact. The focus would shift from picking up the pieces after the fact to maintaining the integrity of the individual, group, or community before the fact.

## Use of PIE in Medical Settings

The PIE system is used much the same in a medical setting as in any other setting, except that Factor IV, Physical Health Problems, usually assumes greater importance in assessment and planning. This difference requires that the practitioner has a good working knowledge about the physical disorders that affect the client. A practitioner employed in a health care setting will probably be familiar with a wide range of physical disorders and their consequences or have access to other health care providers (physicians, nurses, physical or occupational therapists, among others) who can easily furnish enough medical information for the social worker's purposes.

Description of the client and his or her problem proceeds most easily if the practitioner moves systematically from Factor I to Factor II. Factors III and IV may usually be taken in either order; however, it is important to know whether or not any items listed on Factor IV, Physical Health Problems, may be causing an organic mental dysfunction so that Factor III, Mental Health Problems, will be accurately described.

The following is an example of the kind of situation that might arise in an ambulatory care outpatient setting.

---

## Case Study I

Sara was referred by her physician because her daughter, who lives in another state, has expressed concern about Sara's ability to remain in her home alone. Sara is a 79-year-old widow who is seen at the Senior Health Center for Parkinson's disease, mild hypertension, and scoliosis, which causes her considerable pain. She has lived in her home for more than 50 years; however, the neighborhood has been deteriorating over the past few years and Sara is concerned for her safety. In addition, she has increasing difficulty taking care of the house because of her Parkinson's disease. Although Sara has a niece living in the same town and many concerned neighbors, her only child lives in another state and there is no one else to care for her.

When the social worker talked with Sara, she learned that Sara is mentally alert and aware of her diminished abilities. Her social contacts have decreased over the past few years, largely because of "embarrassment" about her increasingly stooped posture and shuffling gait. Sara told the social worker that she used to be quite proud of her posture and was able to move like "a house afire." She also hates having to depend on others for anything and frequently made reference to her reluctance to impose on their busy schedules. Sara also made frequent reference to her fears that she will soon be forced to go to a nursing home, which she equates with rapid physical deterioration and subsequent death. She also fears that "someone will break into the house and rape me in my bed," that she "will fall and no one will find me for days," or that when she goes to a nursing home she "will be left to lie in my own filth and be robbed blind." She talked about her daughter's invitation to come and live with her, but Sara felt that she would be a burden and that she "will probably need to be in nursing home soon anyway." The social worker believes Sara could benefit from in-home care services, but these services were eliminated from the community three months ago because of funding cuts.

## PIE Assessment

On Factor I, Sara is experiencing a Worker Role–Home Problem of a mixed type (dependency and loss), as she lives alone and is experiencing her most immediate problems in relation to the change in her ability to be a capable, self-sufficient individual. The severity of this problem is very high, the duration is from one to five years, and her coping ability is somewhat inadequate.

On Factor II, Sara is experiencing a problem in the Health, Safety, and Social Services System, specifically the absence of adequate social services, because what she needs are in-home care services that no longer exist in her community. This problem is of very high severity and has been going on for one to six months.

Sara is also experiencing a problem in the Health, Safety, and Social Services System (violence or crime in neighborhood), of very high severity, which has been going on from one to five years.

She is also experiencing an Affectional Support System Problem, absence of affectional support system. This problem is moderate in severity and the duration is from one to five years.

Sara has no mental disorders to be recorded on Factor III. On Factor IV, her physician has diagnosed her as having Parkinson's disease, mild hypertension, and scoliosis.

The complete PIE listing on Sara follows:

Factor I      3280.524      Worker Role–Home, mixed type (dependency and loss), very high severity, one to five years' duration, somewhat inadequate coping skills

| Factor II | 8301.54 | Health, Safety, and Social Services System, absence of adequate social services, very high severity, one to six months' duration |
| | 8201.42 | Health, Safety, and Social Services System, violence or crime in neighborhood, high severity, one to five years' duration |
| | 10102.32 | Affectional Support System, absence of adequate affectional support system, moderate severity, one to five years' duration |

| Factor III | | |
| Axis I | V71.09 | No diagnosis |
| Axis II | V71.09 | No diagnosis |

| Factor IV | | Parkinson's disease (by physician) |
| | | Mild hypertension (by physician) |
| | | Scoliosis (by physician) |

---

## Case Study 2

The following is an example of the kind of situation that might arise in an acute care inpatient setting: Robert has been hospitalized for bleeding as a result of severe gastritis, which has been diagnosed as a complication of alcohol use. Until this hospitalization, Robert and his family had not admitted that his drinking was creating either physical or psychological problems for the family.

When the social worker talks with Robert, she learns that he is a 32-year-old Hispanic male who lives with his wife and three children, ages 12, 9, and 2. Robert is currently employed as a law enforcement officer, a job that he feels allows him to contribute substantially to his community. He is particularly proud that he can be a role model to young Hispanic men who might otherwise become involved in gang activity. He is one of the few Hispanic officers on the force and over the past 10 years he reports he has experienced numerous incidents of racist comments directed at him by his fellow officers.

Robert says he began drinking about five years ago as a way of "relieving the stress" caused by his job. At first, this took the form of an occasional "night out with the boys" but has since become a nightly routine in which he drinks "about a six-pack" whether or not he "goes out with the boys." As a result of his drinking, in the past nine months, Robert has had repeated absences from work, has failed to provide adequate "back-up" to a fellow officer, and was accused of using excessive force in the arrest of a juvenile suspected of selling drugs. Last week, he was officially reprimanded and told that he must seek treatment for his drinking and its subsequent job-related problems; his boss has said that he is worried that Robert may be fired if he does not "straighten up." In addition, Robert says that he has become increasingly short-tempered with his wife and children. He hit his wife on several occasions following arguments about his drinking. He is afraid that he may hit his children, and his 12-year-old daughter has told him that she does not like him when he drinks.

The combination of the gastritis, deteriorating job performance, and family problems has made Robert believe that he needs to consider treatment for his "drinking problem." However, he is concerned that his fellow officers and some members of his family may think he is "not a man" because he cannot "hold his booze."

---

On Factor I, Robert is experiencing a Worker Role–Paid Economy Problem, responsibility type, because of the major problems his alcoholism is causing in his job. This problem is of very high severity, has been going on for six months to a year, and his coping ability is somewhat inadequate. An additional Factor I problem for Robert is a Spouse Role Problem, power type, because his conflicts with his wife have escalated to the point of spousal abuse. This problem is of very high severity, has lasted from one to six months, and he has inadequate coping skills to deal with this problem.

On Factor II, Robert is experiencing a problem with discrimination on the basis of ethnicity, color, or language in the Economic/Basic Needs System, because of the racist remarks he has endured. This problem is of high severity and has been going on for more than five years.

On Factor III, Robert has a diagnosis of alcohol dependence on Axis I and no diagnosis on Axis II. On Factor IV, Robert has a diagnosis made by his physician of severe gastritis.

The PIE statement for Robert would appears as follows.

| Factor I | 3130.54 | Worker Role–Paid Economy, responsibility type, very high severity, one to six months' duration, somewhat inadequate coping skills |
| | 1210.545 | Spouse Role Problem, power type, very high severity, one to six months' duration, inadequate coping skills |
| Factor II | 5602.41 | Economic/Basic Needs System, discrimination on the basis of ethnicity, color, or language, high severity, more than five years' duration |
| Factor III | | |
| Axis I | 303.90 | Alcohol Dependency |
| Axis II | V71.09 | No diagnosis |
| Factor IV | | Severe gastritis (by physician) |

## Case Study 3

The following is an example of the kind of situation that might arise in an emergency room setting: Kim is brought to the emergency room by the paramedics for an apparent suicide attempt. She has taken an aspirin overdose.

Kim is a 29-year-old woman who moved here from Korea 10 years ago to marry her husband, a man 15 years older than she. They have two children, ages 9 and 6. Her husband's family owns a liquor store in an African American part of the city where gang activity and other violence occur daily. Kim says that she is expected to work in the store at least 20 to 30 hours per week, including evenings, and that she is frightened, especially after another Korean store owner was assaulted nearby about two months ago. However, her husband is unsympathetic about her concerns and says that everyone must "do their share" so that the family can "get ahead" in the United States. Kim has never felt very comfortable in this country and misses her family in Korea. She does not speak English very well and does not socialize much outside of her church activities. Although her husband's family treats her well, she does not feel close to any of them. She has a few Korean women friends in similar circumstances with whom she feels a sense of camaraderie. She says that despite her husband's unsympathetic attitude toward her fears, he is otherwise a good man and they have a satisfying family life. She says that she does not want to die and that she took so many aspirin because she was experiencing constant severe headaches.

Although some practitioners might argue that Kim's primary Factor I problem is Worker Role–Paid Economy, a more appropriate designation would probably be Immigrant Role–Legal, isolation type. Most of her problems seem to stem from her discomfort living in a foreign country. She misses her family of origin and has not adjusted well in the United States. This problem is of high severity, has been going on for more than five years, and Kim has a somewhat inadequate coping ability.

On Factor II, Kim has a Health, Safety, and Social Services System problem dealing with violence or crime in the neighborhood. The seriousness is very high and the duration is from one to six months.

On Factor III, Kim appears to have an anxiety disorder on Axis I and no problem on Axis II. On Factor IV, Kim has a medical problem of overdose of aspirin.

A PIE statement on Kim would appear as follows:

| | | |
|---|---|---|
| Factor I | 4660.414 | Immigrant Role–Legal, isolation type, high severity, more than five years' duration, somewhat inadequate coping ability |
| Factor II | 8201.54 | Health, Safety, and Social Services System, violence or crime in neighborhood, very high severity, one to six months' duration |

Factor III
   Axis I             Anxiety Disorder
   Axis II   V71.09   No diagnosis

Factor IV              Aspirin overdose (by physician)

## Comments

In 1910 Abraham Flexner conducted a study of medical education. In 1915 he addressed the National Conference on Charities and Corrections on the question: "Is Social Work a Profession?" He applied the same criteria that he had used in his medical study and found that social work, then in its beginning stages of development, could not qualify as a profession. Flexner found five areas in which social work was lacking:

1. basic preparation in the social sciences
2. definite educational and professional qualifications tested under state supervision
3. professional organizations
4. a code of professional practice
5. a body of exclusive and distinctive knowledge and a transmissible professional technique.

Flexner placed his greatest emphasis on the lack of a transmissible professional technique. As a result of this critique, the social work profession may have moved too quickly to affiliate itself with an ideology, psychoanalytic theory, that was only partially compatible with its origins in social action. This affiliation occurred because at the same time that the newly emerging profession was searching for a method of practice, the impact of psychoanalysis was being felt. More than 35 years ago Cohen (1958) raised the question of whether social work, in its haste for professional status, grabbed onto the psychoanalytic methodology, thus closing itself off from its origins in the social sciences. This discussion continues today, even as the profession moves away from its close association with psychoanalytic theory.

Since 1915, Flexner's first four concerns have been decisively addressed. There is no question that preparation for the master of social work degree includes a solid foundation in the social sciences, social workers are licensed in most states, and the National Association of Social Workers (NASW) provides the professional social worker an organization with an enforceable code of ethics.

The area that has remained problematical is that of a body of exclusive and distinctive knowledge and a transmissible professional technique. Since its beginnings, the social work profession has engaged in an ongoing effort to define itself, including its areas of expertise. The public has often had an inaccurate or incomplete picture of social workers and their role. This is also true in medical social work practice settings. Medical social workers find that their areas of expertise overlap with those of nurses, the clergy, and a variety of counselors. Occasionally, medical social workers find that they must confront other members of the health care team because the client wants something that is quite different from the team's recommendations. This means that social workers may have to put themselves in opposition to those with whom they work closely. To be taken seriously, the social worker needs to operate from the position that he or she possesses knowledge and skills on which a judgment or action is based.

The PIE system goes a long way toward demonstrating that the profession does possess a body of exclusive and distinctive knowledge, and to the extent that social workers can demonstrate the validity and usefulness of such a system, they will find that they are accepted as an integral part of the health care team and that their area of professional expertise is considered vital in developing a comprehensive plan for patients and their families and significant others. The use of a practical codified system of diagnosis is a strong indicator of a mature profession.

Although social workers often engage in the assessment and treatment of individuals with an identifiable mental disorder, the profession's body of exclusive and distinctive knowledge is that of assessing and treating persons whose problems exist in the environment in which they live. Sometimes the social worker treats the person and sometimes he or she "treats" the environment. The PIE system can help clarify the problem and provide a framework within which to begin planning.

For social workers who have had experience working with the *Diagnostic and Statistical Manual of Mental Disorders, Fourth Edition* (American Psychiatric Association, 1994), the use of PIE will feel more familiar than for those without such experience. However, the PIE system uses an entirely different means of assigning a code number in Factors I and II, one more congruent with social work practice and principles.

As with learning to tap dance or knit, learning to use a new system is sometimes frustrating and awkward and leaves the beginner feeling clumsy. For those who want to incorporate PIE into their practice, a minimum of a month or two is needed before losing that sense of frustration and awkwardness. During that time, it will probably be necessary to carry the *PIE Manual* so that the system and its recommended use are readily at hand. It is particularly important to be rigorous and exact in the use of the system so that its reliability remains intact across the profession. Regular use of the PIE system, including Factors III and IV, can provide a comprehensive picture of the needs of the client. In situations such as Sara's, where the initial assessment was mixed type, the practitioner can see that he or she must develop a more concise definition of the problem as well as the areas where problems lie.

In a medical setting the PIE system lends itself to a concise formulation of the patient's and his or her significant others' problems. This is important because health care team members will not read long, rambling chart notes, and oftentimes the social worker can provide information others are unaware of that is essential in planning for the patient. As with any social worker, the medical social worker's goal is a plan that meets the expressed wishes and best interests of the client.

Because the PIE system is in its first exposition and will now be used by legions of practitioners in a wide variety of settings, unforeseen situations will certainly arise, causing a revision of the system within a few years. As with any new system as ambitious as this one, that is to be expected and even desired.

Social workers in a medical setting historically have had to fight an uphill battle because they practice in a host setting where role blurring is an inescapable fact of life. These two factors are certainly the most problematic considerations in a medical setting. The PIE system has the ability to facilitate easing the restrictions these limitations pose. Medical social workers should be encouraged to participate in using the system as part of a professionwide effort to standardize and enrich its body of exclusive and distinctive knowledge.

## References

American Hospital Association. (1985). *The role of the social worker in discharge planning*. Chicago: Author.

American Psychiatric Association. (1994). *Diagnostic and statistical manual of mental disorders* (4th ed.). Washington, DC: American Psychiatric Press.

Cohen, N. E. (1958). *Social work in the American tradition*. New York: Holt, Rinehart & Winston.

Deficit Reduction Act of 1984, P.L. 98-369, 98 Stat. 494.

Flexner, A. (1915). *Is social work a profession?* Paper presented at the National Conference on Charities and Corrections.

Joint Committee for the Accreditation of Hospitals. (1993). *Accreditation manual for hospitals, vol. 1: Standards*. Oakbrook Terrace, IL: American Hospital Association.

Social Security Act, P.L. 95-292, 92 Stat. 307–316.

Social Security Amendments of 1972, P.L. 92-603, 86 Stat. 1329.

# 6.

# The Role of PIE in Employee Assistance Programs and Managed Behavioral Health Care

Paul M. Saxton

*Employee assistance programs (EAPs) have provided a significant professional opportunity for social workers since early in the development of the profession, and one that is uniquely suited for application of the PIE system. A review of the history, characteristics, and operations of EAPs illustrates the usefulness of PIE in this setting. The evolution of EAPs into managed behavioral health care organizations and the challenges this raises for the social work orientation of PIE are explored.*

An employee assistance program (EAP) is a service an employer offers to its employees to help alleviate problems that interfere with an employee's job performance. The formal definition of EAPs was established in *Standards*, published by the Employee Assistance Professionals Association (EAPA) in 1990:

> An employee assistance program is a worksite-based program designed to assist in the identification and resolution of productivity problems associated with employees impaired by personal concerns including but not limited to: health, marital, financial, alcohol, drug, legal, emotional, stress, or other personal concerns which may adversely affect employee job performance. (p. 31)

EAP services may be provided internally to the employer organization in the human resources or medical department, or may be contracted to an external provider who serves a number of employers. Similar services are sometimes offered by unions, either internally or externally, and are known as member assistance services. EAPs are usually funded or purchased as prepaid services at a contracted charge per employee per month.

## History of EAPs

The origin of EAPs can be traced to the role of "welfare secretaries" who were employed by corporations near the end of the 19th century. Charged with attending to the family and survival issues that

impinged on worker productivity, these early social workers laid
the groundwork for the occupational social workers of today. With
the rise of unions, which assumed some of these functions in a less
paternalistic way, and as the attention of the profession turned to
other interests, social work involvement in the world of work
tended to lessen until the mid-1930s when social workers were occasionally placed in personnel departments as counselors or case
finders (personal communication with E. Pye, 1982).

In the 1940s and later, corporations assumed an increasing interest in the development of occupational alcoholism programs, often
under the direction of their medical departments and staffed by
self-identified recovering employees. This development culminated
in the 1960s with sponsorship of planning and training endeavors
by the National Institute on Alcohol Abuse and Alcoholism for individuals who formalized the beginnings of the EAP field itself (Bickerton, 1990). Although relatively few social workers were involved
in these developments, social workers in the U.S. Army, originally
trained by the National Institute of Mental Health, focused their attention on enhancing the psychological well-being and productivity
of troops and units throughout the service and demonstrating models of what has come to be known as the EAP.

In the early and mid-1970s, a few visionary and entrepreneurial
social workers from community mental health, private practice, and
industrial bases launched the forerunners of today's EAPs, either as
private companies or as departments in major corporations. Since
the 1980s social workers have been prominent in the EAP field. The
last two presidents and the long-time executive director of the
EAPA were social workers, and the National Association of Social
Workers (NASW) has recognized the field of "occupational social
work" as a major programmatic focus. The prevalence of social
work in the EAP arena lies largely in the congruence between the
underlying perspective, values, and strategies of the social work profession and the EAP setting.

## EAP Operations

Employees and often their family members can usually contact the
EAP on their own initiative when they feel distress that affects the
employee's job performance. Less often, supervisors, managers, or
union representatives may refer the employee on a voluntary or
even involuntary basis as a condition of continued employment.
The EAP staff then engages in a number of processes that are not
unlike those undertaken by social workers in a variety of settings.
The EAPA definition describes these functions:

> The specific core activities of EAPs include (1) expert consultation and
> training to appropriate persons in the identification and resolution of
> job performance issues related to the aforementioned employee per-
> sonal concerns; (2) confidential, appropriate, and timely problem-
> assessment services; (3) referrals for appropriate diagnosis, treatment,
> and assistance; (4) the formulation of linkages between workplace and

community resources that provide such services; and (5) follow-up services for employees who use those services. (EAPA, 1990, p. 31)

Reflecting their traditional view of EAPs as growing out of and still needing to attend primarily to alcohol-related problems, Roman and Blum (1985) offered their classic listing of six EAP core steps:

1. identification of the employee's behavioral problems based on job performance
2. consultation with supervisors, managers, and union stewards on how to take the appropriate steps in using the EAP
3. use of appropriate and constructive confrontation
4. establishment of microlinkages with counseling and other community resources
5. creation and maintenance of macrolinkages between the work organization and community resources
6. maintenance of the program focus on the employee's alcohol problem.

## The PIE System in EAP Operations

The social worker in an EAP setting focuses on behavioral problems as the determinant of intervention. Psychopathology is not mentioned as the criterion; to do so would imply that the existence of such pathology renders employees unable to function productively. If that were the standard, American organizations would be immobilized because much productive work is accomplished by essentially well-functioning people who nonetheless have characteristics that could be labeled as demonstrating psychopathology. Social or role dysfunction is the impetus to seek help in most settings, and EAPs were created to address role performance problems. Thus, the usual psychiatric nomenclature is inappropriate to catalog the distress experienced by EAP clients.

Instead, most EAPs devise their own listing of problem areas for which clients are referred. These lists have little compatibility between organizations and use categories that are seldom tightly constructed or useful with good interrater reliability. In contrast, the PIE system provides a uniform, tested, shared way to describe and categorize precisely the kinds of role and performance dysfunctions that lead clients to seek help from EAPs. PIE thereby facilitates reporting, research, accountability, and time-limited problem-focused interventions for the professional working in an EAP setting.

## Case Study 1

Carlos is a 53-year-old Latino man, referred to the EAP by his supervisor at a large manufacturing company because of his increasing irritability, physical distress, and declining productivity. He reported that a recent physical examination found no medical basis for his continuing stomach pain or headaches.

Carlos denied abuse of alcohol or drugs and reported that his domestic life felt like a haven from the tension he felt at work. Carlos explained with pride that for the past 35 years he had operated a 50-year-old stamping machine that he had "inherited" from its original operator. He enjoyed repairing and nursing this machine, which was central to the functioning of the factory. Recently, however, the plant had been acquired by new owners who incurred substantial debt in the takeover. As a result, they had raised production quotas and substituted less expensive raw materials without the consensus-seeking efforts of the previous administration. Shortly thereafter, the stamping machine began to break down frequently and Carlos could not keep it in service despite heroic efforts. Carlos was almost in tears as he lamented his frustrating and embarrassing failure, explaining that he must be "over the hill." Brief exploration revealed that the machine was not built to handle the new demands and no amount of tinkering would make it do so. With this discussion, Carlos was able to distinguish his personal capabilities from the changed work situation, to begin to defend his performance to his supervisors, enlisting the aid of his union representative, and to place responsibility in its proper place. With this empowerment, Carlos's symptoms subsided in the course of a week, and he reported renewed delight in turning his creative energies and sense of accomplishment to his cactus garden.

---

The *Diagnostic and Statistical Manual of Mental Disorders, Fourth Edition* (DSM-IV) (American Psychiatric Association, 1994) would allow only a client-oriented diagnostic description of Carlos's problem, implying that he is the problem. The PIE system, in contrast, allows the EAP worker to describe the locus of the problem, its nature, and its effect on Carlos. Thus, the PIE statement for Carlos clearly reflects his situation.

| | | |
|---|---|---|
| Factor I | 3130.343 | Worker Role–Paid Economy Problem, responsibility type, moderate severity, one to six months' duration, adequate coping skills |
| Factor II | 5304.44 | Economic/Base Needs System Problem, other employment problem (change in technology), high severity, one to six months' duration |
| Factor III | | |
| Axis I | 309.82 | Adjustment Disorder with physical symptoms |
| Axis II | 799.90 | Diagnosis deferred |
| Factor IV | | Functional stomach and muscle pain (as reported by client) |

PIE clearly displays the nature of the problem and its effects on the client. On Factor II, however, there is room to elaborate the categories to make PIE more precise. First, the kinds of problems or characteristics of the work environment could be amplified to clarify the corporate dynamics or culture the problem is occurring in. Categories such as merger/downsizing, expansion/growth, restrictive discipline and role boundaries, and unclear role boundaries would be useful. EAPs might also find useful a listing of the types of industry, or the types of departmental or functional settings.

By using PIE the EAP staff can report more accurately to their client, the employer, about the problems for which its employees sought help than if they had used traditional diagnostic schemes or the idiosyncratic listings of referral issues that EAPs currently use. When several cases such as Carlos's are aggregated, the EAP has powerful data to use when consulting with the employer about systemic organizational issues that need administrative attention.

---

### Case Study 2

Randy is a 32-year-old Anglo man referred to the EAP by his supervisor because of his erratic attendance, uncooperative attitude toward fellow employees, and substandard production in his food services job. Despite these performance problems, the supervisor did not require Randy to consult the EAP. He did indicate that if Randy did not demonstrate specific improvement, the progressive disciplinary process that ultimately could result in his termination would begin.

At the assessment session, Randy presented himself as distraught, disorganized, and eager for help. He described frustration about his inability to support his wife and newborn son on his marginal income, but was at a loss to imagine how he might seek a better job. He reported his reluctance to ask his parents for assistance although they were quite able to help. Randy credibly denied any substance abuse, but because of his disorganization, seeming depression, tangential and disconnected patterns of speech and thought, the social worker referred him to the psychiatrist associated with the employee health department for further evaluation.

---

This physician diagnosed Randy as having a borderline personality disorder, telling his parents that Randy had a mental age of three, was suited only for sheltered employment, and would require parental supervision for the rest of his life. The EAP social worker was then confronted with a dilemma because the psychiatric diagnosis was correct insofar as it purported to describe the employee's psychopathology. The diagnosis did not, however, account for the fact that Randy had graduated summa cum laude from a university, and had had a self-supporting career as a rock musician for several years, including leadership and management of a band on a cross-continental tour. He had taken his current job to provide some stability for the support of his infant and had opted for independent employment rather than a job in his father's company. Randy's PIE profile takes more into account than psychopathology.

| Factor I | 3130.343 | Work Role–Paid Economy Problem, dependency type, high severity, one to six months' duration, somewhat inadequate coping skills |
|---|---|---|
| Factor II | 5302.41 | Economic/Basic Needs System Problem, underemployment, high severity, more than five years' duration |

Factor III

| Axis I | 300.40 | Dysthymia |
|---|---|---|
| Axis II | 301.83 | Borderline Personality Disorder |

| Factor IV | | Within normal limits (by client report) |
|---|---|---|

This profile suggests substantial problems in the workplace but the problem may be one of fit. Although the employee had significant preexisting problems, the notation of underemployment suggests that those problems do not necessarily reflect his competence or potential. Again, expansion of Factor II might clarify the nature of this lack of congruence. For example, a category such as "employment relevant to skill and training not available in the community" suggests an important characteristic of the social environment that Randy faced.

The social worker referred Randy for psychotherapy with a private practitioner who understood and built on the considerable strengths of Randy's psyche, enabling him to understand and accommodate to the demands of the more regimented workplace in which he found himself so he could accomplish his stated goals. At a six-month follow-up, Randy was still employed and the supervisor reported that his performance was adequate though not stellar. The PIE system allowed the social worker to assess all dimensions of Randy's psychosocial functioning, including his strengths, and to make interventions based on that more complete assessment in a manner consistent with the history and education of the profession.

## Case Study 3

Another case demonstrates both the strength of the PIE system and its limits as a descriptor of functioning rather than as a way to account for the roots of the observed behaviors in the way a classic diagnosis suggests.

Jim is a 45-year-old Caucasian man who has been a coach and administrator at an urban high school for about 20 years. He works and lives in the community where he grew up and experienced his own athletic glory and maintains friendships with his college fraternity brothers and high school teammates. His wife, a teacher, maintains friendships with her college cheerleading partners and the members of her court as homecoming queen. Jim came to the EAP reporting concern about his increasing sullenness and lack of enthusiasm at work, his anger at his teenage sons and his wife, and his increasing use of alcohol. The social worker used PIE to assess Jim's situation.

| Factor I | 3120.523 | Worker Role–Paid Economy Problem, ambivalence type, very high severity, one to five years' duration, adequate coping skills (primary problem) |
| | 1240.424 | Spouse Role Problem, dependency type, high severity, one to five years' duration, somewhat inadequate coping skills |
| | 1110.523 | Parent Role Problem, power type, very high severity, one to five years' duration, adequate coping skills |
| Factor II | 10102.32 | Affectional Support System Problem, support system inadequate to meet affectional needs of client, moderate severity, one to five years' duration |
| | 5304.32 | Economic/Basic Needs System Problem, other employment problem (political and social changes in the workplace), moderate severity, one to five years' duration |
| Factor III | | |
| Axis I | 305.00 | Alcohol Abuse |
| | 300.40 | Dysthymia |
| Axis II | 799.90 | Diagnosis deferred |
| Factor IV | | Within normal limits (as reported by client) |

## Case Study 3 (continued)

Additional assessment revealed that whereas Jim had previously been most successful as a coach and had reveled in his role as a teacher, advocate, and role model for teenagers, the tragedy of contemporary inner-city life made his task impossible now. Fewer than 15 boys out of 300 in his school were academically eligible for sports and were free of drug involvement. Racial politics and the school system's fight for survival rendered his job virtually meaningless to him, yet his commitment to the community and the students made changing to a suburban district unthinkable. Meanwhile, his own sons had reached adolescence and were experiencing the ordinary and appropriate attempts to assert their own autonomy. Jim found himself transferring his hopes for his teams to them and their resistance infuriated him. Because of her sons' increased independence and her own developing professional recognition, Jim's wife was becoming more assertive, experiencing a newly autonomous sense of herself, and experimenting with new ways of relating to Jim that he did not understand. Jim found himself reacting to changes in the behavior and relational style of his wife with confusion, frustration, and a sense of isolation. He found his family and home, previously a refuge and source of pride, to be an alien environment, unresponsive to what he perceived to be his pain and isolation.

Again, specification of the types of strains or changing patterns of gender role dynamics and family interactions in contemporary relationships would make PIE a more powerful descriptive tool.

Explication of these issues with the social worker and a focus on what Jim wanted for himself in these transitions allowed him to discontinue the use of alcohol and to use his professional knowledge and skills to relate in more satisfying ways to his sons. He was unwilling to discuss changes in his relationship with his wife and the implications of those changes for his own sense of self. The social worker referred Jim to an ongoing professionally led group for men exploring gender roles and new styles of coping.

In summary, the PIE system is not only congruent with but facilitates the functions of a social worker in the setting of an employee assistance program. The EAP, with its structural focus on role performance, can benefit from a scheme that focuses the attention of its clinicians on the multiple involvements and dimensions of the lives of the employees it serves. Additionally, the PIE system allows for simplified reporting and evaluation processes in the EAP. These advantages will become increasingly important in the next few years as EAPs come under increasing pressure from two sources. First, the demographics of the U.S. workforce are changing dramatically. More women, people of color, immigrants, and younger and older workers will increase the strain on traditional role definitions and workplace relationships and arrangements. The PIE system offers an effective way to catalog and attend to these issues. With this tool, EAPs can provide better service to the employees they serve and demonstrate that service and its results to the employers who are their clients. The second major challenge to EAPs is the impending change in the organization of the health care delivery system. This change has already begun with the emergence of managed behavioral health care activities, which can overlap, enhance, or intrude on the traditional domain of employee assistance programs.

## Encroachment of Managed Behavioral Health Care

The crisis in the financing and organization of health care is on the front page of newspapers daily. Awareness of the crisis has been growing during the same era of growth in formal employee assistance programs. Although EAPs have grown out of and been identified with personnel or human resources concerns, they have had a significant relationship to medical and health issues as gatekeepers and monitors. The EAPA definition of EAP services and functions (1990) and the listing of EAP core technologies by Roman and Blum (1985) define EAPs as points of entry for clients seeking assistance where they can receive an initial assessment and be directed to appropriate treatment resources. It remains the responsibility of the

EAP staff to follow up on the client after referral to ensure that appropriate treatment was received, and that the client has successfully returned to the workplace. Some writers take great care to distinguish between EAP services and treatment. Others recognize that even one session of assessment and intervention can constitute treatment (Masi, 1993) and have recommended that EAPs move aggressively into offering short-term psychotherapy. This conflict was highlighted in 1987 by the California Department of Corporations, which issued regulations declaring that externally contracted EAPs that offered more than three sessions of assessment and referral services were operating as prepaid health plans subject to the financial and administrative requirements governing health maintenance organizations. To initially comply with these regulations is prohibitively expensive (Cagney, 1987). At the same time, health insurers and payers were noting that the fastest growing segment of costs were those for mental health and chemical dependency treatment. Previously considered a backwater of secondary concern, behavioral health care costs began to be subjected to the kind of scrutiny that medical and surgical costs had endured for a decade. Similar mechanisms were imposed and a new type of organization emerged, designated the behavioral managed care firm, sometimes as an extension of employee assistance programs themselves. To understand the potential for the PIE system in this newer context, a discussion of the similarities and differences between EAPs and managed behavioral health care organizations (MCOs) will be helpful.

MCOs are a natural evolution from progressive EAP functions (Jones, 1988). The clients or customers of MCOs and EAPs are the employers who purchase health care benefits for their employees and their families, who in turn are the consumers of both MCO and EAP services. To ensure accountability for cost control and service quality, MCOs engage in many of the same processes as EAPs, including contracting with a network of institutional and individual providers to offer services at negotiated rates, requiring authorization of services before and during the course of treatment, and actively participating in decisions about the level, focus, and duration of treatment through active case management. MCOs are usually staffed by experienced mental health clinicians, often master's-level social workers, and like EAPs focus intervention on the problems that are of primary concern to the payer client and the employee consumer. Therefore, the focus is usually on the alleviation of some experienced or observed role distress or dysfunction. The term and the level of systemic function labeled "managed care" is to be distinguished from "managed competition." The latter term refers to the reorganization of the ways in which health care will be purchased and paid for as proposed by the Clinton administration, and is in contrast to the current "unmanaged" competition and to the "single payer" plan supported by others, including NASW. Virtually all health care, regardless of payment strategies, will soon be "managed" as the term is used here.

But more important for the relevance of the PIE system are the differences between MCOs and EAPs. Managed care is a function of the health insurance system that pays for medical services rendered in the treatment of illness or individual pathology. In each example above, authorization and treatment for the clients could have been obtained from even the most progressive MCO only through a DSM-IV diagnosis, a medical description. Thus, the power to define issues and procedures passes into an arena that is the purview of physicians. In addition, health insurance in the corporate setting is a function of benefits management rather than of human resources management, and often the defining linkage between the actual worksite and the EAP or MCO assessor is lost.

In this hybrid environment, MCOs have begun to recognize that the traditional psychiatric nomenclature is ill-suited to the kinds of problems and diversity of settings they find themselves dealing with. Some have therefore begun to develop languages or diagnostic schemes that focus on problems in living and functioning. For example, Goodman, Brown, and Deitz (1992) offered the Patient Impairment Profile for use in the "justification for treatment" statement required to obtain authorization of services and reimbursement under managed care plans. This scheme fits with the managed care setting because the locus of dysfunction is placed within the patient, rather than being described as an aspect of his or her transactions with the world. Similarly, Kennedy (1992) developed a set of subscales to Axis V of DSM-III-R that categorize the behavioral dysfunctions that indicate the need for treatment more accurately than a diagnosis alone.

Social workers interested in the expanded use of the PIE system will have a formidable task before them as managed care becomes pervasive in the delivery of health care, including mental health services. But the task is possible. MCOs and health care in general seem to increasingly recognize the medical and cost advantages of focusing on maintaining wellness in contrast to only treating disease. Social workers can demonstrate that their services are cost-effective in a managed care environment (Saxton, 1989), and the PIE system enhances their ability to communicate their expertise. Indeed, in so doing PIE gives social workers a marked advantage over the other professions in demonstrating the efficacy of their expertise. Finally, many administrators and clinicians in managed care organizations are social workers and are both a natural market for and advocates of a system that enables them to better do their job. That job, as it is for all social workers, is ultimately to improve the quality of life of clients. The PIE system is an efficient and effective tool to that end.

## References

American Psychiatric Association. (1994). *Diagnostic and statistical manual of mental disorders* (4th ed.). Washington, DC: American Psychiatric Press.

Bickerton, R. (1990). Employee assistance: A history in progress. *EAP Digest, 11*, 1, 34.

Cagney, T. (1987). Knox–Keene regulation and implications for the future of EAP. *Almacan, 17*, 10, 14–18.

Employee Assistance Professionals Association. (1990). *EAPA Exchange, 20*, 31–37.

Goodman, M., Brown, J., & Deitz, P. (1992). *Managing managed care: A mental health practitioner's survival guide.* Washington, DC: American Psychiatric Press.

Jones, O. (1988). Why insurance carriers are taking an interest in the EAP field. *EAPA Exchange, 18*, 26–28.

Kennedy, J. (1992). *Fundamentals of psychiatric treatment planning.* Washington, DC: American Psychiatric Press.

Masi, D. (1993). Occupational social work today. *Employee Assistance, 5*, 42–44.

Roman, P., & Blum, T. (1985). EAP core technologies revisited. *Almacan, 15*, 8–19.

Saxton, P. (1989). Vendorship for social work: Observations on the maturation of the profession. *Social Work, 33*, 197–201.

# 7.

# Use of the PIE Classification System in Welfare Departments

Mehl L. Simmons

*Social workers practicing in welfare department settings lack a universal classification system for describing behavior, for making recommendations to the judiciary for case disposition, or for prescribing suggested treatment plans. In this chapter the potential for use of PIE in this setting is discussed. Two case examples are used to illustrate PIE's potential in child protective services and adult protective services.*

**M**any of the professionally trained social workers who practice in welfare department settings complain about the lack of a universal classification system for describing behavior, making recommendations to the judiciary for case disposition, and prescribing suggested treatment plans. The *Diagnostic and Statistical Manual of Mental Disorders, Fourth Edition* (DSM-IV) (American Psychiatric Association, 1994), is an excellent tool for professionals working in the mental health field, but no equivalent classification system is available in many of the other settings in which professional social workers are employed. Although DSM-IV has two axes that were designed to eliminate some of the gaps found in its earlier versions, the emphasis is still on individual psychopathology. DSM-IV also lacks the specificity needed to develop a case plan for a typical welfare service case that might include court action or environmental manipulation or both. In the *Diagnostic and Statistical Manual of Mental Disorders, Third Edition–Revised,* (DSM-III-R) (American Psychiatric Association, 1987), Axis IV attempted to measure the severity of psychosocial stressors and Axis V addressed psychological, social, and occupational functioning using measurement on the Global Assessment of Functioning scale. DSM-IV changes Axis IV by adding nine factors of ". . . Psychosocial and Environmental Problems" that may ". . . affect the diagnosis, treatment, and prognosis of *mental disorders*" [italics added] (p. D:4). Although this is a step toward recognizing social factors, the major focus of DSM-IV understandably remains that of the client's mental disease, a focus that is most appropriate for the provision of mental health services and for which the model was designed. Additionally, although the DSM-IV is used to justify reimbursement within the mental health system, no such methodology for reimbursement is required of welfare agencies.

## Welfare Department as a Social Work Setting

Welfare departments across the United States have been assigned the task of protecting both children and adults from victimization. Most states have programs that are generally termed child protective services (CPS) and adult protective services (APS). Professional social workers are often employed in these programs, although frequently the professionals are in the minority, working side-by-side with many employees who lack formal training but are called social workers or caseworkers. Neither the professional nor the paraprofessional protective services workers have a classification system to describe client behavior in any universally understood manner. Most departments have designed bureaucratic models that consist of policies and procedures for processing clients, whether they are victims, perpetrators, or families. Although these procedures may support the departmental and judiciary needs, many workers complain that they do not provide an assessment tool that can measure social as well as personal functioning, lead to a treatment plan for all parties, and clearly communicate disposition recommendations for the custody of children or adults.

The second division in most welfare departments is the income maintenance division. Most lay people think only of the income maintenance or public assistance function of the welfare system when they think of welfare. Unfortunately, little if any social work takes place in most income maintenance sections. In California, for example, state regulations draw a distinction between the duties assigned to eligibility workers and the duties to be performed by social workers, making it clear that the eligibility workers should not do social work.

A brief sketch of how welfare departments have changed in the past several decades might be helpful in understanding how this situation came to be. In the 1968 revisions to the Social Security Act, social services and public assistance were formally separated. Before the revisions, welfare departments used staff often called social workers, but few of whom were trained professionals with a master's degree. These social workers were asked to administer public assistance (financial aid) as well as to provide social services (counseling and casework) to the recipients to enable them to become self-supporting. The assumption underlying the provision of the social services was that anyone on aid must have some problems that social services could remedy. At that time, the prevalent concept of poverty was that poor people could not hold a job because of personal problems. Very little thought was given to the more systemic causes of poverty, wherein most people are needed to work at the peaks of an economic cycle, and fewer are needed to work during the downturns. The revisions to the Social Security Act codified the new assumption that one did not need to have problems, personal or otherwise, to be poor. Hence, one did not necessarily need services just because one was poor.

This change occurred when Americans woke up to discover that the War on Poverty had been lost. While the war was being waged, the clarion call on the lips of many social services administrators was "just give me a social worker for every 60 public assistance cases and we will solve poverty." Social services administrators were not so bold as to actually say this, but that had been the message of the 1961 revisions. When social services and income maintenance were separated, there were too many social workers and too few eligibility workers. The separation was very traumatic to the system and to the social workers, many of whom had to revert to the much lower status and pay of the eligibility technician. The system adjustments were just as disruptive. Very few clients (who were now called recipients) volunteered for social services other than community work and training. The people who became eligibility technicians quickly realized that their jobs were almost entirely clerical and administrative, and any chance of retaining even a modicum of social services provision was summarily eradicated by government regulation. Some of the social workers were transferred to social services positions that already existed within the typical welfare department. Most welfare departments, whether state or county administered, retained a special social services section devoted to the provision of child protective services, usually called foster care. Some departments attempted to retain information and referral sections, along with small adult services divisions, but for the most part, social services for the impoverished aid recipient were eliminated.

At the same time, there was an increased sensitivity to the problem of child abuse. The old foster care sections of welfare departments were significantly upgraded by the implementation of the Child Welfare Act, which authorized the use of social workers instead of probation officers to operate the child protective services system. When Title XX (the social services section of the Social Security Act) money was made available for welfare departments to fund the provision of CPS, most states and counties transferred their abuse prevention effort from the probation department to the welfare department.

## Use of PIE in Welfare Departments

Because 98 percent of eligibility workers' tasks are clerical and these workers frequently carry a caseload that experiences rapid clientele turnover, the helping relationship hallmark of social work simply does not exist. Most eligibility workers have overwhelming caseloads and do not have the luxury of knowing the recipients. Thus, the use of the person-in-environment (PIE) system or any other classification system is, at the present time, irrelevant to the provision of public financial assistance.

There is great need for a universally understood classification system within the social services divisions of welfare departments. The need is especially great when an adult or family receiving protective services moves from one county or state system to another. Today when a case file is transferred, the new worker must start over because the terms used to develop the diagnosis and treatment plan are not comparable from jurisdiction to jurisdiction. Rarely will there be much similarity in the documentation used by the two agencies. Most often the situation is one in which all of the data describing the problems of the adult or family is useless for anything other than anecdotal information. The validity and reliability of descriptive narratives across multiple agencies are low. Clients may actually suffer secondary abuse by the system as a result of ineffective communication.

The profession of social work has not embraced a disease model for describing human problems. It has preferred instead to take a view of human problems that includes the complex interaction of psychological, biological, social, and environmental factors. The PIE system addresses these factors in its approach to assessment. To demonstrate this, two case examples will be presented using the PIE classification system in the welfare setting.

---

## Case Study I

Kathy first became known to the CPS agency when a neighbor complained that Kathy's 10-month-old son was "not being well cared for" much of the time. On further discussion with the complainant it was clarified that the neighbor had noticed that Donny appeared to be very underweight and often crawled around the apartment complex with a dirty diaper or no clothes at all. The neighbor was very worried about the child because "the mother is only a child herself." The caller felt that the mother was unable to care well for the child. The neighbor had volunteered to help Kathy care for the baby and had babysat on some occasions. It was after one of these sessions that Kathy had admitted to the neighbor that she often felt overwhelmed at the prospect of many years of motherhood, because she had never learned how to care for a child.

Kathy later revealed to the CPS worker that her own family had not been stable, and that her mother had been diagnosed as mentally ill and had spent much of Kathy's childhood in an institution. Kathy stated that she had lived with her father and his second wife, but she felt that she was unwanted in that setting. Kathy had gone to school through the second year of high school. She then became involved with a boy in the senior class with whom she fell in love. She became pregnant and the boy wanted to marry her. Within three months of the marriage, Kathy's husband left her and the baby to obtain employment in another state. Kathy's husband later called her and stated that he felt they were just too young to stay married, and he filed for a divorce. So at the age of 17, Kathy found herself divorced with a very young and demanding baby, on the welfare program Aid to Families with Dependent Children, and talking to a CPS worker. Kathy admitted to the worker that she "didn't feel up to taking care of Donny." However, Kathy said she wanted to keep Donny, but needed "a lot of help learning how to be a mother." Kathy was sincere in her desire to raise Donny, even though she also admitted to sometimes feeling "that I had no childhood of my own." She would like to take a parent education class but the only agency in her town providing these classes lost its funding eight months ago.

---

Using the PIE system the worker notes that on Factor I, Parent Role is the primary problem area (11XX.XXX), with the type of problem being that of responsibility (1130.XXX). The severity of the problem is very high (1130.5XX), because the problem could result in the removal of the child by the juvenile court. The duration of the difficulty is six months to one year (1130.53X), because Kathy began to have difficulty caring for the child as soon as he was born. Kathy is coping at an inadequate level (1130.535).

Kathy would like to take a parent education class to help with her Parent Role Problem but these classes have not existed in her community for eight months. So on Factor II, noting problems in the community, this problem would be called a Health, Safety, and Social Services Problem, with the specific problem being the absence of adequate social services (8301.XX). The severity is very high (8301.5X), and the duration is six months to a year (8301.53).

Kathy does not suffer from any mental health problems, so the Factor III statement would be V71.09, no diagnosis on both Axis I and Axis II.

Kathy does not suffer from any significant physical health problems, so the Factor IV statement would read no problem, by client report.

Kathy's formal PIE description follows.

| Factor I | 1130.535 | Parent Role Problem, responsibility type, very high severity, six months' to one year's duration, inadequate coping skills |
|---|---|---|
| Factor II | 8301.53 | Health, Safety, and Social Services System, absence of adequate social services, very high severity, six months' to one year's duration |
| Factor III | | |
| Axis I | V71.09 | No diagnosis |
| Axis II | V71.09 | No diagnosis |
| Factor IV | | No problem (by client report) |

The use of the PIE multifactorial statement would certainly fulfill the desire of a universally understood descriptive system if applied to Kathy's child protective services case. If Kathy were to leave her county for any reason, any worker in another agency could understand the previous worker's description, if both workers knew the PIE nomenclature. Additionally, a judge or referee of the juvenile court would have to understand the PIE system, but could learn easily by using a template or the *PIE Manual*.

The use of PIE for CPS cases is somewhat limited, because PIE is designed to describe only the problems of adults. Not once in Kathy's PIE report was her son Donny mentioned directly, although the presence of a child is inferred. The lack of grandparent or family support was not noted, although the PIE system does allow for this. Yet, Kathy's problem in parenting was clearly shown as the primary reason for the referral to CPS. If Kathy had mastered the skills of parenting, the probability is high that she and Donny would never have appeared on the steps of any social services agency. To describe Kathy's problems with PIE is to clarify the focus for intervention in this particular case and to bring about a positive result.

PIE should be tested by all units of the system that protects children. Would other professional and untrained workers find PIE useful? Would the judiciary accept PIE? These are questions that must be answered if the PIE system is to be adopted in CPS.

## Case Study 2

Ted is a 75-year-old widower who came to the attention of the local county welfare department's APS unit when a bank official called to inform the APS office of an attempt by Ted's son to withdraw all the funds from Ted's bank account. The bank official stated that it would be necessary for the son to obtain a written power of attorney to take more than $10,000 from the $300,000 account, even though the son's name was on the account. A further check of the account records indicated that over the past year since Ted had placed his son's name on the account, the son had been systematically taking money out of the account, which once contained more than $500,000. The bank official believed that Ted was possibly being abused by his son and asked APS to investigate. The APS worker thanked the bank official and asked to be informed if there were further attempts to take money from the account.

The APS worker immediately called Ted's home to make a home visit, only to have the phone answered by the son. The worker indicated that a complaint had been registered and had to be investigated and asked for an appointment that same day. Despite numerous attempts by the son to find out the circumstances of the complaint, the worker adamantly refused to discuss the specifics until a face-to-face meeting was held.

At the home visit the worker was met at the door by a well-dressed man in his thirties who rather grudgingly invited the worker into a well-kept, modest home. The worker asked to see Ted and was told that he was asleep in his room. The worker asked to be allowed to view Ted in his room without disturbing him. When the door to Ted's room was opened, he was wide awake, sitting up in bed. Ted appeared to be in his early seventies. He was attired in a neatly fitting pajama outfit and robe, with matching slippers. Ted said hello and asked what the complaint was all about.

The worker then told Ted and his son that there was a concern noted by an anonymous complainant that the son had attempted to take money out of Ted's bank account. The son's face reddened, and he sputtered that his dad "knew all about that withdrawal, but the busybody bank teller" had prevented him from making the transaction. Ted intervened and said that he had authorized his son to "take some money out" that day. The worker asked Ted if he knew how much money he had left in the bank. Ted laughingly said, "Oh, there is plenty for my old age." The worker attempted to ask Ted how much money he thought he had left, but the son interrupted, saying, "What business is it of yours how much my dad has in the bank?" The worker clarified that her role permitted her to investigate complaints of possible adult abuse. Ted said that he was not abused, and the son agreed, and they both laughed. The worker then indicated that if there was no abuse, there should be no problem getting some simple information from both of them.

She then asked again how much money Ted thought he had in the bank. Ted replied, "Oh, about half a million, I guess." The worker asked Ted to clarify how much he had authorized his son to withdraw from the bank. Ted said, "We have some normal expenses that we have to cover, so I told him to take out whatever he needed to meet our obligations." Before the worker could ask whether Ted knew the amount his son had tried to withdraw, the son interrupted. He explained to Ted that he had inadvertently "forgotten" to tell his dad that he wanted to move the total account from the bank to a savings and loan that paid more interest. A look of suspicion came over Ted's · face, and he said that he expected to be kept informed in advance of any transaction. With growing anger and suspicion, Ted asked the worker, "Just how much did my son attempt to take out of the account today?" When the worker said that the son had tried to remove all of the money, Ted said sarcastically, "Oh yeah, so he could transfer it to another place." Ted then asked the worker how much money was left in the bank. When he was told that little more than $300,000 remained, Ted's face went ashen. Ted turned to his son and said, "Well, it is a good thing that 'busybody' bank teller stopped you from taking all my money." Ted turned to the worker and thanked her for bringing the situation to his attention and stated that he would take care of his own money from now on. At that point the worker left Ted and his son alone, judging that the problem was solved.

The worker called the banker and indicated that the situation had been successfully concluded, but that if Ted's son attempted to take any sizable amounts of money out of the account, the worker would appreciate a call. The banker called back the next day to let the worker know that Ted had come into the bank and had his son's name removed from the account.

---

In this case, no court intervention was necessary, so a case plan was not needed. Only a narrative statement, much like this rendition, was recorded. Using the PIE system, two PIE statements may be completed, one for Ted and one for his son.

## PIE Assessment: Ted

The Parental Role Problem is noted for Ted (<u>11</u>XX.XXX), who obviously has a problem in his relationship with his son. The type of Social Role Problem is one of dependency (11<u>40</u>.XXX), wherein Ted's son took advantage of Ted's dependency on him. The severity of the problem is high (1140.<u>4</u>XX), given the ultimate possibility that all of Ted's life savings could have been lost. The duration was six months to one year (1110.4<u>2</u>X) because Ted arranged for his son to manage his account approximately a year ago. Ted's coping ability was outstanding (1110.46<u>1</u>), given his take-charge attitude once he became aware of the problem presented by his son's behavior.

No environmental problems (0000.00 is the coding) affecting the Parent Role Problem are observable.

Ted does not suffer from any mental health problems, so the Factor III statement would be V71.09, no diagnosis on both Axis I and Axis II, although the worker is not clear what motivated Ted to have his son manage his finances.

Ted does not suffer from any known physical health problems, so the Factor IV statement would read no diagnosis, by client report.

Ted's complete PIE statement follows.

| | | |
|---|---|---|
| Factor I | 1140.421 | Parent Role Problem, dependency type, high severity, six months' to one year's duration, outstanding coping skills |
| Factor II | 0000.00 | No problem |
| Factor III | | |
|    Axis I | V71.09 | No diagnosis |
|    Axis II | V71.09 | No diagnosis |
| Factor IV | | No problems (by client report) |

## PIE Assessment: Ted's Son

Although APS may not routinely complete an assessment of the son because the father is seen as the client, doing such an assessment is useful. A diagnostic sketch of the perpetrator as well as the victim of abuse, whether adult or child, helps clarify the interaction that may have occurred between the two. The discovery of the perpetrator's behavioral determinants may prevent future abuse, as well as assist in treatment planning for the victim. To complete the PIE description of Ted's son, further information is required on Factors II and III.

The son is manifesting difficulties with the Child Role (<u>13</u>XX.XXX) and may have attempted to misuse his power (13<u>10</u>.XXX) or be victimizing (13<u>20</u>.XXX) by stealing from his overly trusting or dependent father. The severity of the role problem is high (1310.<u>4</u>XX), the duration is six months to one year (1310.4<u>2</u>X), and the son's coping ability is inadequate (1310.42<u>5</u>). In a subsequent follow-up visit, the social worker discovers that, even though Ted's nest egg is sufficient to support both of them, because of the son's recent systematic draining of funds and Ted's growing suspicion that his son is conning him, there may be serious future problems for the son. His father is seriously considering kicking him out and ending his dependent role. If this happens, a revision of the son's Factor I listing may be called for. No environmental problem currently (0000.00) seems to be affecting the son's Child Role Problem.

In subsequent visits without Ted present, the son revealed that he was frequently very depressed and self-medicated with alcohol. After he was referred to and attended several sessions with a clinical social worker, it was determined that his depression was quite serious, and that he had planned suicide after his thievery was discovered. He felt like a "sponger" as a result of his financial dependency on his father and his own lack of ambition. He had a college degree in communications but had never sought employment. To assuage his self-image of being worthless, he began to drink excessively after his father lost trust in him and planned his suicide but couldn't go through with it, saying, "I'm even too chicken to do that." Using the PIE schema the worker noted the son's Factor III mental health problems were Major Depression, single episode, severe (296.23) and Alcohol Dependence (303.90) on Axis I and no diagnosis (V71.09) on Axis II. Upon referral to a physician, it was determined that he had no current physical health problems.

The complete PIE assessment for Ted's son now appears as follows:

| | | |
|---|---|---|
| Factor I | 1340.425 | Child Role Problem, dependency, high severity, six months' to one year's duration, inadequate coping skills |
| Factor II | 000.00 | No problem |
| Factor III | | |
| Axis I | 296.23 | Major Depression, single episode, severe |
| | 303.90 | Alcohol Dependence |
| Axis II | V71.09 | No diagnosis |
| Factor IV | | No problems (by client report) |

The PIE system as applied in this case is quite useful in describing, classifying, and coding not only the original problem but also the problems as new information was received. Another social worker assigned to the case could readily understand the situation. Because PIE was designed to deal with adults in their social environment, the system was ideally suited to culling out the peripheral problems (such as the son's victimization) and focusing on the problem for which the intervention was intended: helping Ted regain control over his finances. In short, the intervention plan flowed from the PIE description and seemed to facilitate the resolution of the problem. The treatment of the son, an offshoot of the original case plan, shows how PIE can be used in working with a couple or several members of a family.

## Conclusion

Although the PIE system appears to be useful as a tool to describe, classify, and code the problems of social functioning, further experimentation is necessary to prove its usefulness in the public welfare social services setting. It would be desirable to implement a controlled study of PIE in CPS and APS units within welfare departments. The effect of using PIE could be measured against the use of traditional local systems (or lack thereof) to determine which system resulted in more effective internal processing of clients and in better case outcomes. If the profession is ever to find a way out of our current morass of jumbled descriptions of client behavior and situations, if we are to communicate clearly with each other and with other professions, if we are to understand the impact of the environment on the clients we serve, we must begin now. Welfare departments should seek a piece of the PIE now.

## References

American Psychiatric Association. (1987). *Diagnostic and statistical manual of mental disorders* (3rd ed., rev.). Washington, DC: American Psychiatric Press.

American Psychiatric Association (1994). *Diagnostic and statistical manual of mental disorders* (4th ed.). Washington, DC: American Psychiatric Press.

# 8.

# Using the PIE System to Classify the Problems of Mentally Ill People in Recovery from Addiction

Elizabeth A. Irvin and Walter E. Penk

*This chapter describes how PIE was combined with a social support inventory to document social interaction problems and environmental problems in a group of severely and persistently mentally ill adults enrolled in a state hospital-based addiction recovery program. Results from the Community Survival Skills Project (CSSP) substantiate the importance of maintaining a person-in-environment perspective in recovery planning and the importance of improving the social resources of people who are addicted and mentally ill.*

Substance abuse, a major public health problem in the United States, is found disproportionately among persons with a serious mental illness. Persons with a diagnosis of schizophrenia, for example, are 10 times more likely to develop alcohol abuse disorders and are 7½ times more likely to develop drug use disorders than the general public (Drake, McLaughlin, Pepper, & Minkoff, 1991; Mueser et al., 1990). Forty-seven percent of individuals with a lifetime diagnosis of schizophrenia or schizophreniform disorder have met criteria for some form of substance abuse or dependence. Reports of alcohol and drug-related disorders among persons who are severely mentally ill have increased in the literature since deinstitutionalization began in the United States in the 1970s. In surveys among clients of the Massachusetts Department of Mental Health, for example, where a community-based service delivery system is well established, 59 percent of all adults admitted to state-sponsored mental hospitals met criteria for psychoactive substance use disorder (Penk & Irvin, 1994). The term "dual diagnosis" has been used in recent scientific literature to designate the group of adults who struggle with both addiction and mental disorders. This term will indicate the co-occurrence of psychoactive substance use disorder (recent or current) and a serious and persistent mental disorder such as schizophrenia or manic depressive illness.

Although psychiatric, medical, or alcohol and drug-induced problems most often occupy the attention of clinicians, social problems can contribute significantly to the emergence and maintenance of addiction disorders among the seriously and persistently mentally ill. Psychotic adults with co-occurring addiction disorders are more likely than not to have significant impairments in social adjustment (Drake et al., 1991). People with dual disorders frequently face problems with living conditions, employment, homelessness, nutrition, housing instability, and a loss of social support systems (Drake, Wallach, & Hoffman, 1989). The frustration and emotional turmoil that accompanies problems in these areas can be intense. Indeed, many cases of treatment failure that are perceived as resistance to treatment and denial may actually represent the failure of treatment providers to recognize the impact of a patient's deteriorated social situation.

## The Recovery Process

The challenges to recovery for persons suffering from both addiction and major mental illness are enormous (Minkoff, 1989). Mentally ill persons in recovery from addiction must simultaneously evolve recovery strategies that acknowledge and plan for the problems associated with both disorders. Recovery planning concurrently addresses three primary issues: (1) developing relapse prevention strategies that address specific symptoms of both the addiction and the mental disorder; (2) identifying social environments that support and sustain recovery goals; and (3) identifying and resolving environmental factors associated with relapse.

Planning for recovery should involve a realistic appraisal of the social and environmental resources in the recovery environment (Mee-Lee & Hoffman, 1992). However, strategies for assessing these factors among addicted mentally ill people have gone largely unexplored (Penk, Irvin, & Frost, 1993). To address this problem, the Community Survival Skills Program (CSSP) used the person-in-environment (PIE) system to classify problems in the environments of addicted mentally ill persons.

## Community Survival Skills Program

CSSP was designed to equip mentally ill persons in recovery from addiction with relapse prevention skills for both disorders. CSSP was originally developed by the Commonwealth of Massachusetts Department of Mental Health through a National Institute of Mental Health treatment outcome grant. The program was designed to evaluate the effectiveness of relapse prevention skills training (Marlatt & Gordon, 1985) and social skills training (Liberman, 1987) on relapse among dually diagnosed clients in a state mental health system.

Only patients who met criteria for current major mental illness (a psychotic level disorder) and current psychoactive substance use disorder were eligible for the program. The typical CSSP participant was an unmarried, economically disadvantaged, unemployed white man or woman in his or her early thirties with a diagnosis of schizophrenia and alcohol abuse. The first 50 program participants are reported on here: 30 percent were women ($n = 15$) and 70 percent were men ($n = 35$). They were a relatively young group, averaging 34.6 years of age, and most were modestly educated and had incomes below the poverty level. The most common living arrangement before program enrollment was a community-based halfway house or other supported setting (30 percent, $n = 15$). Twenty percent of the participants ($n = 10$) lived alone, 20 percent ($n = 10$) lived with parents or other family, 12 percent ($n = 6$) were homeless, 6 percent ($n = 3$) lived with a friend, and the remaining 12 percent ($n = 6$) were hospitalized.

Alcohol abuse/dependence was the most common addiction problem identified among program participants (88 percent, $n = 44$). Illicit drug use of marijuana or cocaine was most frequently reported by those with a diagnosis of schizophrenia.

Licensed clinical social workers staffed the program. Patients were contacted early in their hospitalization to assess potential interest and start the engagement process. Patients who agreed to participate in the program began training in relapse prevention skills as soon as withdrawal was complete. This training continued in the community with the same staff, who also provided case management services.

## Evaluating Social Resources

In addition to standard psychiatric and addiction assessments, all program participants cooperated with an evaluation of their social situation. Using the PIE System's Factor I role categories, CSSP participants were asked to consider their own personal situations and to identify their interpersonal role difficulties, their coping resources, the type of difficulty they were having, and how long the difficulties had existed. This self assessment provided several kinds of important information: It informed the treatment team about how participants perceived their situations with regard to difficulties in important interpersonal relationships and roles; it drew attention to environmental factors that were affecting adjustment; it provided an opportunity to clarify when a participant's and program facilitator's perceptions varied with regard to the nature of difficulties encountered in social adjustment; and it provided a concrete system for classifying findings for later reference.

Each concern identified during the evaluation was reviewed with participants for its relevance in constructing a recovery plan. Tim was one of the CSSP participants.

## Case Study

Tim is a 34-year-old single man who lives in congregate housing with other adults who are mentally ill. He was admitted to the hospital after being arrested for dangerous behavior in the community. He broke several storefront windows and was drunk and probably delusional the night of admission. He wanted to get even with his boss for sending him home from work the previous day. Tim has a part-time job preparing fish for sale at a fish market, and he had apparently become loud and somewhat disorganized at work. He reports that he and his boss "had a few beers together" while discussing the problem and then Tim was asked to leave work for a few days.

Tim was first diagnosed with manic-depressive disorder at 19, was hospitalized at age 20, and has been hospitalized at least yearly since age 23. He has never been treated for a substance use disorder despite evidence on chart review that alcohol abuse was implicated in almost all of his previous admissions.

Tim provided the following information about his social situation. He described himself as lonely and without many friends. He does not like living at the halfway house and feels that most of the people there are "crazier than I am." He has a girlfriend whom he sees intermittently. They have known each other for seven years and have a sexual relationship. They usually go out drinking when they get together. She would like to get married, but Tim doesn't think he can handle living with her all of the time, and he doesn't have a job or a place to live.

Tim's father is an alcoholic. Tim is not allowed in the family home to visit because he and his father get into verbal and physical fights, especially when both have been drinking. Tim visits occasionally with his mother at a coffeehouse near her home, but it is difficult to arrange because public transportation is not available and Tim must get a ride from someone. He does not see his brothers or sisters much because "they have their own lives." Tim indicates that although he would prefer to live in an apartment of his choice rather than the halfway house, he can't get his case manager or therapist to support this goal. He does not perceive his drinking as a problem and thinks the police overreacted by arresting him and putting him in a psychiatric hospital.

Tim agreed to meet with the social worker to discuss his situation and to consider entering the CSSP program. He reported that his doctor advised him that he had to do something about his drinking problem or he couldn't be discharged from the hospital. Tim was also told by his court-appointed attorney that getting sober would probably help his pending court case.

The CSSP social worker used PIE to clarify Tim's problems and suggest some possible interventions (Exhibit 1).

Another goal of the CSSP was to learn more about the social supports of dually diagnosed program participants. How many people are in their world? Do particular network members support or im-

*Exhibit 1*
**PIE Analysis of Tim**

| Assessment Findings | | Recommended Interventions |
|---|---|---|
| **Factor I** | | |
| 4290.515 | Inpatient/Client Role Problem, other type (denial), very high severity, more than five years' duration, inadequate coping skills | CSSP |
| 3180.66 | Worker Role–Paid Economy problem, mixed type, catastrophic severity, two weeks' or less duration | CSSP |
| 1330.514 | Child Role Problem, responsibility type, very high severity, more than five years' duration, somewhat inadequate coping skills | CSSP |
| 2130.223 | Lover Role Problem, responsibility type, low severity, one to five years' duration, adequate coping skills | CSSP |
| 2360.424 | Neighbor Role Problem, isolation type, high severity, one to five years' duration, somewhat inadequate coping skills | CSSP |
| **Factor II** | | |
| 10102.41 | Affectional Support System Problem, support system inadequate to meet affectional needs, high severity, more than five years' duration | Case management<br>Al-Anon for mother and siblings<br>Alcoholics Anonymous for father |
| **Factor III** | | |
| Axis I | | |
| 296.43 | Manic Depressive Disorder, most recent episode manic, severe without psychotic features | Hospitalization<br>Medication |
| 303.90 | Alcohol Dependency | Alcoholics Anonymous |
| Axis II | | |
| V71.09 | No diagnosis | |
| **Factor IV** | | |
| | No problem (by client report) | |

NOTE: CSSP = Community Survival Skills Program.

pede abstinence goals and behaviors of participants? Is substance abuse also a significant problem for members of the support network? A risk inventory (Irvin & Penk, 1991) was used to gather information about the size and support characteristics of network associates and to identify persons in the network who may contribute to the continuation of addictive behaviors. Participants were asked to identify associates in their social network on whom they had relied for support, companionship, or advice during the previous six months. In addition to identifying associates, program participants rated each network member's frequency of alcohol and drug use and indicated if they shared drugs or alcohol with that person.

## Program Findings

Evaluation findings were aggregated to provide program staff with a picture of the general array of problems encountered by program participants. The findings were also used for research purposes and to inform staff of training needs. The number of associates in the support network of dually diagnosed adults is very small, averaging only three persons. For most program participants, more than half of their support network consisted of close family members. One-third of those in the network were listed as friends, and the rest were considered casual acquaintances such as work associates or neighbors. Professionals appear to provide an important source of support for this population. When professionals were added to the network counts, participants identified an average of six persons or associates in their support network.

The substance use patterns among associates were also of interest. One-half of all program participants ($n = 25$) identified at least one important person in their support network who abused alcohol, and 24 percent ($n = 12$) of program participants indicated that at least one associate abused drugs. This is particularly important when the average participant had three or fewer nonprofessional associates in their support network. In addition to concerns that few persons were available for support, 84 percent ($n = 42$) of program participants indicated that they shared alcohol with at least one valued associate, and 40 percent ($n = 20$) indicated that they shared street drugs with associates. Thus, not only were social support networks quite small, support activities often took place in the context of alcohol and drug use.

When the PIE descriptions from the first 50 program participants were aggregated, almost all participants reported significant role problems, as illustrated in Tim's case study. On average participants indicated that they had problems in at least three different domains (Table 1). Familial role problems were the most frequently mentioned by both men and women. In general, the severity of women's role problems was rated significantly higher than those reported by men. Women not only reported more severe role difficulties in their families, they relied more heavily on their families for social support than did the men, who had somewhat larger friendship networks. Women also tended to report more alcohol abuse in their families than did men. Participants also reported difficulty in occupational roles and other interpersonal roles. Most of the problems identified through PIE were chronic and lasted several years or longer.

## Treatment Implications

Persistently mentally ill adults are known to have small support networks and to rely heavily on family members for support. This project demonstrated that mentally ill substance abusers also have very

*Table 1*

**Role and Environmental Problems Reported by Addicted Mentally Ill Clients Enrolled in an Addiction Recovery Program**

| Problem Areas | Males (n = 35) | | | Females (n = 15) | | | Signifi-cance* |
| | N | Mean No. Problems Reported | Mean Severity Score | N | Mean No. Problems Reported | Mean Severity Score | |
| --- | --- | --- | --- | --- | --- | --- | --- |
| Total role problems identified | 33 | 2.88 | 3.07 | 15 | 3.27 | 3.16 | NS |
| Familial | 25 | 1.40 | 4.00 | 13 | 1.76 | 5.76 | 0.05 |
| Other interpersonal | 18 | 1.67 | 3.72 | 7 | 1.00 | 3.57 | NS |
| Occupational | 28 | 1.00 | 3.18 | 12 | 1.17 | 3.58 | NS |
| Special life situation | 14 | 1.00 | 2.64 | 5 | 1.00 | 2.00 | NS |
| Affectional support system problems | 25 | 1.00 | 3.24 | 15 | 1.00 | 3.69 | NS |

NOTE: NS = not significant.
*2-tail t-test comparing severity scores of men and women.

few persons to whom they can turn for advice and support. And, for the first time, the support network was characterized in terms of known risk factors to relapse. Program participants not only had small networks, but it was common for networks to share alcohol and drugs. Almost all participants shared alcohol or drugs with at least one important person. Drug abuse and alcohol abuse was prevalent in at least one-third of support network members. Such substance use may further compromise an already easily overburdened group of friends and family members. Small and burdened social networks may afford limited assistance in coping with the social and environmental difficulties reported by participants. PIE provided a useful structure that staff and program participants could use to discuss interpersonal difficulties in the recovery environment, and the classification system offered an opportunity to spot problems common to most persons referred to the program.

Results from this pilot study in the use of the PIE system have a number of treatment implications, which those readers already immersed in recovery planning can readily infer. Briefly mentioned here are a few of the many conclusions drawn from initial clinical experiences in administering PIE.

First, there are questions about the validity or veracity of the self-reported information. Clinicians using PIE must develop personal indicators about how accurately persons in turmoil report their view of their internal state and their external circumstances. The issue of veracity should not be trivialized, nor should patients be grilled about what is or is not accurate. Rather, clinicians should adopt the stance that if a treatment relationship is formed, accuracy of assessment will improve. It is this improvement in the accuracy of the patient's view of his or her social situation that is the barometer of change in the patient's personal life. Clinicians should develop external indicators about the client's alcohol and drug use. Particularly with dually diagnosed clients, clinicians should develop external sources of information with which to compare the patient's perception (such as random urine screening or contacts with the client's family and friends).

Furthermore, clinicians should repeat the PIE assessment at selected intervals, and then set up a system with the client to compare the differences across time. When clinicians and patients work together to compare responses across time, important gains in social interactions are often registered and the goal of improving treatment outcomes is clarified. Repeated administrations of PIE can help improve treatment engagement and foster treatment outcomes.

Second, PIE readily makes manifest that which clinicians intuit about social relationships among dually diagnosed clients. Namely, dually diagnosed clients have few relationships and their sense of isolation and of being alone is severe. To threaten such a socially impoverished person with the loss of yet another person because that friend or relative may be alcoholic or a drug user is simply too great a loss for the patient to sustain. When beginning treatment the clinician is better advised to focus on adding new relationships, not cutting the patient off from existing relationships. The clinical goal in the early stages is to increase the number of social contacts and social relationships that do not involve drugs or alcohol. Later, when the patient has improved social engagement skills and has demonstrated the capacity to add new, enduring, and sustaining relationships, the issue of choice about friends who use alcohol and drugs can be addressed.

Third, PIE is useful for administrative purposes, particularly in quality assurance. Because the diagnosis of substance abuse among seriously mentally ill persons is based on criteria that include indicators about social impairment, PIE can be readily used to empirically demonstrate which problems the patient had when entering treatment, which problems improved with treatment, which new problems emerged as treatment progressed, and which problems persist and need to be resolved. Because social problems are graphically presented by the system, PIE itself could be used as a quality assurance tool. Quality assurance is not limited to reports for the clinician's agency or his or her supervisor. Rather, all clinicians should develop objective monitors for self-evaluation of the clinician as an agent of change. Using PIE to evaluate one's own effectiveness is perhaps one of the more difficult tasks to undertake, but it is an important way to foster clinician self-awareness.

## References

Drake, R. E., McLaughlin, P., Pepper, B., & Minkoff, K. (1991). Dual diagnosis of major mental illness and substance disorder: An overview. In K.

Minkoff & R. Drake (Eds.), *Dual diagnosis of major mental illness and substance disorder* (pp. 3–12). San Francisco: Jossey-Bass.

Drake, R. E., Wallach, M. A., & Hoffman, J. S. (1989). Housing instability and homelessness among aftercare patients of an urban state hospital. *Hospital and Community Psychiatry, 40*, 46–51.

Irvin, E. A., & Penk, W. E. (1991). *RISK scale for assessing substance use and co-dependence in the social network.* (Available from the Massachusetts Department of Mental Health, 25 Stanford Street, Boston, MA 02114)

Liberman, R. (1987). *Psychosocial rehabilitation.* San Francisco: Jossey-Bass.

Marlatt, A., & Gordon, J. (1985). *Relapse prevention.* New York: Guilford Press.

Mee-Lee, D., & Hoffman, N. G. (1992). *Level of care index: Adult-admission form, American Society of Addiction Medicine.* St. Paul, MN: CATOR/New Standards.

Minkoff, K. (1989). An integrated treatment model for dual diagnosis of psychosis and addiction. *Hospital and Community Psychiatry, 40*, 1031–1036.

Mueser, K. T., Yarnold, P. R., Levinson, D. F., Singh, H., Bellack, A., Kee, K., Morrison, R. L., & Yadalam, K. G. (1990). Prevalence of substance abuse in schizophrenia: Demographic and clinical correlates. *Schizophrenia Bulletin, 16*, 31–56.

Penk, W. E., & Irvin, E. A. (1994). *Findings on addiction and trauma among the severely mentally ill.* (Available from the Massachusetts Department of Mental Health, 25 Stanford Street, Boston, MA 02114)

Penk, W. E., Irvin, E. A., & Frost, A. (1993, August). *Dual diagnosis: A review of the literature.* Paper presented at the 100th Annual Meeting of the American Psychological Association, San Francisco.

# Section III

# Use of the PIE System in Other Countries

*One of the tests for the validity of the PIE system is its universality, that is, whether it describes the social functioning problems of humans regardless of the political or cultural conditions under which they live. As a result of several journal articles published about PIE, we were fortunate enough to receive several unsolicited reports of the application of PIE in countries other than the United States. We invited several of these social workers to write about their experiences for this book. Mandiberg and Miyaoka discuss their experience using PIE in teaching social work skills in Japan, Walsh and Ramsay present a Canadian field test of PIE, and Hoekstra discusses her experiences with PIE in teaching about social work's ecological perspective in the Netherlands. We believe that the content of this section will give the reader a clearer perspective on how PIE might translate into other cultures and political systems.*

# 9.

# Using the PIE System to Teach Social Work Skills in Japan

James M. Mandiberg and Kyoko Miyaoka

*This chapter explores the background of Japanese social work and social work education and reports on an experimental training process using PIE as a training tool for teaching inexperienced undergraduate social work students how to think through their work with clients.*

Social welfare services and university courses about social welfare have existed in Japan for many years. However, formal and professional social work in Japan is a post–World War II phenomenon. Its development coincides with the formation of the Japanese welfare state, which was heavily influenced by American and other Western ideas during the postwar Allied occupation of Japan. Consequently, formal social work education in Japan is a relatively recent development that relies a great deal on Western concepts and methods. It is primarily characterized by formal classroom instruction about social work systems and theories. However, Japanese social work education is much weaker in its teaching of practical social work skills and methods. This chapter explores the background of Japanese social work and social work education and reports on an experimental training process using the person-in-environment (PIE) system as a training tool for teaching inexperienced undergraduate social work students how to think through their work with clients.

## Sociocultural Background

Before its development as a welfare state, Japan had a long tradition of indigenous local and neighborhood mutual aid for those in need. This tradition was similar to that in other countries before the formal development of rationalized services (Gitterman, 1986). Historically, mutual aid traditions in Japan have been based primarily on the extended family, rural cooperatives, family affiliations with neighborhood Buddhist temples or Shinto shrines, or employee benefits from the workplace.

## Extended Family

Japan shares some fundamental social traditions with other Asian cultures, based on Chinese notions of family association and responsibility. Historically, social identity and social responsibility have been defined by the family structure. The family is the basic social unit for the individual. Traditionally, the extended family has been responsible for all family members, including providing for their welfare. It was the family's duty to assure that all social obligations were fulfilled, and to retain responsibility if family members had or created problems in the wider community. In this sense, the family unit was responsible for the acts of each family member. The individual also was expected to follow the "wishes" of the family, which usually meant following the wishes of the acknowledged male head of the family, defined by age and by oldest son lineage.

In the post–World War II constitution, most of the legal requirements imposed on the extended family for the welfare of individual family members were eliminated. Additionally, the social traditions of the extended family eroded gradually as Japan moved from a pre–World War II rural peasant society to a postwar urban industrial society. However, many of the social expectations of the extended family still influence social welfare practice.

## Rural Cooperatives

Although Japan today appears to be one of the most urbanized countries in the world, with 77.4 percent of its population living in cities, this is a relatively recent phenomenon. Traditionally, Japan was a rural peasant society. In rural areas, cooperatives were an important source of mutual aid. This cooperative-based social welfare included assistance to families in need; cooperative banking, insurance, and retirement services; formal and informal in-home services; cooperative-owned farming equipment; and cooperation in work. Today, it is not unusual to see neighborhood cooperatives offer educational, social, and recreational programs as well as other benefits for members in need.

## Religion

An additional feature of traditional Japanese society is the function of the local Buddhist temple or Shinto shrine. Shinto, the native Japanese religion, is a polytheistic religion based on the worship of nature spirits, which in more modern times has incorporated features of Confucian ancestor worship and Buddhism. Buddhism was brought to Japan from China, via Korea, in 538 A.D., and has flourished alongside Shinto. Unlike Western religions, Shinto and Buddhism are not in conflict with each other. Many Japanese people practice both Shinto and Buddhism and do not see this as a contradiction.

Although many Western religions have established large central-ized and formal welfare institutions, Buddhism and Shinto have largely kept their welfare services at the local level. Thus, shrine- or temple-based social welfare often appears more like the mutual aid of the rural cooperative, something neighbors do for neighbors, rather than the formalized and often doctrine-based Western reli-gious welfare institutions. Specific shrines and temples have be-come important to distinct high-need groups, and various formal and informal social services have emerged at these places to help meet their needs. In addition, local shrines and temples have tradi-tionally been places where poor, sick, or disabled people gathered and informal systems of assistance from worshipers, priests, and monks grew to serve their needs.

### Workplace

The workplace has also been an important source of social welfare benefits. Historically, the Japanese concept of the business was based on the family. Until fairly recently, a business was small and family based. As they got larger than could be managed within the family, male nonfamily members were invited into the business to participate as equal family members. This often included formal adoption by the family and assumption of the family's name, or marriage to one of the daughters in the family. Consequently, early "employee benefits" were equivalent to the benefits that any family member received.

Although businesses began to get much larger, especially in the intensive development period during the Meiji era (1868 to 1912), the concept of familial responsibility to employees still formed the basis for employer–employee relations. In the concept's positive form, the Western tradition of employer–worker conflict was miti-gated by a sense of employer responsibility for the worker. In its negative form it created paternalistic control and provided a conve-nient way of manipulating workers (Kawamura, 1989). Many of these positive and negative attitudes can still be seen in employer–employee relationships in Japan and in the creation of employee and employee family benefits, which are an important source of ben-efits parallel to social welfare benefits.

### Emerging Social Welfare System

In addition to this extensive indigenous system of social services, Japan started to pass social welfare legislation during the Meiji era. This was a period of intensive effort to modernize government, in-dustry, education, and other social infrastructures so Japan could compete with, and not be dominated by, other industrialized coun-tries (Reischauer, 1991). Many ideas were brought to Japan from the developed West, including ideas of state responsibility for the daily welfare of its citizens. An early Meiji law, the 1894 Indigent Person Relief Regulation (*Jukkyu Kisoku*), mandated that families and neighbors care for the physically disabled, the frail elderly, the physically ill, and children. If this was not possible, the law also established formal government-sponsored relief. This law was later supplanted by a series of more specific laws: the 1929 Poor Relief Law (*Kyugo Ho*), the 1933 Law Concerning Cruelty Prevention to Children, the 1937 Maternal and Child Law (Mother's Aid Law), the 1938 Social Work Law, and the 1941 Medical Protection Law. The 1938 Social Work Law also established the Ministry of Health and Welfare, the government agency responsible for medical and social welfare services (Ichibangase & Takashima, 1981; Japanese National Committee, 1986; Nakamura, Kojima, & Thompson, 1981; Nakamura, Miura, & Abe, 1983; Takahashi, Miyazaki, & Sadato, 1981).

However, although significant laws were enacted, many of their provisions were not implemented. Japanese military activity in the 1930s and 1940s further weakened implementation of formal social welfare services and shifted their focus to caring for war-related problems. This shift included, for example, the 1937 Military Assistance Law that provided benefits for war widows and their children.

In addition to social welfare legislation, social welfare institutions were created during the Meiji era, including orphanages, the Salvation Army, and movements to eliminate prostitution. In 1917, Okayama prefecture, one of 48 prefectures in Japan, began a volunteer welfare system (*homen-iin*) that by the 1920s had become a nationwide movement. This system was replaced in 1946 by another volunteer system (*minsei-iin*), which continues to play an important part in Japan's welfare system.

After World War II Japan's rapid development as a welfare state was influenced by the Allied occupation of Japan, which strengthened concepts of state responsibility for its citizens. Before this development, Japan retained the traditional structure of family responsibility for its members, with citizens owing allegiance to the state but with the state's responsibilities toward its citizens unclear. As the Allied occupation was phased out, Japan passed social welfare legislation that formed the outline of the current social welfare programs. These laws were based on Article 25 of the Japan Constitution, which states "all people shall have the right to maintain minimum standards of wholesome and cultured living," and "the state must make effort to promote and expand social welfare, social security and public health services to cover every aspect of the life of the people." These laws include the Daily Life Security Law (Public Assistance Law) of 1946 and 1950; the Child Welfare law of 1947; the Law for the Welfare of Physically Handicapped Persons of 1949; the Social Welfare Service Law of 1951; the Law for the Welfare of Mentally Retarded Persons of 1960; the Law for the Welfare of the

Aged of 1963; and the Law for Maternal (widows) and Child Welfare of 1964 (Japanese National Committee, 1986; Takahashi et al., 1981).

Today, Japan's social welfare system exists at a very sophisticated level. Similar to the West, welfare structures exist for most dependent populations. Yet there are issues which, from a Western social welfare system perspective, seem problematic.

Being in any way identifiably different is highly stigmatizing in Japan, even more so than in Europe and North America. Being different places one outside of his or her peer group, and peer group affiliation is key for both self-identity and social identity. Although inclusion criteria for peer group membership are often wider than in the West (Tobin, Wu, & Davidson, 1989), exclusion from the peer group carries severe social consequences. Some have proposed that Japanese social relationships are formed primarily on the basis of group membership and one's age-based superior–inferior standing in the group (Nakane, 1970). Thus, individuals who fall outside of recognizable peer groups have an ambiguous status that makes social participation very difficult.

Additionally, families are often still held responsible for a family member who is different. This responsibility exists at both the social and formal legal levels. The *Hogo Gimusha* system for people considered to be mentally ill is an example of this (Mandiberg, 1993a). *Hogo Gimusha* specifies that the family is legally responsible for any problems, including property damage, caused by a person considered mentally ill. This has led families to keep their family members in psychiatric hospitals for indefinite periods of time.

Social welfare institutions for people with physical disabilities, elderly people, people with mental health services needs, people with developmental disabilities, children, and other client populations exist at advanced levels. However, the institutions themselves are very often in remote locations, far from commercial or residential areas. This runs counter to Western concepts of normalization and social integration (Brown & Smith, 1992; Flynn & Nitsch, 1980; King Edward's Fund, 1980). Although social welfare institutions exist at a sophisticated level, their community-based counterparts are very undeveloped. This is changing for certain populations, such as elderly people, but for many other populations there are still social, legal, financial, and economic barriers to the development of community-based programming.

This difficulty has led some to assert that Western concepts of how to develop community-based alternatives might not work in Japan and other Asian societies. For example Lin (1991) proposed that in Asia hospitals might make a better base for community mental health services than the small community agencies or freestanding mental health center models of the West. This proposal was a result of the Asian culture's greater respect for and trust in institutional symbols, the somatization of symptoms that in the West are

expressed psychologically, and the respect for historical continuity
of existing community and social institutions.

## Social Work and Social Work Education

Although there were some state and religious welfare institutions
before World War II, those persons working in the institutions had
limited identity as social workers. Rather, the administrators were
generic civil servants and many of the workers were community volunteers. In that sense, social welfare in prewar Japan was not unlike
the evolution of social welfare in America and Britain (Trattner,
1989).

Allied occupation authorities brought American social workers to
Japan in the immediate postwar period. They assisted Japanese authorities to implement social welfare programming, first at the direction of the occupation General Headquarters and later at the
direction of Japanese government officials (Social Workers' International Club, Japan, 1958).

Some social workers' descriptions of this period seem naive and
paternalistic from a 1990s perspective. The descriptions abound
with the moral responsibility to bring to Japan enlightened concepts
of democracy, Christian charity, Freudian theory, and other culture-
laden concepts, and often sound like descriptions of 19th-century
social Darwinism (Dessau, 1958; Lamb, 1958). However, North
American and British social welfare concepts provided the main influence on the early development of social work and social work education in Japan, with the cultural issues left untouched or seen as
problematic nonconformity with correct Western ideas.

Because the number of people trained as social workers was limited as Japan was aggressively building its welfare state, untrained
workers were used for many of the positions that would be filled by
trained social workers in the West. Untrained workers are still used
today in some areas of social welfare; and although this staffing is
sometimes attributed to the lack of an adequate number of trained
social workers, there are seeming contradictions to this explanation.
For example, practical nursing or care work, most often viewed as
unskilled or semiskilled work in America, is often done by trained
social workers in Japan. On the other hand, counseling is seen as
highly specialized work in America, but in Japan it is often assigned to career civil servants based on seniority and assumed
good judgment, with no relationship to training. Although this
seeming contradiction might be a result of social choices and values
(care work seen as more important than counseling, age, and experience seen as more important than training), there are other indica-
tions that it may be a reflection of a social welfare system still
searching for definition.

It is not unusual for new graduates of social work training programs to be the first social worker hired by an employer. Social

workers in these circumstances report that employers often do not know what social workers do, and so assign them to clerical and even maintenance work. One new social work graduate, hired by a psychiatric hospital, was assigned the titles of both psychiatric social worker and clinical psychologist, although it was unclear to this person what a clinical psychologist did!

Before World War II, few universities awarded degrees in social welfare, which was strictly an academic subject, perhaps leading to government work, but not leading to social work practice. During the Taisho era (1912 to 1926), some universities began to add social welfare courses to their curriculum. In 1921, the Japan Women's College added a Faculty of Social Welfare, with 30 students graduating four years later. From 1926 until 1945, during the Showa era (1926 to 1989), several other colleges and universities also created departments of social welfare.

After the war, social welfare education was more oriented to social work practice. The Japan Social Work School was organized in 1946 as a training school, changed to a professional school in 1947, and again changed to a junior college in 1950. The Ministry of Education officially allowed the creation of faculties of social work in 1947, and new faculties were added to colleges and universities around Japan. The first master's degree course in social welfare was created in 1950 at Doshisha University in Kyoto (Kikuchi & Sakano, 1980).

Four social work degrees are given in Japanese universities, junior colleges, and professional schools. The most basic degree is a junior college degree that qualifies the graduate to do various kinds of care work, including in-home care of elders and people with disabilities. The Japanese Association of Schools of Social Work (JASSW) currently recognizes 15 junior colleges and seven professional schools that award two-year degrees in social welfare. The professional level degree is the bachelor's of social welfare, which most practicing social workers have. There are 40 JASSW-recognized colleges and universities awarding bachelor's degrees in social welfare. Traditionally, the master's level degree has been considered the academic degree, qualifying the person to teach at the university level. In this respect, social work is similar to other fields in Japan, especially social science fields, in which it is rare to find a professor who holds a doctoral degree. Currently, 20 JASSW-recognized universities award master's degrees. Recently, 11 JASSW-recognized universities have begun to award doctoral degrees in social welfare. A doctorate in Japan is usually awarded for significant contributions to the field and as such is considered recognition of mature scholarship. This is in contrast to American doctorates, which are most often awarded as the first step in an academic career. Because the best scholars in Japan continue to hold master's degrees as their highest degree, possessing a doctorate is not seen as a necessity.

Most two-year social work graduates find work as care workers for elderly people and people with physical disabilities. Their coursework tends to be practically oriented for working with various service-dependent populations. Many four-year graduates find applied work in social welfare fields. However, many also find jobs outside of social welfare. Regardless of the major, a four-year degree provides entry to many business jobs. Different aspects of the four-year social work curriculum are regulated by the Ministry of Education, the Ministry of Health and Welfare, and by the Japanese Council on Social Work Education.

Applied social work is not emphasized in the four-year social work programs. Some have referred to the university programs as departments of social welfare theory. Students get extensive lectures in social work history, social work theory, methods, and different fields of practice. However, skill development and applied work are mostly restricted to the required four weeks of field work, called practical work, and a yearlong related course in social work skills in the third year. The field work experience is typically the most contact students have with client populations before getting jobs, although some students also have contact with clients through student clubs in which they study sign language, autism, children's problems, and so on.

Consequently, new graduates are often at a loss about how to define the problems of clients, how to prioritize clients and client needs, how to structure the initial social work relationship with clients, and where to begin in their work with clients. Mature social workers are usually highly skilled and sophisticated, but this is a result of many years of on-the-job training and supplemental continuing education.

## Current Social Work Practice

In Japan today, social work means institutional social work. Most social workers work in various social welfare institutions, including institutions for people with developmental disabilities, children, people with physical disabilities, and in hospitals, nursing homes, and psychiatric hospitals. Community-based social welfare programs are growing, but there are still relatively few. Recently Japan has become increasingly concerned with the aging of its population. Currently, 12.1 percent of the Japanese population is older than 65, and this is estimated to increase to 25.4 percent in 2025 (Japanese Health and Welfare Statistics Association, 1991). The elder population is increasingly becoming a focus of concern and more noninstitutional, community-based responses are being developed for them. This emphasis has both a positive and a negative influence on other social welfare programs. On the positive side, the focus on community care has a spillover effect on other populations. On the negative side, social welfare programming for seniors is seen as a priority for the limited social welfare budget.

The overwhelming focus on institutional solutions to social welfare problems also influences the thinking of social work students. Students are exposed to Western concepts of community-based social work, and they are often well read about various Western models of community-based programs. However, the students frequently have trouble conceptualizing community-based responses to social welfare needs in Japan. The problem may be because of the lack of exposure to the effective community-based programs that do exist in Japan and the cultural inappropriateness of some of the Western models (Mandiberg, 1993b).

As a "new profession" in Japan, social work has not had a long period in which to establish its identity, its theoretical base, and its training institutions and methods. In addition, because professional social work training in Japan is at the bachelor's degree level, students are young and have little life experience with many of the populations social workers help as clients. In these circumstances, teaching students how to help their clients is difficult.

## PIE as a Teaching Tool

The PIE system was selected as an experimental vehicle for teaching students where to begin and how to prioritize their work with clients. Because PIE systematically leads the user through different potential problem areas for clients, it had promise for orienting inexperienced social work students in their work with clients. In addition, PIE is relatively culture free as a training instrument, with the major theoretical orientations being social role theory and the PIE orientation (Karls & Wandrei, 1992b). Social role theory is itself highly culturally adaptable (Biddle & Thomas, 1966). Furthermore, the person-in-environment orientation is not highly culture-bound, allowing adaptability to different environments and views of the person. Thus, the potential usefulness of PIE as a training instrument is heightened for social work education in non-Western cultures.

PIE was not developed as a training instrument but as a classification system and assessment tool (Karls & Wandrei, 1992a, 1992b; Williams, Karls, & Wandrei, 1989). However, because assessment or problem definition is the first step in the helping process (Meyer, 1993), using PIE as a training instrument seemed appropriate. PIE's strength for this purpose was its systematic listing of social roles and potential environmental problems, and its ability to assist in setting priorities based on perceptions of severity, duration, coping skills, and strengths.

PIE's multiaxial approach was seen as helpful by itself, because it was an approach already known through the *Diagnostic and Statistical Manual of Mental Disorders, Third Edition* (DSM-III) (American Psychiatric Association, 1980) and the *Diagnostic and Statistical Manual of Mental Disorders, Third Edition–Revised* (DSM-III-R) (American Psychiatric Association, 1987). DSM-III and DSM-III-R are well known in

Japan by psychiatric social workers, but not by social workers in general or by social work students. However, the advantage of a multiaxial approach is that it allows for viewing several factors in the same process. Given the complexity of the problems social workers deal with, this is obviously an advantage.

## PIE Training Procedure and Results

A 90-minute training session orienting students to PIE was developed. This session used short videotaped and live vignettes depicting three different kinds of social work clients and problems in Japan. The training was given to a class of 111 mostly third-year undergraduate social work majors. The students were shown the first vignette, after which an anonymous pretraining questionnaire was administered. The questionnaire asked for demographic information; the amount of past exposure to client populations; areas of interest in social work; and the student's perceived ability to know, analyze, and prioritize client needs. After completing the questionnaire the students were given an overview of PIE, viewed the second vignette, and using this vignette were told how to use PIE. They were then shown a third vignette and heard an explanation of how PIE would be used in that case. Finally, students were shown the first vignette again and were asked to use PIE by themselves. Students were then given an anonymous posttraining questionnaire with the same series of nondemographic questions as in the pretraining questionnaire, along with multiple choice and free-form opportunities to comment on the usefulness of PIE and the training.

This was the first experience for most of the students with videotaped case examples. Student comments were very positive about this method of vicarious exposure to simulated social work interviews. However, the training time was far too short for students to achieve any level of competence in PIE. The goal in this training was exposure to and not competence in PIE, and the training had to fit in a busy class schedule. Many students commented on the desire for a longer training period, additional training, or some additional supervised exposure to PIE.

Comparison of the pretraining and posttraining questionnaires revealed some interesting changes among the students. On the question "I can identify clients' needs and problems," only 24 students (21.6 percent) agreed or strongly agreed on the pretraining questionnaire. However, on the posttraining questionnaire 88 (79.3 percent) agreed or strongly agreed. On the question "I am confident that I will know which of my many clients to help first," 20 (39.7 percent) of the 63 students who answered "maybe" in the pretraining questionnaire changed to "agree"; and 18 (66.7 percent) of the 27 students who answered "disagree" in the pretraining questionnaire changed to "agree" or "maybe."

The multiple choice and free-form comments on the training and PIE were also informative. Ninety-five (85.6 percent) of the students commented positively on the usefulness of the PIE training. Thirty-three (29.7 percent) of the students commented that PIE clarified the problems of the client more so than thinking about the cases without the PIE structure. Twenty-one (18.9 percent) of the students commented on the usefulness of the assessment skills taught through PIE. Nineteen (17.1 percent) students commented that the training helped to clarify their self-knowledge, especially their need for additional skills. Twelve (10.8 percent) of the students commented on the usefulness of the training as social work training. However, 13 (11.7 percent) of the students commented that the training was not useful. These comments included not understanding PIE, not understanding the vignettes, the difficulty of PIE, and the lack of contact with real clients in the training.

Many students commented that they felt the training was too short for them to become competent in PIE. Others commented that PIE highlighted their lack of skills, confirming our impression from the data analysis. However, 11 (9.9 percent) of the students had comments that agreed with the critique of Kirk, Siporin, and Kutchins (1989) that the PIE system lost too many client details in an effort to classify.

## Discussion

We used PIE as a training instrument for undergraduate social work students to learn to think through a structured approach to better understand clients and their problems in their person-environment interaction. Thus, our use of PIE was slightly different from its intended use as a classification scheme. However, given some of the recent criticism about PIE (Kirk et al., 1989; Mattaini & Kirk, 1991; Meyer, 1993), some comment is necessary.

The multiaxial nature of the PIE system is not an obvious way for students to think about clients' problems. Because Japanese social work students are not familiar with DSM-III or DSM-III-R, they must learn the multiaxial method for the first time through PIE. Thus, one question resulting from this study would be, "Is there a benefit to thinking about clients through a multiaxial or PIE framework?" This is different from and in addition to the issues about PIE's familial relationship with DSM-III and DSM-III-R.

There is a great deal of controversy about the DSM system. Areas of controversty include questions about the desirability of labeling and diagnosis using DSM-III (Brown, 1990; Weiss, 1989), the political nature of DSM-III (Kirk & Kutchins, 1992; Klerman, 1987; Kutchins & Kirk, 1986), the validity and reliability of DSM (Kirk & Kutchins, 1992), and the DSM's reliance on vague definitions of crucial terms (Kirk et al., 1989). But PIE is not DSM. PIE results in no label, it uses both categorical and dimensional approaches (Mattaini & Kirk, 1991), and it is not clear whether it produces a political advantage through professional mystification.

A multiaxial system itself is potentially an effective way of thinking through the complex and multidimensional social problems clients face. The problem of reductionism exists with PIE. However, this problem exists in any attempt to turn complex phenomena into description, or classification, and even the critics agree that a descriptive/classification system is desirable. PIE's use of the multiaxial system does not result in a label, but it does categorize problems. For confused students, this is rather an advantage. Furthermore, PIE has a dimensional aspect when it calls for looking at severity and duration. This aspect helps students to think through prioritizing among the various problems individual clients might have, and among various clients. Thus, as a way to conceptualize and prioritize service delivery, PIE is vastly more useful than a multiaxial-based diagnostic system. Although it has been criticized by Meyer (1993) as overly elaborate and difficult to use, PIE's thoroughness is exactly what makes it attractive in teaching students how to critically think through their work with clients. PIE's somewhat awkward numbering system was unnecessary when using PIE as a training instrument. However, it should be noted that some numbering system is necessary if a classification system is to be useful for research and other data collection purposes. Without a specific social work system researchers are left to rely on inappropriate systems from other perspectives, such as DSM-III-R and the *International Classification of Diseases-Ninth Revision-Clinical Modification* (ICD-9-CM) (U.S. Department of Health and Human Services, 1991).

Using PIE effectively does require training and familiarity. Thus, it should be compared with other practice-oriented structures for its relevance and usefulness. Numerous resources are available in English to help students learn general helping skills (Anderson, 1988; Benjamin, 1987; Brill, 1990; Carkhuff, 1987; Cournoyer, 1991; Egan, 1990; Epstein, 1988; Shulman, 1981, 1984). However, few of these provide concrete assistance in actually delineating and prioritizing areas for intervention.

Some (Anderson, 1988; Shulman, 1981, 1984) follow Schwartz's (1971) schema of teaching skills based on phases of the social work process. However, these skills relate more to the important issues around the social work relationship than to concretely defining interventions. Others present useful tools for understanding complex phenomenon (Hartman, 1978; McGoldrick & Gerson, 1985), but do not themselves point to specific areas of intervention. Still others present helpful assessment outlines (Cournoyer, 1991; Meyer, 1993), but are less schematic and thus require a greater level of sophistication and familiarity with client populations. Finally, some (Franklin & Jordan, 1992) are overly oriented to single client or practice populations (such as mental health).

In their review of social work assessment techniques, Mattaini and Kirk (1991) reviewed several categorical, dimensional, behavioral, and computer-based systems. PIE, although criticized in the article, is the only assessment technique reviewed that is not specific to some client population or problem.

Although the theories used to design PIE appear to be relatively culture neutral, translating PIE for use in non-English speaking countries and in non-Western cultures does involve some adaptation (Miyaoka, 1992). PIE's social roles of Member and Consumer assume a cultural orientation. This orientation can be taught, but is not itself obvious in a non-Western context. Furthermore, there has been some controversy in international social welfare circles about whether Western-based concepts such as these should be taught at all (Midgley, 1981; Nagpaul, 1972). Additionally, PIE's Occupational Roles category leaves unclear the role of full-time, part-time, or occasional worker in a family business or farm. These are common roles in Japan and other Asian societies. PIE seems to straddle all three possible choices. Some of the types of social-functioning problems assume an orientation that may not be shared by social workers in non-Western countries. Dependency and victimization may be seen as very different issues in a non-Western context. Finally, the category of Discrimination in PIE's Environmental section reflects a Western cultural bias that is shared by many social workers trained in Western social work theory, but often not by the wider society.

These are not insurmountable problems, but there certainly is a problem in importing Western social work theories and techniques to non-Western cultures. However, the domination of Western-influenced social welfare systems and social work education in Japan means that using an assessment instrument that is adaptable is attractive. Because PIE is still in process, it is hoped that it can be refined to be more culture neutral.

Our experience in using the PIE system with students yielded some surprises. We expected that students would almost immediately find PIE helpful in thinking through the needs of clients. Thus, we expected PIE to strengthen students' confidence that they could begin to deal with clients' problems. It was surprising, then, that PIE initially seemed to decrease the students' confidence. In retrospect this makes sense. PIE was taught to a class of primarily third-year students in the middle of their first semester. These young students enter the social work program with limited client contact and limited life experience. For most students, their first structured contact with clients comes in the vacation period between the first and second semesters of their third year.

Comments collected from first-year students at the end of the year indicate that this limited client contact tends to produce a bimodal distribution of student attitudes about clients, with some students having an unrealistically optimistic picture of clients and their problems, and some students having an unrealistically pessimistic picture. Cnaan and Bergman (1990) reported a similar "loss of optimism" as students become more exposed to the reality of clients' social problems. The PIE training, and the PIE system itself, tends to force students to view clients in realistic ways. Thus, it reduces students' false confidence that they are knowledgeable about clients.

## Conclusion

As a training instrument with naive students, PIE was very effective. It gave the students a more realistic impression of clients and of the multiplicity of potential areas of intervention. Additionally, PIE concretely exposed the students to their own strengths and weaknesses and pointed to specific knowledge and skill areas in which they needed study. Although the multiaxial process in PIE might be seen as cumbersome to an experienced social worker, it was quite helpful for naive students in leading them through the social work thinking process.

PIE is not a perfect instrument for training or assessment purposes. However, as the best effort yet to establish a unique social work assessment, it can be very useful in training students who have limited experience with clients and for assisting students in structuring their social work thinking. This is especially true in social work training programs that are able to offer only limited supervised exposure to clients.

In addition, as a work in progress, it is hoped that PIE can be modified to remove some of the culture-bound limitations that were found in using it in a non-Western culture. Furthermore, because PIE's use outside of North America divorces it from issues around the hegemony of DSM, PIE can perhaps be viewed in a more dispassionate way for its own value.

## References

American Psychiatric Association. (1980). *Diagnostic and statistical manual of mental disorders* (3rd ed.). Washington, DC: American Psychiatric Press.

American Psychiatric Association. (1987). *Diagnostic and statistical manual of mental disorders* (3rd ed., rev.). Washington, DC: American Psychiatric Press.

Anderson, J. (1988). *Foundations of social work practice.* New York: Springer.

Benjamin, A. (1987). *The helping interview.* Boston: Houghton Mifflin.

Biddle, B. J., & Thomas, E. J. (1966). *Role theory: Concepts and research.* New York: John Wiley & Sons.

Brill, N. (1990). *Working with people: The helping process* (4th ed.). New York: Longman.

Brown, H., & Smith, H. (1992). *Normalisation: A reader for the nineties.* London: Tavistock/Routledge.

Brown, P. (1990). The name game: Toward a sociology of diagnosis. *Journal of Mind and Behavior, 11,* 385–406.

Carkhuff, R. R. (1987). *The art of helping: VI.* Amherst, MA: Human Resources Development Press.

Cnaan, R. A., & Bergman, S. (1990). Constructs of social problems by social work students. *International Social Work, 33,* 157–174.

Cournoyer, B. (1991). *The social work skills workbook.* Belmont, CA: Wadsworth.

Dessau, D. (1958). Social work today in Japan. In Social Workers' International Club, Japan (Ed.), *Glimpses of social work in Japan* (pp. 1–11). Kyoto, Japan: Nippon Kanko Bijutsu Shuppansha.

Egan, G. (1990). *The skilled helper: A systematic approach to effective helping* (4th ed.). Pacific Grove, CA: Brooks/Cole.

Epstein, L. (1988). *Helping people: The task centered approach* (2nd ed.). Columbus, OH: Charles E. Merrill.

Flynn, R. J., & Nitsch, K. E. (Eds.). (1980). *Normalization, social integration and community services*. Baltimore: University Park Press.

Franklin, C., & Jordan, C. (1992). Teaching students to perform assessments. *Social Work Education, 28,* 222–241.

Gitterman, A. (1986). *Mutual aid groups and the life cycle*. Itasca, IL: F. E. Peacock.

Hartman, A. (1978). Diagrammatic assessment of family relationships. *Social Casework, 59,* 465–476.

Ichibangase, Y., & Takashima, S. (Eds.). (1981). *Kozashakai fukushi: Shakai fukushi no rekishi* [*Lecture on social welfare number 2: The history of social welfare*]. Tokyo: Yuhikaku.

Japanese Health and Welfare Statistics Association. (1991). *Kosei no shihyo: Kokumin no fukushi no doko* [*Journal of Health and Welfare Statistics: The Trend of Health and Welfare*], *38*(12).

Japanese National Committee, International Council on Social Welfare. (1986). *Social welfare services in Japan*. Tokyo: Japanese National Committee, International Council on Social Welfare.

Karls, J., & Wandrei, K. (1992a). The person-in-environment system for classifying client problems. *Journal of Case Management, 1,* 90–95.

Karls, J., & Wandrei, K. (1992b). PIE: A new language for social work. *Social Work, 37,* 80–85.

Kawamura, N. (1989). The transition of the household system in Japan's modernization. In Y. Sugimoto & R. E. Mouer (Eds.), *Constructs for understanding Japan* (pp. 202–227). London: Kegan Paul International.

Kikuchi, M., & Sakano, M. (1980). *Nihon kindai shakaijigyo shi no kenkyu* [*Research of the history of modern social work education in Japan*]. Tokyo: Aikawashobo.

King Edward's Fund. (1980). *An ordinary life: Comprehensive locally based residential services for mentally handicapped people*. London: King Edward's Hospital Fund for London.

Kirk, S. A., & Kutchins, H. (1992). *The selling of DSM: The rhetoric of science in psychiatry*. New York: Aldine de Gruyter.

Kirk, S. A., Siporin, M., & Kutchins, H. (1989). The prognosis for social work diagnosis. *Social Casework, 70,* 295–304.

Klerman, G. L. (1987). Is the reliability of DSM-III a scientific or a political question? [Letter]. *Social Work Research & Abstracts, 23*(4), 3.

Kutchins, H., & Kirk, S. A. (1986). The reliability of DSM-III: A critical review. *Social Work Research & Abstracts, 22*(4), 3–12.

Lamb, J. (1958). The influence of Christian charity on social work. In Social Workers' International Club, Japan (Ed.), *Glimpses of social work in Japan* (pp. 164–169). Kyoto, Japan: Nippon Kanko Bijutsu Shuppansha.

Lin, T. Y. (1991). The changing role of mental hospitals in Asian cultures. In T. Y. Lin, K. Asai, & T. Takahashi (Eds.), *Mental hospitals as a base for community mental health in Asian cultures* (pp. 133–148). Tokyo: Keimei Publishing Company.

Mandiberg, J. M. (1993a). Between a rock and a hard place: The mental
    health system in Japan. In J. M. Mandiberg (Ed.), *Innovations in Japanese
    mental health* (pp. 3–12). San Francisco: Jossey-Bass.
Mandiberg, J. M. (1993b). Editor's notes. In J. M. Mandiberg (Ed.), *Innova-
    tions in Japanese mental health* (pp. 1–2). San Francisco: Jossey-Bass.
Mattaini, M. A., & Kirk, S. A. (1991). Assessing assessment in social work.
    *Social Work, 36,* 261–262.
McGoldrick, M., & Gerson, R. (1985). *Genograms in family assessment.* New
    York: W. W. Norton.
Meyer, C. H. (1993). *Assessment in social work practice.* New York: Columbia
    University Press.
Midgley, J. (1981). *Professional imperialism: Social work in the Third World.* Lon-
    don: Heinemann.
Miyaoka, K. (1992). Introduction of PIE (person-in-environment): A system
    for describing, classifying, and coding problems of social functioning.
    *Shikoku Gakuin University Treatises, 81,* 157–170.
Nagpaul, H. (1972). The diffusion of American social work education to In-
    dia: Problems and issues. *International Social Work, 15,* 3–17.
Nakamura, Y., Kojima, Y., & Thompson, L.H. (Eds.). (1981). *Shakai fukushi
    Eiwa–Waei yogo jiten [Social welfare and related services glossary: English–
    Japanese Japanese–English].* Tokyo: Seishin Shobo.
Nakamura, Y., Miura, F., & Abe, S. (Eds.). (1983). *Shakai fukushi kyoshitsu
    [Lecture on social welfare, revised].* Tokyo: Yuhikaku.
Nakane, C. (1970). *Japanese society.* Berkeley: University of California Press.
Reischauer, E. (1991). *Japan: The story of a nation* (4th ed.). New York: Alfred
    A. Knopf.
Schwartz, W. (1971). *Social groupwork: The interactionist approach.* In R. Morris
    (Ed.-in-Chief), *Encyclopedia of social work* (16th ed., Vol. 2, pp. 1252–
    1263). New York: National Association of Social Workers.
Shulman, L. (1981). *Identifying, measuring and teaching helping skills.* New
    York: Council on Social Work Education.
Shulman, L. (1984). *The skills of helping individuals and groups* (2nd ed.).
    Itasca, IL: F. E. Peacock.
Social Workers' International Club, Japan. (1958). *Glimpses of social work in Ja-
    pan.* Kyoto, Japan: Nippon Kanko Bijutsu Shuppansha.
Takahashi, S., Miyazaki, S., & Sadato, T. (Eds.). (1981). *Social work wo kan-
    gaeru [Thinking of social work].* Tokyo: Kawashima Shoten.
Tobin, J. J., Wu, D.Y.H., & Davidson, D. H. (1989). *Preschool in three cultures:
    Japan, China and the United States.* New Haven, CT: Yale University
    Press.
Trattner, W. I. (1989). *From poor law to welfare state* (4th ed.). New York: Free
    Press.
U.S. Department of Health and Human Services. (1991). *International classi-
    fication of diseases–9th revision–clinical modification* (4th ed.). Washington,
    DC: U.S. Government Printing Office.
Williams, J.B.W., Karls, J. M., & Wandrei, K. (1989). The person-in-
    environment (PIE) system for describing problems of social function-
    ing. *Hospital and Community Psychiatry, 40,* 1125–1127.
Weiss, K. M. (1989). Advantages of abandoning symptom-based diagnostic
    systems of research in schizophrenia. *American Journal of Orthopsychia-
    try, 59,* 324–330.

# 10.

# The PIE System: A Canadian Field Test with a Multidisciplinary Mental Health Team

Karen Walsh and Richard Ramsay

*After a brief history of social work in Canada focusing on community mental health services, a description of mental health services in Alberta is presented. An informal field test of PIE was conducted to obtain feedback on the feasibility and potential acceptance of the PIE system in a multidisciplinary community mental health setting as a complement to the standardized assessment format requirements of the agency.*

This chapter will discuss an informal field test of the PIE system in a Canadian setting with a multidisciplinary team of mental health professionals. The objective was to obtain feedback on the feasibility of introducing a separate social work classification system to complement the use of the *Diagnostic and Statistical Manual of Mental Disorders, Third Edition–Revised* (DSM-III-R) (American Psychiatric Association, 1987) and to test the interest of non–social work mental health professionals in using this system.

This system was informally field tested in 1991 with the multidisciplinary rural team of the Calgary region in southern Alberta. Before describing the field test process and outcomes, some background is provided on social work in Canada, the field of community mental health, Alberta Mental Health Services and its clients, and the role of social work in serving the needs of clients.

## Brief History of Social Work in Canada

Social work has been a professional discipline in Canada since the beginning of the 20th century. The roots of Canadian social work are easily traced to European social welfare initiatives, social reform movements, social settlement houses, and Charity Organization Societies in the 18th and 19th centuries. However, the establishment of privately funded Charity Organization Societies and social settlement houses did not have the same effect on the early development of Canadian social work as they did on the development of social work in the United States. Apart from the efforts of various humanitarian and religious groups to serve the "worthy" poor before the turn of the 20th century, early forms of social work in Canada are generally attributed to citizen-initiated social reform activities that are said to have been "spearheaded by the urban reform movement, the Social Gospel movement and muckraking journalists" (Wharf, 1991, p. 20). Other social reformers, identified as social workers, were activist women fighting for the rights of women. The results of these reform activities led to the establishment of government or government-supported social services to protect children or assist the poor. The employees of these services were trained to provide casework services and often were curtailed in their ability to continue social reform activities. There were, however, a few pioneer social workers who continued in the tradition of social reform. These socially conscious individuals, whose ideas were subsequently supported by senior members of the federal Department of Health and Welfare, "were the architects of much of the existing social security system in Canada" (Wharf, 1991, p. 21).

The early education of social workers closely corresponded to the apprenticeship training of Charity Organization Society workers to function as friendly visitors or caseworkers in helping individuals and families under personal and social stress. At the National Conference of Charities and Corrections in 1897, Mary Richmond, a leading figure in the charity organization movement in the United States, was one of the first to call for university-affiliated training schools in applied philanthropy. This was a conscious decision by Richmond to advance the socialization work of charity-based philanthropy into a new age of science-based philanthropy.

By 1904 university-affiliated schools of social work were offering yearlong programs in New York, Boston, and Chicago (Dinerman & Geismar, 1984). The Eastern schools had a strong emphasis on practice wisdom and fieldwork experience. The school in Chicago focused more on research and social reform. The first program in Canada was the Toronto School of Social Services (now the Faculty of Social Work), established at the University of Toronto in 1914. The early curriculum of the Toronto school tried to balance, within a Canadian context, the British focus on the theory of social work and social organization and the American East Coast focus on practical social work methods (Hurl, 1983). Canadian social workers, like their American counterparts, recognized the practice domain, or area of investigation, of their professional work to be the interaction of person and environment, even though the profession invested considerable time and energy into developing method specializations before full acceptance of this broad-based domain occurred in the late 1960s and 1970s.

Similar to developments in the United States, the profession in Canada divided and specialized along several clinically oriented fields of practice (child welfare, family psychiatric, medical, school

social work, and so on) and method specializations (including social casework, social group work, and community work). However,
unlike early developments in the United States, the profession did
not organize into method-specialty associations. A single national
association, the Canadian Association of Social Workers (CASW),
was established in 1926 and operated for almost 50 years as an individual member organization with a nationwide network of provincial and regional chapters (Gowanlock, 1984). In 1975, the
association was restructured into a federation allowing for the autonomous operation of 10 provincial and two territorial associations. Individual members belong to their respective provincial or
territorial associations. CASW, with a membership base in the provincial and territorial associations of more than 13,000 individuals,
is a charter member of the more than 50 national associations that
belong to the International Federation of Social Workers.

## Field of Community Mental Health

The provision of noninstitutional mental health services by Alberta
social workers is rooted in a 70-year history of government-
supported services in the field of community mental health. The
mental hygiene movement of the 1920s provided the impetus for
the establishment in 1929 of part-time, traveling child guidance
clinics outside of mental health hospitals. The first permanent
community-based child guidance clinic was opened in 1947. This
program quickly developed into a provincewide network of permanent and traveling clinics. In 1969, the Blair Report recommended
the deinstitutionalization of long-term mentally ill people and the reintegration of this population into community settings (Blair, 1969).
This shift began when the child guidance clinics were expanded in
1973 to accommodate the follow-up needs of long-term mentally ill
adults.

Naturally, these changes affected the practice of social work in
the field of community mental health and its mental health services
delivery system in the province. In the child guidance clinics, social
workers had practiced exclusively with children and their families.
The nature and scope of presenting problems was usually related to
the child's behavior or academic performance. Social workers had
specific roles and functions on the child guidance teams. They were
responsible for completing social histories at intake and providing
follow-up on their young clients as assigned. As the scope of social
work broadened in the 1960s, the social worker members of a child
guidance team had a professional mandate to work toward alleviating clients' social functioning problems, with a central focus on the
person-in-environment nature of these problems. However, when
the program expanded to include long-term mentally ill people, the
nature of social work changed in all aspects of this redefined field
of practice. Social workers became primary therapists to clients

with diagnosed mental disorders. Many of these clients were treated with psychotropic medications. The role of social workers seeing adult clients shifted to a narrower medical model of illness and treatment, with a reduced mandate to focus on the person-in-environment nature of client problems. With the introduction of DSM-III and its revision, DSM-III-R, social workers had to become oriented to a diagnostic and classification system that was primarily focused on the diagnosis and treatment of mental disorders. Although the newly published *Diagnostic and Statistical Manual of Mental Disorders, Fourth Edition* (DSM-IV) (American Psychiatric Association, 1994) does deal more with social functioning factors in Axis IV, the overall emphasis is still governed by a medical model approach. Also, the general increase in acuity and severity of outpatient problems that resulted from a lower rate of hospitalization required social workers to be well versed in identifying the potential or immediate mental disorder risks that clients could present to themselves or others. Social workers were also required to be well versed in appropriate treatment strategies.

Overall, the practice of social work in the field of community mental health in Alberta has been affected in a number of ways. Ongoing societal changes are felt through shifts away from institutionalization toward keeping individuals in community settings. Also, the medical model has emerged as the standard of practice in the treatment of mental disorders. The social work profession has been without a standard classification system of its own to describe and code common social functioning problems in the broad-perspective person-in-environment domain of the profession. In addition, the profession has been unable to obtain exclusive rights to the title "social worker" (although it does have rights to the title "registered social worker") and did not have a defined scope of practice either in the 1969 Social Workers Act or in the Social Work Profession Act of 1992. Clinical social workers at times find their credibility challenged in mental health settings. These mental health settings are increasingly complex; and professional staff are expected to have extensive knowledge about diagnostic classifications, the use of psychotropic medication, and the application of a variety of treatment modalities. As a result, social workers often have limited opportunities to practice in their own right and increasingly feel subsumed by a medical model that does not reflect the entire scope of their training.

## Mental Health Services in Alberta

Alberta is one of 10 provinces and two northern territories in Canada. It is a prairie province located in western Canada with an area of 661,185 square kilometers and a population of approximately 2.53 million people. The province is roughly twice the size of California and has slightly less than one-tenth the population.

Canada itself is characterized by geographical, political, and economic disparity and diversity. As pointed out by a past president of CASW, "to understand social work in Canada is to understand the diversity of Canadians" (Drover, 1984, p. 6). Drover described the country as a land of many contrasts. Canadians live in the second largest country in the world, but it is one of the most sparsely populated countries. Canada's heritage is closely tied to the British monarchy but 60 percent of the people are not Anglo-Saxon. The country has two official languages, French and English, yet most people speak only one language. Canada has one of the highest standards of living in the world but still reports large numbers of people living below the poverty line.

Economically and politically, Canada and its provinces have always been quite interdependent. The country is a federal state that became independent in 1867. The federal and provincial governments are based on the traditions of the British Parliamentary system. The federal government has an appointed upper house, the Senate, and an elected lower house, the House of Commons. The provincial governments have only elected legislative assemblies. The division of power between the federal and provincial governments is distributed on a shared and exclusive basis. The federal government has responsibilities over such matters as defense, currency, and regulation of commerce. Provinces have responsibility for health, education, and social services. However, the once exclusive power of provinces over health, education, and social services is now shared. The federal government uses a transfer payment system to the provinces to ensure that national standards are maintained and that the provinces provide direct services to their citizens. Health care is jointly funded by the federal and provincial governments.

The health care system in Canada is governed by the Canada Health Act of 1985. The fundamental principles of this legislation are universality, portability, public administration, accessibility, and comprehensiveness. The funding of the health care system is complex, involving some federal transfer payments, income from provincial health care premiums, and in some instances provincial taxes. Ratios and components of the funding base vary from province to province.

Mental health services in Alberta are one component of the overall health care delivery system. The Department of Alberta Health operates the Mental Health Services division, which is governed by the provincial Mental Health Act (1990, revised). This act formally recognizes the individual rights protected under the Canadian Charter of Rights and Freedoms and respects the adoption of recent patient rights principles in mental health practice. As a result of 1988 legislation and subsequent revisions, the provincial government has appointed a Mental Health Patient Advocate. The mission of the Mental Health Services division is to promote, preserve, and restore the mental health of Albertans. This mission is to be achieved through the equitable, effective, efficient, and accountable delivery of services and programs in response to the needs of Albertans (Alberta Health, 1992).

The community outpatient component of Mental Health Services provides assessment, diagnostic, and treatment services to Alberta residents of all ages. Alberta has 56 permanent mental health clinics. In addition, rural Alberta areas are served by approximately 44 traveling clinics. Mental Health Services clinics serve approximately 21,000 people annually. There is no charge for service.

Mental Health Services clinics are fully accredited by the Canadian Council for Health Facilities Accreditation as community psychiatric outpatient clinics. The provision of mental health services is part of the larger mental health system that includes hospitals, funded agencies, and private practitioners. The significance of mental health services in current society reflects a fundamental social value of providing such services to all Alberta residents. The Mental Health Services component endeavors to make services readily available to all communities across the province. Having services in the community minimizes the need to seek outside services and may prevent the need for hospitalization, which is more costly and often more disruptive for individuals and their families.

### Mental Health Services Staffing

Mental Health Services clinics operate on a primary therapist model, with new clients assigned to a nurse, psychologist, or social worker as the primary therapist. Clients may also be seen when necessary by a psychiatrist, who is engaged on a contract basis—for example, when a prescription or a diagnostic opinion is required.

Primary therapists function as part of multidisciplinary teams that are organized by geographic areas, such as rural areas, or by specialized programs in urban centers, such as child, adolescent, or adult programs. Wherever possible, assessment and treatment plans are discussed by a multidisciplinary team that includes a clinical supervisor and consulting psychiatrist. Assessment, diagnostic formulation, and treatment plan formats are standardized throughout Mental Health Services clinics in Alberta. The initial assessment must conform to Provincial Quality Audit Standards, which sets out nine mandatory headings. These headings are identifying data, intake information, presenting problem, history, present functioning/mental status, risk assessment, formulation, diagnosis, and treatment plan. DSM-III-R is used by primary therapists in the formulation of a diagnosis. Treatment goals are identified by the client and therapist, then worked on as agreed. Treatment modalities could include individual or group therapy; psychotropic medication; and referral to residential, vocational, or community programs and treatment plans.

## Mental Health Clients

The client population served by Mental Health Services covers the full age spectrum of Alberta residents. Service priority is assigned to children, elderly people, people chronically disabled by mental illness, aboriginals, people with mental handicaps and mental disorders, people affected by family violence, and immigrants and refugees. The clients of Mental Health Services clinics must freely agree to receive services.

The diversity of the client population, as well as geographic and demographic variations, makes the delivery of mental health services complex. Consequently, there is no typical client profile. However, clients are often similar in their multiproblem presentations. Clients with severe mental disorders frequently experience difficulties in daily living. Lack of shelter, need for financial assistance, family or relationship problems, and the need for vocational rehabilitation are prevalent among many clients. Therefore, clients with mental disorders in community settings must be assessed in the context of their overall biopsychosocial functioning, taking strengths and weaknesses into consideration.

## Role of Social Work on a Multidisciplinary Team

Social work is one of the professional disciplines in the multidisciplinary team model. Social workers operate as primary therapists to mental health clients. Each of the professional disciplines on the multidisciplinary team is valued in the sense that each profession contributes the specialized knowledge and expertise achieved through their professional education and training. The client benefits from the input of a broad-based treatment team through consultation and conferences.

The combination of professional disciplines (nursing, psychology, psychiatry, and social work) assigned to multidisciplinary teams in community mental health clinics broadens the spectrum of professional expertise offered. In effect, this enriches the services received by clients. However, the shift of mental health services from hospital to community settings is relatively recent, as is the broad acceptance of DSM-III-R. In some respects social workers are still in the process of defining their role within this milieu. Social workers, by virtue of their training and orientation, readily recognize the complexity of difficulties and needs presented by clients with mental disorders. The interaction of social functioning and environmental factors is the domain of social work practice. A classification system compatible with DSM-III-R could help to formally establish the role of social workers in the mental health field. The PIE system appears to be a system that might help social workers make Axis IV of DSM-III-R and the new DSM-IV become a more relevant part of assessment and treatment-planning discussions.

## The PIE System

PIE is a four-factor system designed to describe the problems of clients on each of the factors (Karls & Wandrei, 1992). Factor I is used to describe social role and interaction difficulty problems. Factor II is used to describe systemic problems in the social institutions that exist to help the client. These two factors provide the core social work description. Factor III is used to describe mental disorders according to the diagnostic categories in DSM-III-R. Factor IV is used to describe physical disorders according to the *International Classification of Diseases–Ninth Revision–Clinical Modification* (ICD-9-CM) (U.S. Department of Health and Human Services, 1991). All four factors must be described to provide a holistic picture of a client's problems.

## Methodology for a Field Test of PIE

The authors conducted an informal field test to obtain information on the feasibility and potential acceptance of the PIE system in a multidisciplinary community mental health setting as a complement to the standardized assessment format requirements of the agency. The participants consisted of the primary therapist members and consulting psychiatrists assigned to the Calgary region rural team of Alberta Mental Health Services. The field test was conducted as a special addition to regularly scheduled conference intake days. Because the field test was voluntary, team members were not required to participate.

Information about the PIE system was initially presented to Calgary region social workers of Alberta Mental Health Services in October 1990. A draft of the *PIE Manual* (Karls & Wandrei, 1990) was subsequently reviewed and discussed by the Calgary region managers. The managers explored the possibility of field testing the system with their respective multidisciplinary teams.

The rural team volunteered to participate in an informal field test of the PIE system. This team provides mental health services to six rural areas, including several small towns and villages and one midsize city outside Calgary. Each clinic has one or two primary therapists, a secretary, and when possible, a part-time consulting psychiatrist. The rural team meets monthly to discuss cases and attend to organizational business issues.

The rural team has six psychologists, one social worker, and one nurse. Team members expressed an interest in exploring alternate models and believed that the PIE system had potential as a holistic assessment system. The team understood that they would still be expected to comply with the standardized assessment and diagnostic format required by Mental Health Services. The team agreed to conduct the PIE assessment in addition to the standardized assessment, diagnostic formulation, and treatment plan format requirements of Mental Health Services.

Four rural clinic site visits were planned over a six-week period, attended by a clinical supervisor and a University of Calgary Faculty of Social Work consultant familiar with the PIE system. Mental Health Services and the Faculty of Social Work have a contractual agreement for teaching and practicum purposes. The field tests were organized as one-day sessions so that therapists from each clinic could receive a brief training on the use of the system and then use PIE with a client in an intake interview. The faculty consultant conducted the training sessions and observed the client sessions. The draft *PIE Manual* was given to all team members as a reading assignment well before the scheduled site visit.

The field test day was divided into two parts. In the morning, the team members were instructed on how to use the manual and the coding system. All participating staff watched a video from the Social Work Interview Series produced by the University of Calgary (Ramsay, 1977), which was one of the videotaped client interviews used in the pilot PIE reliability study. An informal observation of interrater reliability was noted by the supervisor and PIE consultant. In the afternoon, team members were scheduled to conduct two new client intake interviews. Each therapist obtained the necessary clearance from the client to have team members observe the intake interview. The clinical supervisor, consultant, and other team members observed the interview from a one-way observation room and completed independent assessments using PIE. Each therapist conducted the interview in keeping with the tenets of his or her professional discipline and the standardized formats of Mental Health Services. In addition, each therapist completed an assessment using the PIE classification system. At the end of the interview, the therapist and other team members consulted with each other to determine an acceptable treatment plan to present to the client for approval. In addition, the team discussed the experience of using the PIE system and offered verbal feedback about the value of the system specific to the intake case and generally to the overall merits of using it as part of the standardized format of Mental Health Services.

## Results and Discussion

The PIE system was used with a total of seven client intake interviews. One clinic had a no-show appointment. The participating primary therapists represented the disciplines of psychiatric nursing, psychology, and social work. Only one of the eight participating therapists was a social worker. A consulting psychiatrist observed two of the intake interviews.

There was general agreement from all participants at the end of the training session and at the end of the intake interview that the PIE categories characterized the language and ideas of working in community mental health. The categories describing the social role

and interaction difficulty problems were particularly compatible
with the daily living problems commonly presented to clinic therapists. The system was judged by the participants to be conceptually
sound and to have face validity for use in a community mental
health setting.

A multiproblem case, typical of the type presented to the rural
clinics, was seen at one of the intake sessions.

## Case Study

Julie was a 19-year-old unemployed, single mother with an eight-month-old
daughter. Julie received income support from public assistance. She was referred by her family doctor. The client wanted help in getting her feelings
out about being alone, overweight, and cut off from family and friends. Julie
had a poor work history, was oversleeping, and was eating a lot when alone.
She spent most of the interview expressing angry and depressed feelings
about the lack of love and supportive attention from her family of origin during her childhood and adolescence.

In addition to Factor III and Factor IV assessments that were covered by standardized assessment requirements of the agency, this
case illustrated the value of including Factor I and Factor II descriptions to help with planning and treatment decisions. Julie's primary
Factor I problem was coded as a Child Role Problem with her family of origin of the withdrawal/isolation type (in the last section of
the *PIE Manual*, this has been simplified to the isolation type). This
problem was of high severity, its duration was from one to five
years, and Julie had inadequate coping skills (1360.425). Julie's Factor I problem was compounded by an inadequate Affectional Support System on Factor II. Julie's Factor II problem was of high
severity and its duration was one to five years (10102.42). The secondary Factor I problem was coded as a Parent Role Problem and
frustration with the demands of being an adolescent parent. This
problem was of high severity, its duration was six months to one
year, and Julie had somewhat inadequate coping skills (1130.434).
The Parent Role Problem was compounded by the Factor II problems of an inadequate parenting support system of moderate severity, lasting one to six months (10102.34) and insufficient economic
resources to provide for Julie and her child, also of moderate severity, lasting one to six months (5401.34). The addition of the social
functioning descriptions provides for a broader spectrum of individ-
ualized and social treatment goals that might be identified to deal
with the multiproblem nature of client presentations.

## Findings of the Field Study

The participants in the field study were generally positive about the
feasibility of the PIE system. Some saw the system developing to

the point of sharing the record of information with clients. Factor I
was easy to apply and considered a practical method of describing
the social functioning and interaction problems of clients. Participants found Factor I quite helpful in determining practical next-
step social functioning treatment plans for their clients. Factor I
provided a more enriched description of client strengths and difficulties compared with the diagnostic categories in DSM-III-R. However, participants found it hard to make judgments about the macro
nature of an environmental problem. In general, they did not think
they had enough information about the institutional services in
their community to distinguish which environmental problems were
systemic in the community and which were particular to the individual. Participants were more inclined to describe environmental problems in terms of difficulties facing the particular client. The Factor II
list of environmental problems helped team members to be more
specific about the other participants in the role and interaction problems described under Factor I. The difficulties using Factor II may
be a reflection that only one of the eight team members was a social
worker.

Interrater reliability was tested between the interview observers
and the primary therapist conducting the interview. Discussions at
the end of each interview indicated good rates of interrater agreement across several social functioning problems. The raters were inclined to select more than one social role problem instead of
identifying a primary role problem. There was less interrater
agreement in identifying the type of interaction difficulty associated
with social role problems. Feedback discussion revealed that this
was because of a lack of integrated familiarity with the meaning of
each category. Overall, the raters agreed there was good potential
for interrater reliability to be demonstrated with increased study of
the manual and more practice in using the classification system.

An important value of this field test was conducting it with members of a multidisciplinary team who might be inclined to be more
comfortable than social workers with the medical disease orientation of DSM-III-R. There was a risk that these members would find
the PIE system an unnecessary addition to the demands of an existing standardized assessment format that is already quite lengthy
and comprehensive. The positive feedback about the practical merits of the system from the non–social work members of the team
was encouraging. Their feedback points to the value of developing
the PIE system not only for social workers to use independently or
as members of a multidisciplinary team, but also as a system other
professionals can use to complement the classification and diagnostic systems specific to their own disciplines.

## The Future of Social Work in
## Community Mental Health

The field of practice for social workers in mental health settings is
affected by the constant process of change, new economic realities,

and emerging trends in mental health treatment and care. The future of social work in community mental health settings in Alberta has been a topic of much discussion. Staffing patterns confirm that fewer new social workers are being employed in community mental health clinics despite concerted recruitment efforts. Employers and academics are unable to explain this phenomenon. Social work candidates are simply applying in fewer numbers.

Furthermore, there is a trend in mental health fields toward creating generic mental health workers under a generic job classification system. Generic mental health workers would be required to possess knowledge and skills specific to the needs of the mental health setting.

As with many changes there are potential advantages and drawbacks to this trend. A generic mental health worker model would likely result in pay equity for members of the primary therapist disciplines, which does not exist in the current multidisciplinary team model. However, the inevitable question arises: Would the disciplines eventually lose their unique professional identity within a homogeneous generic model? And, what would the future be for the PIE systems in a generic mental health setting? The feedback received from other professional disciplines involved in this field test indicates the potential for a broader applicability of the PIE system. The mental health field is evolving in the direction of mental health workers becoming more specialized in terms of knowledge requirements, yet at the same time becoming more generic in terms of professional identity. As this trend progresses, the use of a comprehensive biopsychosocial classification system such as PIE could greatly assist current efforts in the mental health field to develop a more standardized, measurable, and accountable method of evaluating the benefits of specialized, multidisciplinary services.

## References

Alberta Health. (1992). *Future directions for mental health services in Alberta.* Edmonton, Alberta, Canada: Author.

American Psychiatric Association. (1987). *Diagnostic and statistical manual of mental disorders* (3rd ed., rev.). Washington, DC: American Psychiatric Press.

American Psychiatric Association. (1994). *Diagnostic and statistical manual of mental disorders* (4th ed.). Washington, DC: American Psychiatric Press.

Blair, W.R.N. (1969). *Mental health in Alberta.* Calgary, Alberta, Canada: Government of Alberta.

Dinerman, M., & Geismar, L. (1984). *A quarter-century of social work education.* New York and Silver Spring, MD: Copublished by the Council on Social Work Education, ABC–CLIO, and the National Association of Social Workers.

Drover, G. (1984). Policy and legislative perspectives. *Social Worker, 51,* 6–10.

Gowanlock, G. (1984). Perspectives on the profession. *Social Worker, 51,* 17–20.

Hurl, L. F. (1983). *Building a profession: The origin and development of the department of social services in the University of Toronto, 1914–1928* (Monogram Series). Toronto: University of Toronto Faculty of Social Work.

Karls, J., & Wandrei, K. (1990). *Person-in-environment: A system for describing, classifying, and coding problems of social functioning.* Silver Spring, MD: NASW Press.

Karls, J., & Wandrei, K. (1992). PIE: A new language for social work. *Social Work, 37,* 80–85.

Ramsay, R. (1977). *The social work interview series, I–IV* (Videotapes). Calgary, Alberta, Canada: University of Calgary, Department of Communications Media.

U.S. Department of Health and Human Services. (1991). *International classification of diseases–9th revision–clinical modification* (4th ed.). Washington, DC: U.S. Government Printing Office.

Wharf, B. (Ed.). (1991). *Social work and social change in Canada.* Toronto: McClelland & Stewart.

# 11.

# PIE's Potential for Furthering an Ecological Perspective for Social Work in the Netherlands

Kathleen O'C. Hoekstra

*In response to the scrutiny the social work profession has received by the Dutch government and the public, Dutch social workers have searched for unity across fields of practice. The author describes her experiences working with the social work faculty of the Hoogschool van Amsterdam to introduce them to the ecological perspective. The Dutch social workers found PIE to be an excellent tool for implementing this perspective.*

The Netherlands has long been viewed as a strong example of a democratic social welfare nation. Thus, among its institutions one might expect to find a strong Dutch social work profession. On the contrary, in recent years the social work profession in the Netherlands has found itself increasingly on the defensive. Earlier popular perceptions were of the social worker as an overly serious and usually female champion for change, reflected in the term "greystockings." This view has been replaced with a less confusing one in which social work is seen as part of the so-called "soft sector" believed by many Dutch people to have systematically undermined national character by promoting overly liberal attitudes and programs. The Netherlands, like other European nations, is rapidly becoming culturally and ethnically diversified while being faced with a high unemployment rate and its accompanying tensions. Just as economic and social factors foster the need for social work services, they also fuel the search for scapegoats. Thus, at this challenging time, the profession may not find the needed level of public support.

The government recently mandated the merger of schools of social work with other technical training schools such as those for health and education into large polytechnic institutes. Many social work educators believe this merger is a reflection of the social work profession's failure to demonstrate its unique training needs and its place among the helping professions. "Social worker" continues to be an unprotected title that may be held by someone trained in teaching, psychology, sociology, and anthropology. Also, because of the requirement that polytechnic faculty have a university education, one regularly finds social work faculty who are trained primarily in these other fields because social work is not yet a university-trained, but rather a polytechnic-trained, profession. Even the recent endowment of the first chair of social work at the University of Utrecht is seen by some social workers as an attempt by outsiders to criticize and dictate to the profession.

Social work is by no means alone in receiving close scrutiny by both government and the public. Across the helping professions, which by American standards receive generous public funding, there is a clear call for accountability. Thus, in addition to meeting the challenge to claim their professional domain, social workers must also be concerned with evaluating the effectiveness of their methods.

One response to this crisis has been a search for unity across fields of practice. In 1987, the Dutch Committee on Professional Questions Regarding Social Work was formed to develop a profile of the professional social worker. In a report (Kessener, Walpot, & Alsem, 1987) informed by input from a large number of social work professionals and organizations, the committee clearly delineated the interface between person and environment as the social work domain. The committee identified the professional tasks to be undertaken in that domain as well as the related teachable skills required for those tasks. Although it is an attempt to cope with crisis, this effort to identify and disseminate a core professional profile can also be seen as a natural developmental step for a relatively new profession. The response is reminiscent of one undertaken in the United States when social work education moved away from the fragmenting fields of practice model toward a generic view of practice.

## Ecological Perspective

The energy created by such a defining step can be seen in some recent activities of the social work faculty at the Hoogschool van Amsterdam (Amsterdam Polytechnic), which has one of the largest social work training programs in the Netherlands. Under the leadership of Karl E. H. Hesser and Anjo van Hout, this faculty has been involved in developing training methods that will prepare professional social workers to work generically in the social work domain. In a search for generic models, several Amsterdam faculty members traveled abroad, especially to the United States, to observe social work education and practice. At the request of Hesser and van Hout, a study tour of several schools of social work and social services agencies in New York was arranged.

As a result of that experience, the Amsterdam faculty became interested in the ecological perspective as it is described in the life model (Germain & Gitterman, 1980). Although the faculty felt that this perspective, on which I have also written (Hoekstra, 1984), was consistent with the systemic approach already familiar to Dutch social workers, they believed that the ecological perspective went beyond systems thinking. Their reaction was similar to Germain's (1978) earlier views on the limitations of systems theory for application to human systems. The Amsterdam faculty felt that the ecological perspective not only incorporated the traditional values of Dutch social work but reflected current thinking about the nature of the problems social work was being asked to address. Thus, in 1990 the Amsterdam faculty invited me to present master classes on the ecological perspective to other Dutch social work educators and practitioners.

In these classes, as well as in other meetings with Dutch social work educators, I described the ecological perspective and provided training in the use of techniques to apply its concepts. The Dutch response to conceptualizing practice ecologically and to applying related techniques such as the ecomap (Hartman, 1978), the genogram (McGoldrick & Gerson, 1985), and transactions in the environment (TIE) (Monkman, 1991) has been extremely enthusiastic. Illustrative of the successful Dutch adaptation of these American social work products is the lead article in a recent volume of the journal *Sociale Interventie,* in which Hesser and van Hout (1992) recounted successful field applications of ecological principles developed by Bronfenbrenner (1979) and elaborated in the life model by Germain and Gitterman (1980).

## Ecological Tools in Dutch Social Work Practice

As my dialogue with the Amsterdam faculty has developed, the need to continue to design and teach techniques for ecologically based social work practice has become clear. As Germain and Gitterman noted themselves, the ecologically based life model does not spell out specific practice principles or provide needed tools. These must be developed as ecological concepts are applied in the field.

The idea of using instruments as social work tools was surprisingly new for the Dutch social work professionals. Such technology has been seen as more natural to the domain of other helping professions such as teaching, psychology, and psychiatry. However, within a year of my introduction of the ecomap (Hartman, 1978) in 1990, Dutch social workers had creatively adapted and applied it in several fields of practice (Hesser & van Hout, 1992). Thus, the transfer of technology by and for American social work was not only smooth but successful. This success has strengthened interest in the Netherlands not only in the ecological perspective generally, but specifically in assessment and evaluation methods and techniques to implement this view of helping.

It was in assisting the Amsterdam faculty to identify such ecological tools that I introduced the person-in-environment (PIE) system

developed by Karls and Wandrei (1992). Because PIE not only assesses problems functionally as role-related interactions between
people and their environments, but also evaluates both person-
based and environment-based coping resources, it provides the
transactional picture we define as the interface, as what we claim to
be the domain of professional social work.

Before PIE was introduced in the Netherlands, it had already
been adapted for use in Liege, Belgium, where it had been translated into Flemish, a language quite similar to Dutch. At St. Joseph's
Hospital, PIE had been adapted by strengthening its ability to identify client strengths, and it was valuable for work with psychiatric
patients. I was unable to secure a copy of this Flemish version in
time for my presentation in Amsterdam. However, the workshop
participants were proficient in English so language was not a significant obstacle.

In August 1991 I presented a full-day workshop on PIE to 18
Dutch social work educators and practitioners. Most of these participants had attended my previous master classes so they had at least
a general understanding of the ecological perspective and the life
model. Thus, they readily saw the potential of PIE for ecological assessment.

A special enthusiasm could be detected among those participants
who were at odds with the notion that social work should be primarily concerned with reflexively providing concrete services to clients. This "entitlement" philosophy, which has characterized Dutch
social work for decades, is now strongly challenged by those who
believe such a conception of practice not only undermines client
coping but also obviates needed broader social change. Several
workshop participants noted that in conceptualizing the person-in-
environment functionally in terms of social role, PIE not only acti-
vated the transactional dual focus that is unique to social work, but
also identified a truly therapeutic mixture, and a dose of intervention, that would permit a client to act in his or her own behalf to
the degree possible, and by this activity, to grow.

Obviously, one day of training, even when the conceptual under-
pinnings of an instrument are adequately understood, is not sufficient to produce skilled application of an instrument of PIE's scope.
Nonetheless, after working in small groups to apply PIE to the case
vignettes developed by Karls and Wandrei (see the case examples
in the *PIE Manual*), the workshop participants were able to produce
valuable oral and written critiques. Overall, participants felt that using PIE stimulated dual-focused thinking more so than the less
structured and often client-only or environment-only interviews
they were more familiar with. As a result, the participants found
that thoughts about specific and purposeful actions came more
quickly. Comparisons were made to TIE in which the client side
of the dual focus is similarly conceptualized in terms of the individual's basic needs but less information for specific action is gained.
Some participants noted that PIE's dual focus not only made it a

good assessment tool, but also an effective multidisciplinary case-conferencing organizer because it encompasses areas of functioning in which other professionals such as physicians and teachers might be involved.

Among the weaknesses noted was that, like many instruments, PIE might promote inequality between client and helper because the helper could be seen as rating or judging the client. In a similar vein, some participants were concerned that applying such a lengthy instrument might inhibit natural conversation or lead to the worker becoming dominant in the relationship. Some participants felt that the instrument did not focus as strongly or specifically as it might have on the strengths of the client, and thus could be seen as continuing in the tradition of the medical model.

## Conclusion

PIE was developed to help American social workers assess problems from the profession's unique dual perspective of individual functioning and related environmental factors. The authors of PIE contend that it is an atheoretical system that can be incorporated into many practice orientations. Because one of the goals of PIE is to provide social workers across fields and orientations with a common language, it was interesting to see that this instrument held such interest for practitioners across different cultures as well. This cross-cultural finding provides strong support for the contention that social work is a professional activity grounded on basic ideas about social functioning. In a world where nations find themselves rapidly diversifying, often at speeds that greatly challenge the ability of traditional institutions to meet critical needs, such findings fuel the hope that our profession will be able to respond adequately. The questions raised by the Dutch social workers about PIE, which were valuable for their potential to strengthen this promising instrument, made it clear that at least across our two cultures, the common language of social work already encompasses shared commitment to values. To paraphrase Mark Twain: To this practitioner, it appears that the news of our demise has been greatly exaggerated.

## References

Bronfenbrenner, U. (1979). *The ecology of human development*. Cambridge, MA: Harvard University Press.

Germain, C. (1978). General systems theory and ego psychology: An ecological perspective. *Social Service Review, 52*, 535–550.

Germain, C., & Gitterman, A. (1980). *Life model of practice*. New York: Columbia University Press.

Hartman, A. (1978). Diagrammatic assessment of family relationships. *Social Casework, 59*, 465–476.

Hesser, K.E.H., & van Hout, A. (1992). Een sociaal–ecologisch perspectief voor hulpverlening. *Social Interventie, 1,* 131–140.

Hoekstra, K. O'C. (1984). An ecological definition of mistreatment of adolescents. *Children and Youth Services Review, 6,* 285–298.

Karls, J., & Wandrei, K. (1992). PIE: A new language for social work. *Social Work, 31,* 80–85.

Kessener, A. W., Walpot, B., & Alsem, I. (1987). *Professional profile of the social worker.* s'Hertogenbosch, the Netherlands: Committee on Professional Questions Regarding Social Work.

McGoldrick, M., & Gerson, R. (1985). *Genograms in family assessment.* New York: W. W. Norton.

Monkman, M. M. (1991). Outcome objectives in social work practice: Person and environment. *Social Work, 36,* 253–258.

# Section IV

# Other Issues

*In this section a variety of important concerns in the development and use of the PIE system are addressed. Karls and Wandrei have contributed a chapter on PIE as a tool in case management. Delewski reports on her use of PIE in teaching social work students. To stimulate readers' critical faculties, there is an essay by Ramsay in which he stretches their thinking beyond the ecological systems model of social work into a futuristic synergistic model on which a future version of PIE might be developed. Williams reports on the testing of PIE and discusses the use of PIE in research. Karls and Wandrei conclude with a chapter on how a computerized version of PIE may make the task of capturing and reporting assessment findings less tedious.*

# 12.

# PIE as a New Tool for More Effective Case Management

James M. Karls and Karin E. Wandrei

*This chapter outlines the application of the PIE system to the classification
of problems that clients bring to case managers. It notes how the PIE
system allows for a clear delineation of the appropriate targets for case
management intervention. The chapter also illustrates the system's use with
three examples: (1) child protective services, (2) chronically mentally ill
people, and (3) older adults.*

**C**ase management has been a method in human services delivery in the United States for more than 130 years. Case management's origins are in the dual concerns of those responsible for helping the poor, sick, and disadvantaged to provide the needed services and yet to conserve the funds allocated for these services. According to Weil and Karls (1985),

> the history of case management is best correlated with the industrialization and urbanization of our society and the growth in size and structure of our country's health and social services systems. It seems fair to speculate that case management would not exist if human problems were singular or simple, if they could be resolved with a single intervention, and if the intervention were readily available and inexpensive. Most human problems are complex and often chronic. The complexity of individual needs coupled with the complexity of services necessitates a clearly worked out case management approach. (p. 10)

Case management is practiced by various human services professionals, among them nurses, psychologists, psychiatrists, rehabilitation counselors, and others. Although the origins of case management theory and practice are in the field of social work, the concepts and practices are readily adopted by other professions. In differentiating case management performed by social workers from

An earlier version of this chapter entitled "The Person-In-Environment System for Classifying Client Problems: A New Tool for More Effective Case Management" by James M. Karls and Karin E. Wandrei was published in the *Journal of Case Management*, 1992, 1(3), pp. 90–95. Reprinted, with changes, with the permission of the Springer Publishing Company.

generic case management, the National Association of Social Workers (1992) defined social work case management as a

> method of providing services whereby a professional social worker assesses the needs of the client and the client's family, when appropriate, and arranges, coordinates, monitors, evaluates, and advocates for a package of multiple services to meet the specific client's complex needs; social work case management addresses both the individual client's biopsychosocial status as well as the state of the social system in which case management operates. Social work case management is both micro and macro in nature: intervention occurs at both the client and system levels. (p. 5)

As a process, case management is an orderly, planned provision of services intended to facilitate a client's functioning at as normal a level as possible and as economically as possible (Weil & Karls, 1985). Weil and Karls identified the essential elements for effective case management as "client identification, assessment of need, service planning, service coordination and linking, and the monitoring and continuous evaluation of the client, of the service delivery, and of available resources" (p. vi).

Most of these terms are self-explanatory. Client identification is reaching out into the community to identify case management candidates and engaging them in the case management process. Assessment encompasses an evaluation of the client's physical, mental, and social functioning problems and of the problems in the community that affect the client. Service planning is the selection of interventions and providers of these interventions. It follows a comprehensive analysis of the problem complex. No case management plan ends at this point for it is the coordination of the delivery of services and the linking of the client to appropriate services that is the task for the case manager. Service delivery is followed by evaluation of the client and the services provided in terms of whether case management goals are being reached.

To provide these essential elements, most case managers and case management agencies have developed a series of procedures to collect and order the array of problems their clients present. Kane (1985) told us that

> many case management efforts have vigorous evaluation components. At times, the evaluation has seemed to drive practitioners into adopting lengthier or more standardized assessment procedures than they would otherwise use. The ongoing tensions between research and practical uses of information may abate somewhat as programs become operational. Unresolved questions will still remain, however, about how much information is needed on what dimensions and how frequently. Case management programs should be able to generate systemwide information that will assist in community planning. But any information system depends on uniform, consistent data collection. (p. 196)

An essential element in case management is the assessment of need or the diagnosis. This is the linchpin for the service plan and the evaluation of client progress. Without a comprehensive biopsychosocial assessment of the individual, a case management plan is likely to be ineffective. Without consensus on the nature and extent of the client's problems, the several agencies or practitioners involved in the helping process are like players on a team who do not know in which direction they are going or what roles they play in reaching a goal.

Identifying and ordering the multiple problems presented by most case management clients is a complex task that can be simplified by using the person-in-environment system. With its multifactorial system and uniform language for describing problems, PIE communicates the problem complex in terms that can be understood by practitioners and clients alike. Although developed initially for social workers, PIE readily lends itself to use among other professions engaged in case management.

The elements and structure of the PIE system have been described in other parts of this book and will not be repeated here. In this chapter the application of the system will be illustrated by three vignettes from case management practice. The first is a child welfare case, the second addresses case management with a chronically mentally ill person, and the third assesses a client of an older adult service. These illustrations demonstrate that the PIE system has the potential for providing a comprehensive description of a client's problem no matter what the setting and that this description can serve as the vehicle for planning, implementing, and evaluating the interventions chosen to address the client's multiple problems.

After the case manager has identified the problems the client is experiencing in social role functioning (Factor I) and identified the contributing environmental problems (Factor II), the mental health problems are then noted (Factor III), and the physical health problems are described (Factor IV). No matter what the agency setting—medical, geriatric, child protection, developmental disability, mental health—these four factors can describe the problem complex and serve as the foundation for a case management plan. After the case manager has made a listing of the client's problems on each of the four factors, the problem complex is clearly presented and the interventions can be chosen to address each of the problems noted. Although it is not demonstrated in this chapter, it is possible to quantify the interventions either in terms of time or expected changes in the identified problem and to monitor the client's progress, or lack of it, for each problem area identified.

## Examples of PIE Assessment

Because of space limitations, the examples that follow do not include all the details required to reach a definitive PIE statement. The numerical codes are included to demonstrate the potential for uniform data collection and for the facilitation of administration in

*Exhibit 1*

**PIE Assessment of a Child Protective Services Case**

| Assessment Findings | | Recommended Interventions |
|---|---|---|
| **Factor I** | | |
| 1180.564 | Parent Role Problem, mixed type (victimization and responsibility), very high severity, two weeks' or less duration, somewhat inadequate coping skills (primary problem) | Parent education classes Psychotherapy |
| 1370.515 | Child Role Problem, victimization type, very high severity, more than five years' duration, inadequate coping skills | Psychotherapy |
| 1220.344 | Spouse Role Problem, ambivalence type, moderate severity, one to six months' duration, somewhat inadequate coping skills | Psychotherapy |
| **Factor II** | | |
| 5201.42 | Economic/Basic Needs System Problem, absence of shelter in a community, high severity, one to five years' duration | Referral to shelter Political advocacy |
| **Factor III** | | |
| Axis I | | |
| 304.20 | Cocaine Dependence, severe | Referral to drug treatment |
| 309.89 | Posttraumatic Stress Disorder | Psychotherapy |
| Axis II | | |
| 799.90 | Diagnosis deferred | |
| **Factor IV** | | |
| | Diabetes (by client report) | Medical evaluation Referral to diabetes association |

larger case management programs. For further information on coding, the reader is referred to chapter 2.

## Case Study: Child Welfare

Anna is a 28-year-old mother of two children, Adam, age three, and Alice, age five. Alice disclosed three days ago to her preschool teacher that she and Adam had been repeatedly sexually molested by Greg, Anna's live-in boyfriend. The teacher reported this to child protective services (CPS). On her investigation, the CPS worker found that Anna had used crack cocaine extensively for the past seven months. Because of Anna's drug usage and her poor

*Exhibit 2*

**PIE Analysis of a Chronically Mentally Ill Person**

| Assessment Findings | | Recommended Interventions |
|---|---|---|
| **Factor I** | | |
| 4230.516 | Inpatient/Client Role Problem, responsibility type, very high severity, more than five years' duration, no coping skills | Supportive casework<br>Medication reevaluation |
| **Factor II** | | |
| 8105.42 | Health, Safety, and Social Services System Problem, absence of adequate mental health services, high severity, one to five years' duration | Political advocacy |
| **Factor III** | | |
| Axis I | | |
| 295.34 | Schizophrenia, paranoid, chronic with acute exacerbation | Medication reevaluation<br>Supportive casework |
| Axis II | | |
| V71.09 | No diagnosis | |
| **Factor IV** | | |
| | No health problems reported | |

salary as a bank teller, there was little food in the house and the gas and electric company was on the verge of discontinuing her service because she could not pay the bill.

Alice's disclosure and the subsequent CPS intervention distressed Anna greatly. She stated that one of the major reasons she smokes crack was because of recurrent memories and nightmares about her own sexual molestation by her stepfather, which had occurred when she was also five. Anna also was diagnosed two years ago as having diabetes.

Greg had come into Anna's life to help with her financial problems. Ever since Anna could remember, there were few jobs available in her community at which people could make enough money to support themselves. For the past three months, however, she and Greg have been fighting a great deal, and she feels that smoking crack allowed her to escape many of her problems. Anna is now worried that she will not be able to pay her bills and will become homeless, because there has been a serious lack of affordable housing in her community for the past four years.

The CPS worker could use the PIE system to clarify Anna's problems and suggest some possible interventions (Exhibit 1).

*Exhibit 3*

**PIE Assessment of an Older Adult**

| Assessment Findings | | Recommended Interventions |
|---|---|---|
| Factor I | | |
| 1250.424 | Spouse Role Problem loss type, high severity, one to five years' duration, somewhat inadequate coping skills | Psychotherapy Widows support group |
| 2250.444 | Friend Role Problem, loss type, high severity, one to six months' duration, somewhat inadequate coping | Psychotherapy |
| Factor II | | |
| 8305.45 | Health, Safety, and Social Services System Problem, other social services problem (threatened elimination of services), high severity, two to four weeks' duration | Political organizing |
| Factor III | | |
| Axis I | | |
| 296.23 | Major Depression, single episode, severe without psychotic features | Psychotherapy Medication referral |
| Axis II | | |
| V71.09 | No diagnosis | |
| Factor IV | | |
| | Arthritis (by client report) | Consultation with physician Arthritis support group |

## Case Study: Chronic Mentally Ill Person

Bob is a 34-year-old man who has been diagnosed as having paranoid schizophrenia for the past 10 years. He was recently hospitalized for the 15th time. As has been his usual pattern, three weeks ago Bob stopped taking his antipsychotic medication because he thought it was an attempt by his psychiatrist to poison him. At that time, he became very aggressive and was thrown out of his board-and-care home. The only board-and-care facility that would accept a client like Bob closed down three years ago. No other board-and-care home in his community will take him in. He has been wandering the streets, talking to himself, and shouting insults at other people. The discharge planner in the hospital refers him to the county's new case management program for people who are chronically mentally ill.

The case manager uses the PIE system to describe Bob's problems (Exhibit 2).

### Case Study: Older Adult

Marcy is a 77-year-woman whose husband of 55 years died 1½ years ago. Her children all live out of the area, and her only close friend died five weeks ago. Marcy has been very depressed since her husband died. She has been crying, is unable to leave her house, and is withdrawing from the world. Her arthritis, which has been worsening for the past year, leads her to visit her physician, who is concerned about her and refers her to a senior center in her community. The case manager at the senior center does an intake assessment on Marcy. He is concerned about his ability to assist Marcy in obtaining other services from the center because the governor has been threatening for the past three weeks to eliminate state funding for the center.

The case manager at the senior center uses the PIE system to describe Marcy's problems and some possible interventions (Exhibit 3).

### Conclusion

These are a few examples of how the PIE system can facilitate case management practice. Although PIE is still a work in progress, it has thus far worked well for those case mangers who have taken the time to study it and adapt it to their case management practice.

### References

Kane, R. (1985). Case management in health care settings. In M. Weil & J. Karls (Eds.), *Case management in human service practice* (pp. 170–203). San Francisco: Jossey-Bass.

National Association of Social Workers. (1992). *Standards for social work case management*. Washington, DC: NASW Press.

Weil, M., & Karls, J. (1985). *Case management in human service practice*. San Francisco: Jossey-Bass.

# 13.

# Training Master of Social Work Students in Clinical Assessment Using the PIE System

Cathie Hanes Delewski

*This chapter reports how PIE was used to teach assessment skills to first-year master of social work students. It tells how students were more likely to conceptualize client problems beyond a traditional casework or psychiatric–mental health model. It shows that students felt that PIE forced them to think more holistically about the individual than from a narrower mental health perspective.*

One of social work's distinctive functions and tasks arises from its social purpose to strengthen coping patterns of people and to improve environments so that a better match can be attained among an individual's adaptive needs, potential, and the qualities of the impinging environments (Gordon, 1969; Schwartz, 1971). Gitterman and Germain (1976) noted that when the human condition focuses on interactions between individuals and their social and physical environments, the interventions developed by the social worker will be more encompassing. Ecological or systems theorists view this approach as being more balanced than the "personality states" or "environmental states" that categorize the understanding of human behavior from various theoretical viewpoints (such as psychodynamic, behaviorism, and so on).

A corollary to using the person-in-environment or ecological perspective is an explicit understanding of the diversity of clients and their environments. This understanding is of paramount importance to the social work profession because one of its driving assumptions is that each individual is unique. If social work is to be "culturally responsive" to its clients, then understanding how the cultural context affects the expression of behaviors becomes an integral part of the assessment and intervention process (Vargas & Koss-Chioino, 1992). As part of the educational process, social work students need to learn the components and importance of diversity in both the client and the client's environment.

## Assessment Process

One of the primary processes in social work practice is assessment. The purpose of assessment is to reach an understanding of the problem, characteristics of the client, the client's situation, and relevant environmental factors so that goals can be formulated and the interventions can be constructed (Compton & Galaway, 1989; Hepworth & Larsen, 1993).

Social work educators can teach the nature of the assessment process from a variety of perspectives. Each perspective is guided by theoretical models such as the psychodynamic, the humanistic, the life model, behaviorism, and problem-solving casework. Assessment in each of these models leads to data that define the nature of the problem, determine the coping capacity of the client, assesses the relevant systems involved, verify resource availability, and estimate motivation of the client (Hepworth & Larsen, 1993). The issues related to the diversity of the client and the environment are included in the assessment to ensure an appropriate intervention. The emphasis placed on each of these components is determined by the model or theory used. Guided by the model, the social work practitioner comes to an understanding of the key elements of the problem from the client's perspective and of the impact of the client's environment on that problem. Relevant interventions are then formulated with the goal of successful problem resolution.

In teaching the assessment process and skills to social work students, all of the critical elements of the process are needed. One of the dilemmas for the profession is the need for a common language in which all social workers could communicate client needs with one another regardless of theoretical orientation.

## Person-in-Environment System

The person-in-environment (PIE) system (Karls & Wandrei, 1992) is one attempt to standardize or develop a common understanding of client problems and strengths that has applicability to the training of social work students. The goal of PIE is to provide the profession a widely adaptable tool that highlights social work's unique understanding of human behavior: addressing clients' needs within their unique and differing environments. Although PIE was developed in response to the criticisms and problems associated with the *Diagnostic and Statistical Manual of Mental Disorders–Third Edition–Revised* (DSM-III-R) (American Psychiatric Association, 1987) it should be clear that PIE was meant to complement the psychiatric model and not replace it. PIE extends beyond the psychiatric model and can be used in a variety of contexts in which social workers practice (family therapy, case management, medical social work, employee assistance, and so on).

PIE is a system that describes, classifies, and codes problems of client functioning. The system is designed for individuals age 18 and older. PIE allows the social work student or practitioner to conceptualize the client along two major dimensions: social functioning (Factor I) and environmental factors that affect the client's social well being (Factor II). PIE also includes the psychiatric diagnosis (Factor III) and the physical conditions that influence functioning (Factor IV). Each factor refers to a different class of information that lead to potential intervention strategies.

The first two factors are viewed as the focus of social work intervention, but all four factors are needed to complete the assessment. For example, if a client's presenting complaint is depression, the practitioner would assess which areas the depression is affecting (such as parenting, work, spouse, and so on). PIE also requires an assessment of which environmental factors could inhibit the client's social functioning (such as work availability, housing, or discrimination). The environmental assessment may lead the worker or client to pursue areas related to resource acquisition, client advocacy, or community action. The client may be referred to a medical professional for medication. The social worker's interventions would focus on improving parenting skills or job training skills or on providing couple's counseling. The DSM-III-R diagnosis of depression is still treated but within the context of the person-in-environment. In essence, PIE reprioritizes problems and interventions. In addition, PIE requires the social worker to pay attention to client strengths and positive environmental conditions that will facilitate the functioning of the client.

## Teaching PIE in the Classroom

Teaching assessment skills in the classroom can be a tedious process based on students' previous clinical experience and knowledge. One of the advantages to using the PIE system is that it provides a comprehensive description of the client problems frequently encountered by social workers in various settings. The overall structure of the system also makes it fairly understandable for people who do not have extensive clinical experience. For these reasons PIE is an excellent tool for teaching clinical assessment for social work students.

One of the challenges of teaching PIE to students is the time allocated to instruction. Because assessment is only part of the social work process, PIE can be taught only as one portion of a clinical course, which includes casework, case management, introduction to direct practice, and so on. This training certainly differs from that of practitioners who attend a multiple-hour training workshop on PIE. Although students receive an introduction to PIE with limited practical experience, this exposure gives students skills that can be applied in the field.

Students should have read the *PIE Manual* before class to familiarize themselves with the structure and content of the system. Within the lecture/lab portion of the class, the system can be reviewed and additional time can be spent describing each factor. On Factor I, clarifying each of the social roles is important. For example, the Child Role is explained as how a client relates to his or her family of origin, not how the client's child relates to him or her as a parent. On Factor II, the existence, availability, and adequacy of certain resources within the client's environment must be emphasized, not the client's use of those resources. For Factors I and II, a discussion and clarification of the Severity, Duration, and Coping Indexes are important. It is critical that students understand how these indexes assist them in determining how to prioritize problems for intervention. The students' familiarity or experience with DSM-III-R will dictate the amount of time spent on Factor III. For beginning social work courses, a description of the psychiatric system and examples of diagnoses may be used rather than an extensive explanation or teaching of diagnostic skills.

After reviewing the system, students need the opportunity to practice. This can be accomplished in several ways. First, the instructor works through a case example with the students. A videotape or written case scenario of a client is provided. Students read or view the case and as a class determine the potential social functioning problems (Factor I), which are listed on the blackboard. For example, a client expresses concerns about being abused by her spouse. The social worker would list Spouse Role as the area of the social functioning problem and for type may list intimidation/victimization (changed to intimidation in the latest edition of the manual). After the social functioning problems and their types are identified, the Duration, Severity, and Coping Indexes are completed. In the previous example, the woman reveals that her spouse has been abusing her for six years (the duration code would be more than 5 years), and that he previously threatened to kill her (the severity code would be extreme). Her coping ability is assessed as inadequate.

The discussion then turns to Factor II, environmental problems. The same process is followed. For example, in the above scenario, a shelter for abused women may not be available. That Factor II problem would be listed as absence of adequate social services. Factor III's DSM-III-R diagnosis would be Major Depression, recurrent, moderate. The physical illness recorded on Factor IV would be none reported by client.

After all factors are listed, a discussion of prioritizing problems occurs. These decisions are made in the context of the duration, severity, and coping ratings. The main problem is then discussed briefly in terms of potential goals or intervention strategies. The numeric codes are not emphasized during the instruction. In general, students find the codes rather cumbersome and confusing at this stage.

Another method of applying the PIE system is to provide the students with the case scenario and then assess the client based on DSM-III-R or another traditional casework assessment method. The PIE system is then applied to the same case in the manner described above. Students then have the opportunity to discuss the benefits and limitations of each method.

After the instructor has worked through the case with the students, students are given additional cases to work on in small groups. The number of cases used will depend on the amount of time allocated. After the groups have had a chance to categorize the client's problems, the groups reconvene and all responses are listed on the board. Any discrepancies are noted and discussed. This type of discussion can lead to issues regarding the reliability of the PIE system. In part, the discrepancies between groups lead to a discussion on the theories or models that may have influenced the students to make their choices.

The final step is to incorporate the PIE system into a case assessment paper in which students assess a client, client problem, goals, and an intervention plan. This exercise requires the student to develop an individual assessment that reinforces classroom learning.

## Assessing the Effectiveness of PIE as a Teaching Tool

To determine how well students understood the PIE system, an exploratory/descriptive study was undertaken to see whether students trained in the PIE system assessed their clients differently from those not trained in PIE. Although PIE has been evaluated with social workers in practice, it has not been systematically examined with students entering the profession. The subjects consisted of first-year master of social work (MSW) students enrolled in a beginning casework course that is required of all first-year students. Because the study was voluntary, students were not required to participate. However, out of a class of 85, only 17 students did not participate.

Approximately one-half of the students were trained in the PIE system along with traditional casework assessment skills (provided by one instructor). The other half received only traditional casework assessment skills (taught by two instructors). It was assumed that students had various degrees of experience in social work, but any significant differences were assumed to be minimal because students were spread over the four sections of the course.

Assessment skills were taught at approximately the same time in the course. Training in the PIE system was given during one two-hour class period. Before class, the students were required to read the *PIE Manual* (actually, a draft of the manual that accompanies this book) to become familiar with the system. An additional lab hour was used to practice the system with a case scenario. The scenario was discussed in detail, and problems and questions about the system were addressed.

Two weeks before the course ended, students in both groups were asked to assess clients presented in two case scenarios. Each scenario was constructed to delineate problems with the social functioning of clients as well as environmental conditions that might interfere with the resolution of the client's social functioning problems. Students were instructed to read each scenario and then to list the concerns or problems they believed were creating difficulties for the client. Students in the PIE-trained group were aware that they were to use the PIE system in evaluating the client. They were then asked to prioritize each problem based on severity. The instrument was given during class time so instructors could assess the time needed to complete the scenarios.

After the scenarios were completed, responses were categorized into discrete categories (similar responses) for ease of analysis. Students were not required to list intervention strategies or goals.

A total of 68 students participated in the study. Twenty-five percent ($n = 17$) of the participants were male, and 75 percent ($n = 51$) were female. The average age of the respondents was 32.9 years. Of those who participated, 64.7 percent ($n = 44$) had previous social work experience, with an average of 3.66 years (the range was less than one year to 13.5 years; mode = 2 years). No significant differences existed between the PIE-trained group and the traditional assessment group on any demographic characteristic.

---

## Case Study I

Jerry is a 32-year-old white divorced male who comes to the local mental health center today complaining of feelings of depression and concerned that he may take his life. Jerry has no specific plan regarding suicide but does feel that if he doesn't get some help soon, he may follow this path. He provides you with the following information:

Jerry has been divorced for six months from his 30-year-old wife of five years. They have a three-year-old son, Jason. Jerry is allowed to see Jason only every other weekend. Jerry feels that he is being deprived of seeing his son and building a relationship with him. His wife was given custody of Jason as well as their home.

Jerry is a pipe fitter. He works full-time as well as three evenings a week at McDonald's as a night assistant manager.

Jerry lives alone in a small one-bedroom apartment. He feels that the apartment is "beneath his standards," but this is all he can afford because he must pay 35 percent of his salary for child support and alimony.

He recently saw a physician who put him on Prozac, an antidepressant medication. He is now sleeping better, although he still wakes up in the middle of the night thinking about his son. He doesn't feel the medication is doing anything for his depressed mood and occasional crying spells.

Jerry's immediate family lives in Nevada. He talks to them infrequently because he cannot afford the phone bills. He states that his brother is the most supportive of the family. He does not get along with his parents. They blame Jerry for the divorce and not being able to see Jason.

Jerry has few relationships with friends, but states that since the divorce, he rarely sees them. He states he misses these individuals but has no time to see them.

He denies substance abuse problems. He states he occasionally has a beer on the weekends. He does not smoke or use other drugs.

Jerry appears depressed. He has poor eye contact and frequently looks at the floor as he speaks. His voice is monotone and at times inaudible. His clothes are neat and clean, and he is cooperative. He genuinely seems to want help and feels overwhelmed by his concerns about his son and finances.

## Assessment

The 33 students in the PIE-trained group overwhelmingly classified Jerry's Factor I problem as difficulties in the Parent Role (93.9 percent, $n = 31$). Other Factor I problems commonly identified included the Child Role (63.6 percent, $n = 21$), and the Spouse Role (60.6 percent, $n = 20$) (Exhibit 1).

When examining the consistency of the type of interactional difficulty in social role, 75.7 percent ($n = 25$) of the PIE-trained students noted that separation/loss was the primary dynamic leading to problems in the Parent Role. In regard to the second social role problem, the Child Role, the most common type of interactional difficulty was listed as conflict/ambivalence (33.33 percent, $n = 11$). This was followed by responsibility/performance expectation (18.2 percent, $n = 6$) and isolation/withdrawal (6.1 percent, $n = 2$). (Because of concerns about the lack of mutual exclusiveness of several of the types, the types have been changed since this study was completed. Conflict/ambivalence is now ambivalence, responsibility/performance expectation is now responsibility, and isolation/withdrawal is now isolation.)

Common Factor II problems identified included nutrition (60.6 percent, $n = 20$) and lack of adequate Affectional Support System (48.4 percent, $n = 16$). The Factor III problem of Depression was listed as a problem by 33 percent ($n = 11$) of the students. The problem list for the 35 students trained in traditional casework assessment was in stark contrast to the PIE-trained group. Eighty percent ($n = 28$) listed depression as the client's main problem. This was followed by poor support systems (57.5 percent, $n = 20$); poor nutrition (45.7 percent, $n = 16$); suicidal thinking (40 percent, $n = 14$); and poor self-esteem (31.4 percent, $n = 11$). The client's concern of visitation with his son ranked sixth in the list (22.8 percent, $n = 8$). (Additional reasons were listed but were not in sufficient numbers to report.)

*Exhibit 1*

**Classification of Jerry's Problems**

| Traditionally Trained Students (N = 35) | | PIE-Trained Students (N = 33) | |
|---|---|---|---|
| Problem | n | Problem | n |
| Depression | 28 | Parent role | 31 |
| Poor social support | 20 | Child role | 21 |
| Poor nutrition | 16 | Nutrition | 20 |
| Suicidal | 14 | Spouse role | 20 |
| Low self-esteem | 11 | Affectional support | 16 |
| Relationship with son | 8 | Friend role | 16 |
| Finances | 7 | Worker–paid economy role | 16 |
| Family relationships | 7 | Depression | 11 |
| Loneliness | 7 | Lack of housing | 10 |
| Insomnia | 6 | Sibling role | 3 |
| Divorce | 6 | Client/consumer role[a] | 1 |
| Medication management | 6 | | |
| Lack of vocational training | 6 | | |
| Few friends | 5 | | |
| Poor relationship skills | 5 | | |
| Poor living conditions | 4 | | |
| Social isolation | 3 | | |
| Lack of motivation | 3 | | |
| Time management problems | 3 | | |
| Life change | 3 | | |
| Communication problems | 2 | | |
| Lack of recreation | 2 | | |
| Guilt | 1 | | |
| Hopelessness | 1 | | |
| Trouble concentrating | 1 | | |
| Helplessness | 1 | | |

NOTE: Totals do not add up to total n for each group because students could pick more than one problem.
[a]The client/consumer role used at the time of this study is now the consumer role.

## Case Study 2

Tina is a 20-year-old Hispanic female who comes into a storefront crisis clinic where the clients are frequently transient and can walk in off the street at any time to ask for assistance. She comes to the clinic on a Wednesday afternoon. She complains that she has nowhere to stay, having recently traveled to the city from New Mexico. She presents the following information.

Tina has been on the street since she was 14 years old. She states she has been a prostitute to make money to live. She travels from state to state when it appears that the authorities have become aware of her prostitution. She prides herself on never having been convicted.

Tina states that she tried to get into the women's shelter four days ago; but they didn't have room, and there was no other place to be referred because the recent snowstorms had caused overcrowding of the shelters. Tina says that she stayed with a couple of truckers over the last few days but doesn't feel this will continue to work because "you know how men are." The only thing Tina wants from the clinic is a place to stay.

She thinks her family still lives in Mexico, just over the border from Texas. She said she left at age 14 because her father frequently physically and sexually abused her. She stated she could "no longer live like that" and left. She has not spoken to her family in six years. She also claims she has no friends.

Tina admits to using cocaine and marijuana on occasion but adamantly denies she has a "problem with drugs."

She denies any medical problems. She has not been tested for the human immunodeficiency virus or other sexually transmitted diseases. She admits to having had two abortions.

Tina is petite and thin. Her clothes are neat, but obviously worn. Her clothing also does not seem appropriate for the climate. She appears to be of average intelligence but is exclusively focused on the here and now. There is no evidence of thought disorder, depression, or other mental illness. She is angry at not being able to get the services she needs.

---

## Assessment

Students trained in PIE listed the Factor II problem of lack of shelter as the number one problem for Tina (87.8 percent, $n = 29$). Other common Factor II problems included lack of an Affectional Support System (51.5 percent, $n = 17$) and lack of appropriate employment (39.3 percent, $n = 13$). On Factor I, students identified the most common problems as Child Role (75.7 percent, $n = 25$) and Worker Role–Paid Economy (27.2 percent, $n = 9$) (Exhibit 2).

In Tina's case, Child Role interactional difficulty type was listed by the PIE-trained students in three major categories: (1) intimidation/victimization (36.3 percent, $n = 12$); (2) conflict/ambivalence (15.1 percent, $n = 5$); and (3) isolation/withdrawal (15.1 percent, $n = 5$). (Since this study, many of these categories have been simplified. Please refer to the *PIE Manual* for the current terms.) There was less consistency in these responses than in the previous case. (The intimidation/victimization type is now the victimization type.)

The traditionally trained students were predominantly concerned about the client's shelter needs. Thirty-two of students (91.4 percent) listed this as the client's main problem. However, problems ranked after shelter took a different course. Drug abuse was the second problem listed (62.8 percent, $n = 22$), followed by poor support systems (57.1 percent, $n = 20$), sexual abuse (45.7 percent, $n = 16$), and food (37.1 percent, $n = 13$).

## Discussion

The overall trend in the traditionally trained group was to focus on psychiatric symptoms or diagnoses rather than interactional social role problems. Students trained in the PIE system were more likely to assess the client in the different social roles in which they participated. Psychiatric disorders or symptoms were not ignored (these

*Exhibit 2*
**Classification of Tina's Problems**

| Traditionally Trained Students (N = 35) | | PIE-Trained Students (N = 33) | |
|---|---|---|---|
| Problem | n | Problem | n |
| Lack of shelter | 32 | Lack of shelter | 29 |
| Drug abuse | 22 | Child role | 25 |
| Lack of support systems | 20 | Lack of employment opportunities | 13 |
| Sexual abuse | 16 | Worker–paid economy role | 9 |
| Lack of food | 13 | Lack of health services | 8 |
| Low self-esteem | 12 | Safety problems | 8 |
| Human immunodeficiency virus | 11 | Immigrant–undocumented | 6 |
| Lack of clothing | 11 | Client/consumer role[a] | 6 |
| Limited work skills | 10 | Lack of economic resources | 5 |
| Medical problems | 9 | Lack of mental health services | 5 |
| Lifestyle | 5 | Friend role | 4 |
| Legal problems | 4 | Discrimination | 4 |
| No money | 2 | Lack of education | 3 |
| Needs mental health services | 2 | | |
| Loneliness | 2 | | |
| Lack of education | 2 | | |
| Out of touch with reality | 2 | | |
| Runaway | 2 | | |
| Refuses to take responsibility | 1 | | |
| Blames others | 1 | | |
| Poor social skills | 1 | | |
| Needs to be in school | 1 | | |
| Lack of options | 1 | | |
| Unemployment | 1 | | |

NOTE: Totals do not add up to total n for each group because students could pick more than one problem.
[a]The client/consumer role used at the time of this study is now the consumer role.

disorders were listed on Factor III), but took less of a priority. Students in the PIE-trained group also listed environmental factors affecting the person's functioning more often than the traditionally trained students.

In analyzing the data, one issue that remained difficult for students was determining if environmental resources were inadequate or unavailable or if the client was underutilizing the resource. This problem was seen in both cases, especially on issues of diet and nutrition. If the client was not eating well, PIE-trained students frequently chose nutrition as a Factor II problem even if there were adequate food supplies in the community. This seemed to be a consistent problem for students during training and in the study. This result may be explained by inadequate training time and a lack of understanding about the community's resources.

### Limitations of the Study

In general, students appeared to exhibit a high degree of consistency regarding the primary problem (based on frequencies, interrater reliability was not calculated within each group). However, the PIE-trained group gave a variety of responses as to the specific type of role problem the client was experiencing. This could be a result of perceived theoretical biases that students brought to the exercise. However, sufficient information was not available to ascertain if theoretical bias influenced student decisions. Additional studies in this area could shed light on this issue.

The second concern expressed by students was the cumbersome coding system. Although they were not required to use the coding system, many expressed concern about the use of the coding and saw it as a major stumbling block.

Finally, because this was an exploratory study, there were several apparent evaluation problems. First, not all students prioritized the problems. This created a gap in information as to which problems would be tackled first. Second, if the instrument responses had been objectively written (as in a closed-ended or multiple-choice format), more analysis and interrater reliability statistics could have been done. Finally, generalizing about the use of PIE for students is limited based on a relatively small sample, although the results are encouraging.

## Implications of the PIE System in Social Work Education

PIE provides an atheoretical framework to address the diversity of clients and their environments while affirming the common needs of all individuals. The PIE system allows the practitioner to examine clients within their specific environments and determine what is culturally relevant. Because the PIE system is not based on any specific theories, it permits the social work educator the flexibility to entertain different theoretical models that determine the dynamics of a problem as well as appropriate interventions. This categorization system reinforces the person-in-environment perspective, with special emphasis on environmental factors influencing social well-being. The emphasis on the environment can also lead to community and social action.

PIE was generally viewed positively by students. Many students had talked about PIE with practicum supervisors who seemed intrigued by the system. However, students expressed concern that because agencies required students to use specific models of assessment, they would never use PIE. Undoubtedly, the only way the PIE system can be beneficial to training students is to have the cooperation and participation of practicum agencies.

## Conclusion

Overall, MSW students trained in the PIE system were more likely to conceptualize client problems beyond a traditional casework or psychiatric/mental health model. It was clear that both social roles and environmental factors were considered important by the students who received the PIE training. The PIE system seems to create an assessment environment in which students can conceptualize problems with issues of client and environmental diversity in mind.

The benefit in using the PIE system, according to students, is that it causes them to think more holistically about the individual than they do when using a narrower mental health/psychiatric perspective.

The PIE system is a new and exciting tool for assessing social work clients from a perspective of diversity. However, like DSM-III-R, it is not without controversy. As the system is used in practice, there will undoubtedly be debate and revisions. To make PIE beneficial, however, educators and practitioners will need to make a commitment to use it, and this will require a great deal of energy and negotiation between agency directors, supervisors, practitioners, and educators to implement. PIE has the potential to be the standard assessment tool used by the profession and to help legitimize our unique understanding of human behavior.

## References

American Psychiatric Association. (1987). *Diagnostic and statistical manual of mental disorders* (3rd ed., rev.). Washington, DC: American Psychiatric Press.

Compton, B. R., & Galaway, B. (1989). *Social work processes*. Belmont, CA: Wadsworth.

Gitterman, A., & Germain, C. B. (1976). Social work practice: A life model. *Social Service Review, 50,* 601–610.

Gordon, W. E. (1969). Basic concepts for an integrative and generative conception of social work. In H. Gordon (Ed.), *The general systems approach: Contributions toward an holistic conception of social work* (pp. 5–11). New York: Council on Social Work Education.

Hepworth, D. H., & Larsen, J. (1993). *Direct social work practice*. Monterey, CA: Brooks/Cole.

Karls, J., & Wandrei, K. (1992). PIE: A new language for social work. *Social Work, 37,* 80–85.

Schwartz, W. (1971). Social group work: The interactionist approach. In R. Morris (Ed.-in-Chief), *Encyclopedia of social work* (16th ed., Vol. 2, pp. 1252–1262). New York: National Association of Social Workers.

Vargas, L. A., & Koss-Chioino, J. D. (Eds.). (1992). *Working with culture*. San Francisco: Jossey-Bass.

# 14.

# Conceptualizing PIE within a Holistic System of Social Work

Richard Ramsay

*In this chapter the conceptualization of PIE is addressed within a broader holistic conception of social work. A geometric model derived from the work of Buckminster Fuller is proposed as a common organizing framework. This framework is shown to accommodate the testing of different theoretical orientations to explain or classify the dynamics of social functioning and to support a repertoire of practice theory interventions that are consistent with the central focus, values, and ethics of social work.*

**D**eveloping the person-in-environment (PIE) classification system is an important step the social work profession should take to establish "its independence and uniqueness among the human services professions" (Karls & Wandrei, 1992, p. 80). The objective is to provide social workers with a classification system that can be used independently or in collaboration with the diagnostic systems of other disciplines, in particular medicine and psychiatry.

"Social well-being" and "person-in-environment" are central concepts of the PIE system. Social well-being is a recognized component of a person's health status, different from physical and mental well-being. Person-in-environment is the concept commonly used to describe the social work domain of practice, and it comes from the profession's long-standing efforts to develop a common conceptual description of the core components of the discipline. Since the inception of the National Association of Social Workers (NASW), its leadership and encouragement of others to participate in the search for a broad perspective conceptual framework has been substantial. Building on the efforts of others, this chapter proposes the use of a common, but somewhat unfamiliar, geometric framework. It also proposes the use of the new scientific paradigms of holism to integrate the PIE system as a core component of a broader holistic conception of the social work profession.

## History of Efforts to Find a Common Conceptual Framework

Before the 20th century, social work in Europe and North America was characterized by a range of voluntary philanthropy in the form of Charity Organization Societies, settlement houses, social reform movements, and women's liberation advocacy. The need for an organized form of "socialization" work was forged during the Industrial Revolution when exploitation of individuals and puritanical beliefs about people in poverty were commonplace. Early concepts of charity and philanthropy were tied to righteous attitudes of moral authority that separated the "worthy" from the "unworthy" poor (Briar & Miller, 1971). Similar attitudes were held by individuals with political and economic power over others who oppressed both minority groups and the less privileged, including women, children, and disabled people.

Charity organization volunteers were initially trained to be "friendly visitors," providing moral reform help to the worthy poor. Social reform and women's liberation volunteers were community activists who took issue with those in power and set out to improve the social well-being of those deprived or denied basic human rights and equal opportunities. Settlement house volunteers were live-in neighbors helping the poor and working-class immigrants to participate in the democratic processes of their communities and to press for social change. In their disparate forms, these activities represented a dual-purpose view of social philanthropy, each with its own champion advocates. Charity organizations in the United States, with strong leadership from Mary Richmond, focused on reforming individuals and families in poverty. Settlement house and reform work, supported by Jane Addams and other pioneer champions of social justice, focused on changing the social conditions of poor housing, child labor, and sweatshop environments in factories.

Settlement houses and charity organizations were lesser factors in the growth of social philanthropy in Canada. The pioneers tended to be early 20th century social reformers like J. S. Woodsworth, who was linked to the Social Gospel movement; crusading journalists like J. J. Kelso, the founding president of the Toronto Children's Aid Society; or women's rights advocates like Nellie McClung and Agnes McPhail (Wharf, 1991).

### 1900 to 1920

The rise of social work as a human services profession emerged from efforts to replace voluntary philanthropy with scientific philanthropy. The moralistic approach was being replaced with a greater concern for the welfare of the individual and a recognition of the influence of the environment, especially economic handicaps. Greater emphasis was placed on the specialized training needed to conduct thorough social investigations on the assumption that by gathering enough facts, a remedy could be prescribed. At the turn of the century, Mary Richmond was a vocal advocate for the establishment of university-affiliated training schools with academic courses and agency field work in applied philanthropy (Dinerman & Geismar, 1984). Not only did Richmond want the volunteers (mostly women) to be better trained, she strongly defended their right to earn a living as a social worker. Because women did not have equal access to mainstream professions such as law and medicine, social work was one of the few accessible career paths open to them.

As university programs were established in the early 1900s, there was a struggle to find a unified conception of the new profession. Richmond had recognized the broad-based "man in his environment" perspective inherent in the range of philanthropy activities, and certainly Addams's argument that the causes of personal social problems were embedded in the environment reinforced the need for the profession to have a social environment focus. The few efforts to conceptualize social work with an integrated person-in-environment domain and a social interaction focus received little support. In fact, the rivalry between Richmond and Addams became so great that the two resorted to denouncing each other's perspective (Franklin, 1986). The pressure to become scientific pushed social work in the direction of Richmond's method specialization perspective, consistent with the prevailing scientific worldview and the bias for specialized, narrow-domain disciplines. For many people, social casework was the profession, casework was the practice, and social caseworkers were the professionals. The swing away from any serious intention to develop a broad conception is generally given to Abraham Flexner's 1915 address—"Is Social Work a Profession?"—to the National Conference on Charities and Corrections, when he analyzed social work against his self-proclaimed criteria for a profession (Austin, 1983).

Flexner was not a social worker, but he was America's most influential expert on professional education, having authored a highly critical study of medical education in the United States and Canada. In 1910 a report by Flexner had a major impact on the medical profession's transformation from an apprenticeship and practice wisdom model of learning to a university-based scientific method, focused on the methodological study of disease. The scientific base of the medical model was the worldview of causal mechanics. A recent review of the Flexner Report showed "the science to be taught and the research to be pursued were firmly embedded in the reductionist biomedical framework; in particular, they [the doctors] were to be dissociated from social concerns, which were considered outside the boundaries of medicine" (Capra, 1983, p. 159). The medical model was grounded in Newtonian principles of fixed determinism, linear predictability, reductionist methods, and observer objectivity. Science was dominated by the metaphor image of the universe as a giant orderly machine.

Flexner concluded that social work met only some of the traits of a profession, thus failing to qualify as an "established profession" (Austin, 1983). He critiqued the social welfare domain as too broad for one professional body. Social work lacked an exclusive knowledge base and framework and did not have a distinctive scientific method to address the complexity of social welfare issues. In other words, social workers did not have a specialized way to make objective observations, discover facts, form a theory to explain the facts, make a prediction from the theory, and test the results of the prediction by another objective observation.

The 1917 publication of Richmond's *Social Diagnosis* identified social casework, with its emphasis on a thorough investigation, diagnosis, and treatment as social work's teachable scientific method. This publication supplied the profession with its first authoritative answer to Flexner's criticism. The fact-finding, case method of study was the profession's first explicitly stated conceptual framework. This case method conception moved the profession toward a specialized focus on individual functioning and a deterministic view of causal factors linked to the mechanical science foundations of the medical model. The causes of human poverty were still seen as in the economic and social order, and treatment was largely in the form of relief work. The form of treatment would change with the effect of World War I and the extension of casework services to people not living in poverty. Postwar needs introduced social work to Freudian psychology and its emphasis on psychic determinism. With the eventual incorporation of this theory into the curricula of schools of social work, social casework switched almost exclusively to an individual unit of study and a search for the mechanisms of psychological causes. Social casework specialties soon emerged in different fields of practice: child welfare, family, psychiatric, medical, and school social work.

### 1920 to 1950

The proliferation of casework practice into separate method or field specializations became a problem. The Milford Conference meetings of social agency leaders concluded in 1929 that social casework practice was a generic entity. The method differences in the separate fields of practice were primarily descriptive rather than substantive. This solved the problem of fragmented field specializations, but it did not stop the trend toward method specialization conceptions of the profession.

Social casework, the first to develop as a method specialization, evolved into two rival schools of thought (the diagnostic and the functional) in the 1930s and 1940s, reinforcing the focus on a method conception of social work (Bartlett, 1970). The diagnostic school was based on Richmond's social diagnosis model, Freudian psychology, scientific determinism, and objectivity in the caseworker–client relationship. The functional school was based on the psychology of Otto Rank, rejection of scientific determinism, and greater participatory involvement in the caseworker–client relationship guided by the function of the agency. In spite of their differences, both assumed that casework was essentially psychotherapy with a focus on intrapsychic relationships (Briar & Miller, 1971). The specializations of social group work and community organization, which had their early roots in the social settlement movement, were developed as separate method conceptions during this same period.

## 1950 to 1990s

By mid-century it became apparent that efforts to conceptualize the profession by method specialties were divisive. The work done in the 1950s by Werner Boehm (1959), chair of the Council on Social Work Education's Curriculum Study, and Harriet Bartlett (1958), chair of the NASW committee on the Working Definition of Social Work, addressed the importance of a common domain of practice across all method specializations and the need for a holistic conception of the entire profession. Out of these efforts came the generic term "social work practice" as a replacement for specialized practice terms such as casework, group work, and community practice.

The importance of conceptualizing a common domain was not widely communicated until the 1970 publication of Bartlett's *The Common Base of Social Work*. Bartlett identified three core components needed for a holistic conception of social work: (1) a social functioning focus, (2) a broad-based practice orientation, and (3) a repertoire of intervention methods. Social work required an "area [domain] of central concern that is (1) common to the profession as a whole, (2) meaningful in terms of the profession's values and goals, (3) practical in terms of available and attainable knowledge and techniques, and (4) sufficiently distinctive that it does not duplicate what other professions are doing" (p. 86).

Social functioning interactions, where individuals and their social environments meet, were identified as the central focus of the profession. The common domain included three essential concepts: people, interactions, and environment, abbreviated into the now familiar concept of person-in-environment. Practically, this meant the primary focus of social work was on the interaction between the coping efforts of individuals, singly or in groups, and the environmental demands they experienced over time. Bartlett argued for a broad orientation to the concept of social work practice, which would include field and practice method specializations. Underpinning this broad orientation would be a common set of values about the nature of human relationships, a body of knowledge, and intervention approaches familiar to all social workers, whether generalists or specialists. The intervention framework was to be broad enough to accommodate a repertoire of intervention methods compatible with the central focus of the profession.

Bartlett's reconceptualization of social work was the forerunner of several general social work practice conceptualizations during the 1970s and 1980s (Germain & Gitterman, 1980; Meyer, 1983; Middleman & Goldberg, 1974; Pincus & Minahan, 1973). The development of these models was aided by the introduction of general systems and ecological theories (Germain, 1979; Hearn, 1959). These theories provided the theoretical foundations for social workers to describe the systemic or holistic patterns of interaction between the different elements of the person-in-environment domain. Also, from a systemic perspective they allowed the review of a range of interactions with people in different social systems arrangements that did not equate the locus of the problem with the target of intervention. In this way problems no longer had to fit the systematic method of practice. The selected method had to fit the problem and the selected interactional approach to the problem. Pincus and Minahan, for example, developed a simple four-part social systems model: (1) change agent system, (2) client system, (3) target system, and (4) action system. This model provided a practical way to map the different people who could be worked with in terms of micro or macro, generalist or specialist, and direct or indirect options of helping someone with a social functioning problem. Middleman and Goldberg developed a similar model using a quadrant structure: (1) work with clients for their own benefit, (2) work with clients to benefit themselves and others like them, (3) work with others to benefit a category of people, and (4) work with others to benefit specific clients. Meyer argued for a conceptual framework with an ecological-systems perspective that would give social workers "a way of thinking about and assessing the relatedness of people and their impinging environments" (1983, p. 29). Meyer's (1990) support for a holistic conception of the profession would "not [be] a unified, professionally agreed-on general theory of people and of practice, but a unified professionally agreed-on perspective of the tasks of social work; a respect for others' commitments to different theories; and a full repertoire of interventions to accommodate the complexity of psychosocial defined cases" (p. 397).

As the 1980s progressed, social workers elevated their critical exploration of the place of science in the evolution of the profession (Weick, 1987; Zimmerman, 1989). Many of the early explorations of science and social work reported by Zimmerman concentrated on attacking the traditional tenets of logical positivism (empiricism) and reductionist methods. Other critics started to look at the development of social work toward a holistic conception in the larger context of the scientific revolutions and consequent paradigm shifts over the past 400 years. As Weick (1987) pointed out, the struggle to let the deep interdependency of relationships between person and environment develop as the legitimate domain of the profession had largely been a result of the "constraints placed on the concept by the mechanistic traditions of classical [Newtonian, Cartesian, Baconian] science" (p. 36). Weick provided considerable evidence to show that the concept is firmly grounded in ancient wisdom and some of the post-Newtonian scientific revolutions of the 20th century.

The emergence of quantum theory (ironically, about the same time that Flexner is claimed to have pushed social work toward a mechanical model) challenged the clockwork determinism of Newtonian science and questioned the scientific premise of observer-controlled objectivity in experiments. This theory and the more recent scientific revolution in the study of chaos (Gleick, 1988; Kellert, 1993) showed the impossibility of separating the parts of any system with the expectation of being able to understand and predict the behavior of the whole system. The new scientific worldviews of the 20th century support the concept of the universe as a deeply interconnected whole rather than a collection of separate systems to be studied or acted upon in isolation from each other.

Weick (1987) was convinced that social workers, as a collective, have always had an intuitive awareness of the inseparableness of the person-in-environment concept. Weick said, "It's as if we have understood that human life exists within a context and cannot be properly understood without reference to it" (p. 44). For the profession to validate a holistic conception of person-in-environment dynamics, there must be a transformation to a new scientific worldview "which may include but [must] go beyond the mechanistic, mathematical assumptions of positivism" (p. 45).

Zimmerman (1989) provided a reasoned warning that the current attacks on the mechanistic paradigm of science should not be used to discard science as a necessary foundation for social work practice. According to Zimmerman, the limits of reductionism and determinism should be acknowledged and replaced by "more contemporary scientific explanations of reality" (p. 59). The scientific requirements of determinism have been trouble for the profession since its earliest efforts to find predictable causes of social functioning problems and transformation in the direction of "scientism" (acceptance of the belief that "true" knowledge is valid only if the event being studied can be empirically observed, confirmed by controlled experiments, and verified by quantitative measurement). Zimmerman favored the less deterministic worldviews of post-Newtonian science and rejected the tenets of scientism as the only method of scientific proof. What is needed are methods to provide detailed and holistic descriptions of evolving networks of person-in-environment relationships. If we were to do this

> such methods [would] imply a deemphasis on traditional "effectiveness" models of research and more intense efforts to describe the pertinent variables in human behavior. In such an approach, there is less emphasis on prediction and generalization and more credence is granted to studies that undertake to describe the relevant characteristics of the states of individuals, families, small groups, organizations, communities, and other systems. (Zimmerman, 1989, p. 59)

Instead of emphasizing the primacy of quantitative approaches to find correlational or causal relationships, social workers would receive instruction on qualitative approaches and the value of using intuitive wisdom. A balanced approach would lead to a more harmonious synthesis of the pertinent variables in a system network.

Considerable progress has been made in moving the conception of social work from that of a narrowly based method specialization to a holistic conception of the profession. In spite of the progress made, the profession is still in search of agreement on a common framework that could model a holistic perspective, and at the same time allow for differential theoretical foundations and a full repertoire of interventions to address the complexity of human social functioning.

## Contributions of Buckminster Fuller

Past efforts to conceptualize social work as a whole system suggest the need for a common framework to provide a conceptual infrastructure for the task. A proposed framework is found in the works of Buckminster Fuller (1969, 1975), one of America's most distinguished scientists, philosophers, and individualists. Fuller extended the understanding of systems concepts beyond the general systems theory of von Bertalanffy (1968) and the ecosystems theory of adaptive fit between organisms and their environments. General systems introduced the idea that all systems, mechanical and organic, are sets of interacting parts. Both general and ecosystems theories address the concept of wholeness, but only as a one- or two-dimensional construct. Even though they are similar, mechanical and organic systems are not the same. Mechanical systems are closed. Organic systems are open. Living organisms can self-renew, self-repair, self-organize, and self-intervene, whereas mechanical systems cannot (Augros & Stanciu, 1988). In this respect, living systems have the capacity to influence themselves and their environments through natural feedback activities and are not subject to entropy or disorder in the same way mechanical systems are. Although general systems and ecosystems thinking have been quite prevalent in social work for nearly 40 years, antisystems sentiments are still widespread, largely because this type of conceptual thinking does not explicitly acknowledge unequal distributions of power, nor does it include prescriptive (how-to) methods of interventions. There is still a strong bias favoring empirical science and the need for mechanical model predictability in the application and results of social work interventions.

Although the development of abstract concepts based on geometric shapes can be traced to Greek antiquity and Plato's scientific philosophy of idealism, science has generally relied on mathematical equations to model realities. Even though the science of chemistry acknowledged, well before the 20th century, nature's use of geometric forms in molecular structures, geometric models were not used by other sciences until after the major discoveries in "new" physics of the 20th century. Fuller capitalized on the systems discoveries in the physical sciences to advance our ability to engage in whole systems thinking—whole-to-part conceptualizing, or the belief that the whole is more than the sum of its parts—instead of the more common reductionist method of part-to-whole thinking, the belief that the whole can be generalized from an understanding of its parts. Fuller's systems discoveries revealed nature's way of organizing whole system structures in the form of simple geometric models without diminishing the complexity of the system. Fuller worked from the assumption that nature likely had one simple and most economical coordinate system to account for its multitude of complex transactions and transformations. He discovered that it takes four totally related events to produce a system. Nature's minimum system is a geometric tetrahedron, a structure made of four parts, four triangular faces, and six interrelated connections. Perhaps the best evidence of this system in nature is illustrated by the "19th century scientific proof of the tetrahedral configuration of carbon, the combining master of chemistry" (Fuller, 1969, pp. 100–101). Using the tetrahedron as a structural model, Fuller showed how the humanities and sciences, and other entities assumed to be opposites (like the physical and metaphysical elements of the universe), could be comprehended as unified whole systems.

Working from the knowledge of whole system structures in nature, Fuller conceptualized the universe as the largest and most comprehensive whole. He then demonstrated how the universe could be multiplied into smaller, special-case whole systems by a process of progressive subdivision. The subdividing instrument of the universe is a system defined as "the simplest physical or metaphysical experience we humans can have" (Fuller & Kuromiya, 1992, p. 124). The system structure of these experiences is the tetrahedral structure found in nature. Fuller discovered the law of structures in which a finite system always "subdivides the universe into two parts: all of the universe inside and all of the universe outside its system" and the system itself is a third part (Fuller & Kuromiya, 1969, p. 95). The tetrahedron system is a free-standing, four-dimensional structure with demonstrable insideness and outsideness. It is the basic subdividing instrument of the universe. It also serves as a holistic model to conceptualize the core components and essential relatedness of any defined whole system. To conceptualize the profession of social work as a whole system, for example, would require, at a minimum, a four-part conceptual model that showed the relatedness of all parts to each other.

An easy way to recognize the tetrahedron as a solid structure is to physically visualize a triangle-base pyramid instead of the more familiar square-base Egyptian pyramid that comes to mind, as shown in Figure 1A. A way to recognize it as a network of interconnected parts is to visualize the structure as four components linked together by six connecting lines. Figure 1B is a drawing of a tetrahedron network with its minimum four parts, six connecting lines, and four triangular faces.

Fuller was a post-Newtonian thinker heavily influenced by Einstein's worldview that the "Universe is an aggregate of only overlapping nonsimultaneous episodes" (Fuller & Kuromiya, 1992, p. 40). This view opposed Newton's conception of the universe as a static structure that could be viewed in its entirety all at one time. Fuller called Einstein's view "scenario universe" because of how it resembled "an ever-changing film script with the threads of new comings and goings interwoven into a complex story" (p. 40).

The classical science separation of the observer from the three-dimensional space of his or her environment surroundings did not fit with Fuller's experiential discoveries. The observer dimension is always interconnected to the three dimensions of space, which makes all observer–space systems four-dimensional and structurally coordinated in the basic shape of a tetrahedron. In a social work context, the term "person-in-environment" represents a four-dimensional construct rather than a person "in" but separated from his or her three-dimensional environment.

Fuller and Kuromiya's (1992) geometric comprehension of holism is based on the principle of synergy that "the behavior of whole systems [is] unpredicted by the behavior of any part of the system when considered only separately" (p. 32). Simply explained, there is nothing in the separate experiences or behaviors of one person that by itself will precisely predict how the sum of the experiences or behaviors of that person will act together in the future. The corollary of this synergic principle is equally important: "The known behavior of the whole and known behavior of a minimum of known parts often make possible the discovery of the values of the remaining

*Figure 1*

**Pyramid Tetrahedron (A) and Network Tetrahedron (B)**

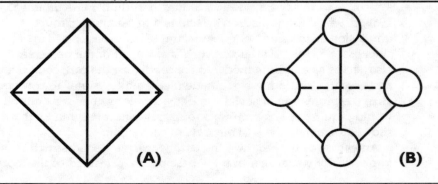

(A)                                            (B)

parts" (Fuller, 1969, p. 73). Applied to social work, this principle recognizes that most social workers start their work with few knowns and multiple unknowns. To have a model that depicts the minimum components of a whole system and the relatedness of each component to the other provides a common structure for locating known information and identifying parts when little or nothing is known about the system. Starting from a whole system conception will minimize the dangers of narrowly pursued investigations and reductionist conclusions.

Fuller's comprehension of synergy neither supports society's long-standing belief in the exclusive importance of separated specializations nor fits the causal mechanical theory and tradition of scientific reductionism, in which parts of a complex system are isolated in an effort to explain the behavior of the whole. It does, however, fit well with the 20th-century's scientific advancements in relativity, quantum physics, and chaos theory which are questioning the viability of the long-held scientific metaphor that the universe operates in the manner of an orderly and predictable machine. Fuller concluded that to learn anything one has to start with the whole system and work one's way to an understanding of how the parts contribute to the functioning of the whole.

Figure 2A shows the unfolded triangle faces of a tetrahedron pyramid lying flat on a two-dimensional plane. As shown in Figure 2B, the triangle faces of a tetrahedral network can be progressively subdivided at their midpoints to illustrate increasing levels of complexity in a system without losing its minimum system structure.

The tetrahedron is basic to synergetic geometry. It is the minimum structural set that acts as a dividing instrument in the universe and can be used to physically demonstrate holistic relatedness in a system. Neither the parts nor their related connections are static. The parts can be changed, modified, or replaced, and the relationships varied without changing the structural configuration. Because a system framework always minimally divides the largest conceptual whole, the universe, into three divisions (the system itself, everything outside the system, and everything inside the system), conceptualizing a system in this way ensures that a whole-system perspective is never lost. No matter how the dividing system is conceptualized—an idea, a person, the person-in-environment, the social work discipline, a nation-state, and so on—it can never be fully comprehended in isolation from its relative connections to other systems, inside and outside. Although many things outside will be too macroscopic, and some things inside will be too microscopic to have any relevant meaning, there will always be "gray" areas inside and outside the system that will move in and out of dynamic relevance. Systems are no longer seen as entities that can operate or be studied separately from their surroundings as they once were but as networks of dynamic, deeply interconnected relationships, consistent with the dramatic shift in the physics view of the physical world that took place in the 1920s.

*Figure 2*
**Unfolded Tetrahedron (A) and Divided Tetrahedron (B)**

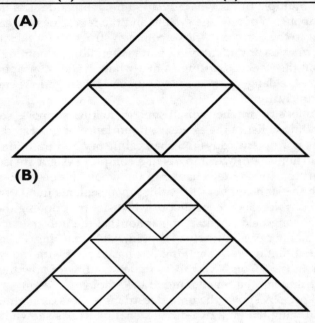

Nature's minimum system structure, the tetrahedron, and the whole-to-part principles of synergetics can be used as a universal organizing framework to construct a minimum four-component conceptual model of social work and a similar model of a progressively more complex person-in-environment component.

## Conceptualizing Social Work

Using the tetrahedron on which to model, a holistic conception of social work can be developed from a common framework. The identification and discussion of what might be core components of the framework can be drawn from previous efforts to conceptualize the profession.

From its earliest beginnings, two concepts stand out as integral components of social work's efforts to become professionally and scientifically credible. These are its domain of practice and its methods of practice. Although some social workers still struggle with whether social work is an art or a science, there is general agreement that social work is a necessary integration of both. Wilber (1985) pointed out that any field can be defined as a science if it has a domain that helps distinguish it from other fields of science (by defining its subject area) and if it has methods of inquiry by which its findings can be tested. He did not specify a particular method for doing this, only that the process be systematic and the findings be open to challenge and refutation. From this, one can conclude that the components of domain and methods reflect the everyday realities of social work practice and should be core parts of how the profession is conceptualized. These components are the same as two of Bartlett's common base components: social functioning within the interactional context of person-in-environment and her recommendation that social work consist of a repertoire of intervention methods. In addition to domain and methods, a third component would identify the basic paradigm of the profession. This component comes from Bartlett's conception of social work as having a broad-based orientation that would embrace general as well as specialized approaches. It would include both direct and indirect strategies of helping people with social functioning problems. This component addresses the need for an enduring group of adherents who coalesce around an agreed-on domain of practice, values, and ethics, and who agree to establish particular modes of professional activity to work within the boundaries of the defined domain. Kuhn (1970) called activities that meet these characteristics "paradigms." A fourth component is not as explicitly stated in social work literature as the first three, and could lead to the conclusion that a three-part conceptual model is sufficient. However, following Fuller's idea that a whole-system structure has a minimum of four parts and knowing three of the conceptual parts can lead to the discovery of the unknown fourth component. The extensive references in social work to the importance of self-awareness and the conscious use of self in practice relationships suggests that the domain of the practitioner should become the fourth component.

The four core components of the holistic conception of social work are demonstrated in Figure 3.

## Domain of Practice

The component of domain of practice depicts the person-in-environment perspective used to define the central purpose of social work practice. The profession holds that its primary focus of

*Figure 3*
**Common Conception of Social Work**

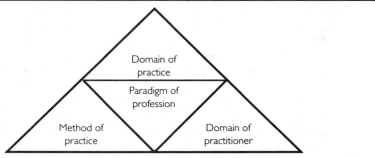

attention is on the transactional patterns between person and environment entities, rather than a dual focus, alternating from one entity to the other. The central purpose of practice is that of changing the social conditions of society and the ways in which individuals achieve their potential. The focus given to the transactions between the individual and society that affect the quality of the whole system is a domain of practice that no other helping profession has claimed. Scientific support for the merit of selecting this transactional focus comes from scientific findings in the 20th century that confirm the nonexistence of solids and show that the property or characteristics of something belong to the relationships between parts of the system, not the parts themselves (Capra & Stendl-Rast, 1991). The component can be progressively incorporated into a tetrahedral model of interacting factors that constitute the person-in-environment system.

## Method of Practice

This component consists of the systematic methods of problem solving and specific intervention procedures that social workers use. Whereas the other components provide a way of thinking about the nature of the parts and their relatedness within a system network, method provides the framework for applying specific skills. The method component provides a way of connecting the experiential networks of the other components into a problem-solving process working toward improved social well-being as an outcome goal. This component can be unfolded and arranged into a methodical map showing the minimum number of phases that the helping process is experienced by the social worker, client, and others.

## Paradigm of the Profession

This component addresses the need of a profession for an enduring group of adherents who have an agreed-on domain of practice, common values and ethics, and established modes of professional activity. Social work, like any other mode of scientific endeavor or professional activity, needs a paradigm component to serve as a vehicle for minimizing disagreements among those who learn the basics of the discipline in the context of different cultures, varied interpretations of the discipline's body of knowledge, and the use of multiple intervention approaches. Having adopted a broad orientation paradigm, social work has come to the position that its professionals can no longer be identified as dual purpose practitioners, specializing only in personal problems or working exclusively on social reform issues. The locus of the problem is no longer assumed to be the primary target of intervention. The basic practitioner is prepared to work with, or arrange for others to work with, a variety of people in different social systems arrangements (including the employing organization) to facilitate goal-defined social relationship changes within a person-in-environment system. This component can also be incorporated into the tetrahedral model to identify practice approach options.

## Domain of Practitioner

The component of domain is used to acknowledge the fact that social workers, like the people they work with, function in their own person-in-environment systems, personally and professionally. The makeup of their own domain in terms of their values, cultural background, affectional support, community resources, and personal well-being influences how they will perceive the domain of the people they work with and how they will apply selected methods of intervention. Because social workers generally identify themselves as primary "instruments of change" and are constantly asked to rise above their personal biases and preferences, they must constantly monitor and evaluate the personal and professional influences that bear on the creative and intuitive ways they use themselves in practice situations. The art of social work is expressed in how these influences are interwoven with the person-in-environment transactions of those being served.

Although each of the four components can be subdivided into progressively more complex detail, and it can be illustrated that they relate together as an integrated whole (Ramsay, 1990), this chapter is limited to a conceptual discussion of the person-in-environment domain of social work.

## Conceptualizing PIE

The person-in-environment domain of practice can be subdivided into its own four-factor system. The tetrahedron was Fuller's adapted-from-nature model for social psychology, the relationship of self and otherness. Fuller described the universe as a "scenario of otherness [environment] and self [person]" (Applewhite, 1977). Fuller contended that life in living systems begins with awareness of otherness. Without otherness there can be no awareness, and without awareness neither life nor thought can exist. He concluded the existence of two kinds of otherness: single and plural. Single otherness means that the living entity, an individual for example, is one of the otherness factors in his or her life. For example, one of the awareness-of-otherness activities of infants is to discover and experience their body extremities, toes, fingers, nose, ears, and so on. Plural otherness refers to the multitude of other otherness experiences in one's life. In the context of the social work domain, single otherness would be part of the person side of the system, and plural otherness would be part of the environment side. This would logically lead to a one-part person, three-part environment conception of the social work domain of practice.

The person part, as a single otherness entity, can be conceptualized in different-size units of attention: individual, couple, family, small group, community, or organization. These units can be further divided into increasing levels of complexity. In the case of an individual, for example, the next level of complexity might include social, physical, mental, and spiritual factors. Relationships with environmental factors will be experienced in two ways. One will be physical (visibly demonstrable), which includes all that is experienced by the senses (smelling, touching, seeing, and hearing) and coordinated through the brain. The other will be metaphysical (intangible, but thinkable), which includes only what is experienced in a cognitive way and processed through the mind. Only the mind can discover and experience relationships that cannot otherwise be experienced by the senses.

The environment parts can be conceptualized to include factors commonly identified as contributing influences to the social well-being of the individual and overall well-being of the defined person-in-environment system. A proposed way to conceptualize the environment factors is the following: personal otherness, resource otherness, and validator otherness. These factors and their relationship to the person factor are shown in Figure 4.

*Personal otherness* describes the informal social support resources and experiences that are intimately or closely related to a person that contribute to or detract from social well-being. The intimate nature of these relationships is expected to provide affectional and personal support grounded in common values, interests, goals, and aspirations. Spousal and intimate friend relationships, close family and kinship networks, and neighborhood and occupational bonds are examples of this type of relationship. The affectional support from this part of the environment is not restricted to relationships with people. The close relationship may be a metaphysical one with a pet, home, job, special memento, and so on.

*Resource otherness* describes a wide range of institutionalized and other less intimate opportunities, services, and resources that can sustain, enhance, or damage the social well-being of persons or those close to them. The term *resource* refers to experiences that can

*Figure 4*
**Conception of Person-in-Environment**

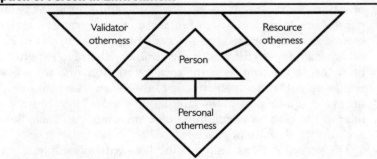

be called upon for aid or support. This factor covers a wide range of institutional supports that should be in place to maximize the social well-being of individuals, groups, families, and community networks. Health, welfare, education, and justice services; employment opportunities; membership associations; and a host of other society-sanctioned, government and nongovernment, for-profit and not-for-profit resources are parts of this factor. Resources include the broader cultural, political, economic, legal, geographic, and natural (including ecological) resources that contribute to or detract from social well-being. Absence or inadequacies in any of the resource systems can negatively affect the social well-being of the system.

*Validator otherness* describes the multisource system of values, beliefs, ideologies, customs, traditions, attitudes, norms, laws, and policies that have sufficient influence to regulate, control, dominate, oppress, incite, socialize, shape, or in some other form validate or invalidate the behavior and responses of people or organizations in the other factors. Some validators are centralized and considered mandatory in the form of unquestioned and loyal allegiance to declarations of fundamental rights, national laws, cultural customs, religious doctrines, family rules, or organizational policies. Others are decentralized, allowing for a diversified, flexible, and even controversial expression of behaviors among members of a person-in-environment system. Examples of this type of validator can be found in civil and political rights to freedom of expression, religion, assembly, and association.

Validator factors expressed in the form of dominant ideologies of a society often function through commonly held expectations people have of each other or through formalized social institutions to ensure desired social integration and social control of its members. In this context, the validator factor is the principal source of inequities, injustices, and unequal distribution of power in relationships among people within their particular person-in-environment systems. Efforts to understand and eliminate the ways dominant interest groups and individuals subordinate others to their discriminatory and oppressive interpretations of social well-being are an integral part of social work practice. However, it has not been common to include this factor as a core element of the social work domain in the same way that resource factors have been identified. This omission has left the door open for critics of systems conceptions to conclude that interactional reciprocity between system factors assumes benevolent mutuality, a condition they rightly claim does not reflect reality in many person-in-environment situations (Wharf, 1991).

When the four factors of the person-in-environment domain are presented as a geometric network as shown in Figure 5, the significance of the social work focus on relationships become clear.

To describe and assess the way the four factors contribute to the individual and collective social well-being of the system, practitioners must be able to focus on the six different relationships that

*Figure 5*
**Domain of Practice Network**

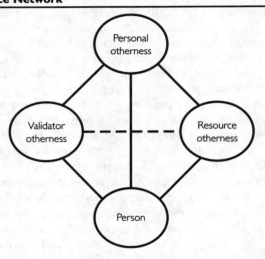

link these factors together. Any time there are four or more interrelated factors, the minimum of relationships linking them into a geometric network will always be considerably greater than the known
number of factors. The actual number of relationships can be quanti-
fied by the formula $r = n^2 - n/2$, where $r$ is the number of relationships and $n$ is the number of known factors (Fuller & Kuromiya,
1992). Consider the following case example.

## Case Study

Mary is a 30-year-old mother of one child, Jane, age 6. Jane disclosed four
days ago to her grade school teacher that she had been physically hurt by
John, Mary's common-law husband. The teacher immediately reported this to
child protective services. The child welfare worker's investigation found that
Mary had a drinking problem, because of her drinking and low salary as a re-
tail clerk there was little food in the house, and her utilities were about to be
cut off because of her overdue account.

In this example there are nine factors: Mary, Jane, John, teacher,
child and welfare worker, dependency on alcohol, low-paying job,
inadequate access to food resources, and demands from the utility
company. Using Fuller's formula, the number of relationship dynamics that may require some level of focused attention is 36 ($9^2 = 81$;
$81 - 9 = 72$; $72/2 = 36$).

Now, add to the scenario Mary's belief system that what goes on
at home is a private matter, John's belief in the old adage "spare the

rod, spoil the child," child protection laws requiring school personnel to immediately refer any sign of social difficulty to child protective services, and the child welfare worker's personal policy of following child protection laws to the letter. The four additional factors more than doubled the number of possible relationship dynamics on which to focus, from 36 to 78 ($13^2 = 169; 169 - 13 = 156; 156/2 = 78$). Without a holistic conception of these relationships within a common framework, it is difficult for specialized practitioners from any discipline to understand how the behavior of the whole system is affected by the complexity of this network.

## Using the PIE System to Classify Domain of Practice

Having developed a whole-system conception of social work's person-in-environment domain, the PIE system can be examined in terms of its conceptual and operational fit with the larger conception of the profession. The conceptual structures of the PIE system and the domain of practice component described above complement each other. The PIE system was developed as "a means for planning and testing social work interventions" (Karls & Wandrei, in press). Limiting the number of factors in the system to four is consistent with developing a holistic conception of social work based on a minimum system framework. As a tool to classify and code problems of social functioning, the PIE system is operationally part of the "method-of-practice" component. It would be used as part of a comprehensive assessment of what needs to be done to bring about a desired change in social well-being.

The PIE concept was initially used to identify interpersonal social functioning problems on the person side (Factor I) and social institution problems that exist in society on the environment side (Factor II). To expand PIE into a broad perspective biopsychosocial assessment model, two additional person-side factors were included: the mental health and the physical health status of the individual (Karls & Wandrei, 1992). The addition of these factors created a basic three-part person and one-part environment classification system to describe a client's interpersonal, mental, and physical health problems. Assessment of the person-side factors of mental and physical health (Factors III and IV) are the formal responsibility of psychiatry and medicine and their respective use of the *Diagnostic and Statistical Manual of Mental Disorders, Fourth Edition* (DSM-IV) (American Psychiatric Association, 1994), and the *International Classification of Diseases* (U.S. Department of Health and Human Services, 1991), known as ICD-9-CM. Social workers who are properly authorized are sanctioned to use DSM-IV within the limits of their professional mandate.

When the PIE system is unfolded to the next level of complexity, and the mental and health factors are set aside, the person-to-environment ratio is more balanced. At this level theoretical orientations are introduced to support the selection of factors used in the person-in-environment construct.

Factor I uses concepts from social role theory to identify and describe the many and various roles people experience in their lives (Karls & Wandrei, 1992). Factor I addresses social functioning problems in four different categories: family roles, other interpersonal roles, occupational roles, and special life situation roles. Social functioning concepts by definition describe a person–otherness relationship and set the stage for a central focus on the person-in-environment interactions between the principals in each category. The role problem types describe the interactional difficulty focus of PIE and identify the types of otherness relationships in the system. Factor I provides a clinical or microlevel person-in-environment context for planning and testing social work interventions.

Factor II was used on a social systems model of community development developed by Roland Warren (Karls & Wandrei, 1992). Warren's view of community was a systemic cluster of people and social organizations found in a boundary-defined location. Factor II addresses environmental problems in five social institution areas and one personal support area that prevent the person's access to these supports: (1) Economic/Basic Needs System; (2) Education and Training System; (3) Judicial and Legal System; (4) Health, Safety, and Social Services System; (5) Voluntary Association System; and (6) Affectional Support System. The social institution and affectional support concepts directly correspond to the resource otherness and personal otherness concepts in the proposed whole-system conception of person-in-environment. Factor II was designed to identify environmental problems that are systemic in a community, affecting whole categories or groups of people in addition to the individual client. This factor provides a macrolevel person-in-environment context for planning and testing interventions of a social policy or social reform kind.

Although each environmental category has a number of subtypes, discrimination is a subtype common to all categories. For example, discrimination in the Economic/Basic Needs System might be a mandatory retirement policy. In the Education and Training System, it might be a college policy not to provide readers for blind students. In the Judicial and Legal System, discrimination might exist in the form of sexist judges. In the Health, Safety, and Social Services System, discrimination could be evidenced by the failure to provide mental health services in culturally sensitive ways. In the Voluntary Association System, it might take the form of a religious denomination not accepting a gay or lesbian subgroup. In the Affectional Support System, discrimination could be family rejection when an unmarried member cohabits with a partner. The discrimination problems that could occur under all of the environmental categories are systemically linked to dominant ideologies, values, customs, norms, private or public policies, family rules, and personal attitudes that sanction the use of discriminatory and oppressive behaviors.

The concepts that give meaning to discrimination behaviors are all part of the Validator Otherness concept in the proposed whole-system conception of person-in-environment. When validator concepts are represented in a whole-system framework, the microlevel and macrolevel effect on both person and environmental categories can be visualized. The conflictive effect of opposing values on a relationship between a 25-year-old woman, for example, who believes in the fidelity of unmarried cohabitation, and her parents, whose religious customs view such relationships as extramarital and wrong, can be visualized in a geometric model of person-in-environment. The problem takes on a macrodimension if there is a parental norm in the community that condemns the unmarried cohabitation of young people.

From an examination of the categories and subtypes in Factors I and II, it is possible to configure the concepts of social role, social institutions, affectional support, and discrimination into a four-factor system, linked together by six relationships representing the interactional strengths or difficulties between all factors. When the core social work description of the PIE system is looked at from this perspective, the comprehensive holistic nature of the system can be observed. It also provides a look at a possible limitation in the PIE system. Discrimination is a behavioral manifestation of prevailing societal values and beliefs that appropriately belongs as a subtype under the social institutions and affectional support categories. If the problems of social functioning are only described in terms of the behavioral manifestations of discrimination or other forms of human prejudice without including the prevailing attitudes associated with them, a holistic description of the person-in-environment scenario is weakened. In a similar vein, the comprehensiveness of the instrument may be strengthened by looking at the direct effect of culture and ethnicity demands on the role performance expectations of an individual in addition to the way they are transmitted to the person through others in their environment.

When the four factors (social functioning, environmental problems, mental health, and physical health) of the PIE system are visually displayed as a whole system network, the relationship complexity among the four factors is graphically illustrated. Any one of the six relationships between factors may have a critical influence on how parts of the system relate to each other. In fact, it no longer seems appropriate to describe the first two factors as constituting the core social work description as currently stated in the *PIE Manual*. The relationships among all four factors are equally important to provide a comprehensive holistic picture of a client's problems from the perspective of a social worker. The expertise of the social worker, especially in a multidisciplinary setting, is not simply to identify and code the social role and environmental category problems but, more importantly, to describe the systemic relationship strengths and difficulties among all four factors in a way that demonstrates the value of a holistic approach to client problem solving.

Overall, the PIE system conceptualization and development into a practical instrument for social workers to use in their method of practice activities represents a progressive move forward in NASW's long history of helping the profession find a unifying perspective and common conceptual framework. The project is on target in its objective to provide social workers with a common language to describe their clients' problems in capsulated form, as a mechanism for clearer communication among practitioners, and as a basis for gathering data for research and program design purposes.

## Future of the PIE System

PIE developers describe the current version as being the prototype of a new system. PIE is an early model of a classification system that has a promising future in social work. It is an exciting and substantial effort by members of the profession to evolve an operational system that can be used independently or combined with classification and diagnostic systems developed by other human services professions. The field test trials and small reliability tests have been positive. The developmental research investment must be stepped up to complete the process of providing and disseminating a universal classification system for the profession.

In the long run, PIE is not the only system social workers need for a holistic model of the social work profession. PIE addresses only one component of a four-component holistic conception of social work. The intervention-planning benefits of PIE can be augmented by the use of similar four-factor systems maps of the other three core components. A system to use the proposed paradigm of the profession component would bridge the gap between a whole-system description of the person-in-environment problems and a holistic description of the people the social worker may interact with in different practice approach alternatives. The systems models developed by Pincus and Minahan (1973) and Middleman and Goldberg (1974) provided examples of the types of social systems interactions that could be identified and integrated with the PIE component. The third system, domain of the practitioner, would allow the social worker to conduct a holistic assessment and ongoing monitoring of his or her own person-in-environment domain as part of the overall effort to improve intervention planning. The fourth system, method of practice, is needed to outline the minimum-phase framework that is necessary to guide the problem-solving process of working with a client or others to bring about goal-identified changes in the person-in-environment domain.

## Conclusion

The geometric tetrahedron model of a minimum system structure is proposed as a common organizing framework on which to build a holistic conception of social work. The framework can accommodate the testing of different theoretical orientations to explain or classify the dynamics of social functioning and can support a repertoire of practice theory interventions that are consistent with the central focus, values, and ethics of the profession. The four-factor tetrahedral structure is a simple and practical way to illustrate the network relatedness of a holistic system. With major paradigm transformations occurring in the basic sciences toward a holistic, less deterministic worldview, the adoption of a minimum four-component organizing framework could help the profession assert its unique and interdependent place among the human services professions. There is no better time than now in the history of social work to be proud of belonging to a broad-view profession. The science of social work can purge itself of the Flexner-haunted need to be grounded in the old science assumptions of mechanical determinism, reductionist methods, and narrow specializations. Empirically based accountability no longer has to be held up as the only truthful measure of practice effectiveness. The new sciences of wholeness and complexity, discovered in the 20th century, provide scientific credibility for the use of intuitive wisdom and synthesis in the human services professions. A holistic conception of the profession can be used to integrate the art–science foundations of social work. The PIE system, grounded in the art and science of social work, is conceptually consistent with the use of a holistic model to help advance the social well-being of individuals, families, and communities.

## References

American Psychiatric Association. (1994). *Diagnostic and statistical manual of mental disorders* (4th ed.). Washington, DC: American Psychiatric Press.

Applewhite, E. (1977). *Cosmic fishing: An account of writing synergetics with Buckminster Fuller.* New York: Macmillan.

Augros, R., & Stanciu, G. (1988). *The new biology: Discovering the wisdom of nature.* Boston and London: New Science Library.

Austin, D. (1983). The Flexner myth and the history of social work. *Social Service Review, 57,* 1357–1376.

Bartlett, H. (1958). Toward clarification and improvement of social work practice. *Social Work, 3,* 5–7.

Bartlett, H. (1970). *The common base of social work.* New York: National Association of Social Workers.

Boehm, W. (1959). *Social work curriculum study.* New York: Council on Social Work Education.

Briar, S., & Miller, H. (1971). *Problems and issues in social casework.* New York: Columbia University Press.

Capra, F. (1983). *Turning point: Science, society, and the rising culture*. New York: Bantam Books.

Capra, F., & Stendl-Rast, D. (1991). *Belonging to the universe*. San Francisco: Harper.

Dinerman, M., & Geismar, L. (1984). *A quarter-century of social work education*. New York and Silver Spring, MD: Copublished by Council on Social Work Education, ABC-CLIO, and National Association of Social Workers.

Flexner, A. (1910). *Medical education in the United States and Canada* (A report to the Carnegie Foundation for the Advancement of Teaching, Bulletin 4). New York: Carnegie Foundation.

Franklin, D. (1986). Mary Richmond and Jane Addams: From moral certainty to rational inquiry in social work practice. *Social Service Review, 60*, 504–525.

Fuller, R. B. (1969). *Utopia or oblivion: The prospect for humanity*. Woodstock, NY: Overlook Press.

Fuller, R. B. (1975). *Synergetics: Exploration in the geometry of thinking*. New York: Macmillan.

Fuller, R. B., with Kuromiya, K. (1992). *Cosmography: A posthumous scenario for the future of humanity*. New York: Macmillan.

Germain, C. G. (1979). Introduction: Ecology and social work. In C. G. Germain (Ed.), *Social work practice: People and environments*. New York: Columbia University Press.

Germain, C. G., & Gitterman, A. (1980). *The life model of social work practice*. New York: Columbia University Press.

Gleick, J. (1988). *Chaos: Making a new science*. New York: Penguin Books.

Hearn, G. (1959). *Theory building in social work*. Toronto: University of Toronto Press.

Karls, J., & Wandrei, K. (1992). PIE: A new language for social work. *Social Work, 37*, 80–85.

Karls, J., & Wandrei, K. (in press). Person-in-environment. In R. Edwards (Ed.-in-Chief), *Encyclopedia of social work* (19th ed.). Washington, DC: NASW Press.

Kellert, S. (1993). *In the wake of chaos*. Chicago: University of Chicago Press.

Kuhn, T. (1970). *The structure of scientific revolutions* (2nd ed., enlarged). Chicago: University of Chicago Press.

Meyer, C. (1983). *Clinical social work: An ecological perspective*. New York: Columbia University Press.

Meyer, C. (1990). Commentary: The forest or the trees. In L. Videka-Sherman & W. J. Reid (Eds.), *Advances in clinical social work research* (pp. 394–399). Silver Spring, MD: NASW Press.

Middleman, R., & Goldberg, G. (1974). *Social service delivery: A structural approach to social work practice*. New York: Columbia University Press.

Pincus, A., & Minahan, A. (1973). *Social work practice: Model and method*. Itasca, IL: F. E. Peacock.

Ramsay, R. (1990). *Toward a comprehensive design science-profession conception of social work*. Paper (revised) originally presented to the National Association of Social Workers, International Chapter, Vienna Symposium: New Frontiers for Families, July 1989.

Richmond, M. (1917). *Social diagnosis*. New York: Russell Sage Foundation.

U.S. Department of Health and Human Services. (1991). *International classification of diseases–9th revision–clinical modification* (4th ed.). Washington, DC: U.S. Government Printing Office.

von Bertalanffy, L. (1968). *General systems theory*. New York: George Braziller.

Weick, A. (1987). Beyond empiricism: Toward a holistic conception of social work. *Social Thought, 13,* 36–46.

Wharf, B. (Ed.). (1991). *Social work and social change in Canada.* Toronto: McClelland & Stewart.

Wilber, K. (Ed.). (1985). *Quantum questions: Mystical writings of the world's greatest physicists.* Boston: New Science Library.

Zimmerman, J. H. (1989). Determinism, science and social work. *Social Service Review, 63,* 52–62.

# 15.

# PIE Research Issues

Janet B. W. Williams

*Presentation of a pilot reliability study of PIE suggests that PIE has likely acceptability and feasibility in practice, and most likely satisfactory reliability, at least for the major role categories. Thus, it is a reasonable system to use in social work research.*

S ocial work has made great strides since the mid-1980s in establishing a scientific base for its theories and practice approaches, as was emphasized by the report of the Task Force on Social Work Research supported by the National Institute of Mental Health (Task Force on Social Work Research, 1991). As this trend continues, a classification system for the variables that are the focus of social work intervention becomes more essential. The current emphasis on the development of practice guidelines in psychiatry and psychology, as well as increasing demands for accountability, will probably make this system inevitable.

*The Diagnostic and Statistical Manual of Mental Disorders, Fourth Edition* (DSM-IV) (American Psychiatric Association, 1994) provides an acceptable framework for classifying mental health problems and is used for clinical communications in most mental health facilities. DSM-IV has become the standard language for mental health research. Physical problems are adequately covered by the *International Classification of Diseases–Ninth Revision–Clinical Modification* (ICD-9-CM) (U.S. Department of Health and Human Services, 1991). The person-in-environment (PIE) system fills in the missing piece—a classification of the social problems that are the primary focus of the social work profession.

In most facilities, social workers report the results of assessment or intake evaluations in lengthy narratives that describe their clients' problems. These generally vary from agency to agency and worker to worker in format, focus, and language. This variation creates a lack of comparability across settings and workers and poses serious problems in data analysis for needs assessments and other research inquiries. The PIE system provides both a common language for describing the problems that are the focus of social work research and social work practice and a system for gathering prevalence data that can be used in needs assessments studies.

With the publication of the *Diagnostic and Statistical Manual of Mental Disorders, Third Edition* (DSM-III) (American Psychiatric Association, 1980), mental health practitioners in the United States were introduced to a new concept in evaluation: a multiaxial system for codifying and recording different domains of information about the people they were evaluating (Williams, 1981; 1985a; 1985b). In DSM-IV this system includes separate axes for recording mental disorders, general medical disorders, psychosocial and environmental problems, and overall level of functioning. The incorporation of a multiaxial system encouraged clinicians to take a biopsychosocial approach to evaluation, paying special attention to each of these three realms of functioning. However, despite the inclusion of separate axes for psychosocial and environmental problems and functioning in the multiaxial system of DSM-IV, these separate social axes provide only brief summary judgments. The very limited features of these two social axes prohibit the identification of social problems in the same way that well-recognized mood disorders, such as major depressive disorder and bipolar disorder, could not be identified as different entities if Axes I and II were limited to summary scales.

The PIE system provides a basis for developing a classification of social work interventions and for studying their efficacy for different kinds of psychosocial problems listed in the PIE classification. PIE may be useful to other health professionals as well because they must also deal with the types of problems included in its classification.

## The Psychometric Properties of PIE

To establish PIE's usefulness for research, its reliability and validity must be assessed. Early pilot studies are summarized in chapter 1; this chapter describes the results of more recent, larger scale studies.

In 1991, a pilot reliability study was funded by a small grant given to the authors by the board of directors of the National Association of Social Workers. This study used videotapes of clinical social work interviews. Most of these tapes were obtained from the video libraries at the social work schools at the University of California, Berkeley, and the University of Southern California.

The videotapes were shown to social workers at four sites: (1) United Charities of Chicago, part of Family Service of America, a nationwide membership organization of accredited family service agencies; (2) the Los Angeles–University of Southern California County Medical Center; (3) the Social Work Department at the New York State Psychiatric Institute, a state-supported research and teaching psychiatric hospital; and (4) the Commonwealth of Massachusetts Department of Mental Health.

Participants were trained by James Karls in the use of PIE. A total of 197 ratings were made across 16 videotapes, with four to 30 raters per tape. Although actors were used in most of the tapes, a substudy indicated that the social workers who participated were unable to distinguish the actors from real clients. Tables 1 and 2 present the initial results from this study.

The intraclass correlation coefficients (ICC) are presented for all Factor I social role problem areas and the two Factor II environmental problem areas that had adequate between-variance estimates (of .05 or larger) to indicate stable figures. Agreement on the specific Factor I roles (for example, Parent, Lover, Student) was generally higher than for the broader categories (for example, familial or other interpersonal). Agreement on the family roles was generally higher than for the other major categories. Agreement on the type of social role problems was examined for each social role. (Since this research was completed, the types were changed in response to the difficulty users reported in differentiating between several of the types.) This analysis was difficult because of the need to take

*Table 1*

**Intraclass Correlation Coefficients of Agreement on Factor I and Factor II Categories**

| Category | ICC | No. of Tapes |
|---|---|---|
| Factor I | | |
| Familial Roles | .80 | 16 |
|   Parent | .77 | 12 |
|   Spouse | .63 | 13 |
|   Child | .70 | 12 |
|   Sibling | .73 | 5 |
| Nonfamilial Roles[a] | .46 | 12 |
|   Lover | .76 | 4 |
| Occupational Roles | .28 | 16 |
|   Worker–Paid Economy | .43 | 16 |
|   Worker–Home | .27 | 10 |
|   Student | .76 | 3 |
| Special Life Situation Roles | .55 | 8 |
| Factor II | | |
| Economic/Basic Needs System | .29 | 14 |
|   Economic resources | .52 | 8 |
|   Discrimination | .60 | 5 |
| Education/Training System | — | — |
|   Education/training | .00 | 4 |
|   Discrimination | .10 | 1 |

NOTE: ICC = intraclass correlation coefficient. ICCs are listed only for categories for which the between-subjects variance estimate is .05 or higher, indicating enough variability to reflect a stable estimate.

[a]The title of this subcategory was changed to "Other Interpersonal Roles" after this reliability test was completed.

*Table 2*

**Intraclass Correlation Coefficients of Agreement on
Types of Social Role Problems**

| Type of Problem | Role | | | | | |
|---|---|---|---|---|---|---|
| | Parent | Spouse | Child | Sibling | Other | Significant Other |
| Control/power | .33 | .10 | — | — | 0 | 0 |
| Conflict/ambivalence | .20 | .15 | .28* | .25* | .28* | .41* |
| Responsibility/ performance expectation | .15 | .09 | .34 | .22 | 0 | — |
| Dependence/reactive | .02 | 0 | — | — | — | 0 |
| Independence/proactive | — | — | — | 0 | — | — |
| Status/status change | .003 | .29 | .41 | 0 | 0 | — |
| Separation/loss | .54 | .63* | .45* | .05 | 0 | 0 |
| Isolation/withdrawal | .01 | 0 | .12 | .38* | — | .25* |
| Intimidation/victimization | .01 | .13 | 0 | 0 | 0 | — |
| Mixed (>3 categories) or other | .09 | .06 | .45* | 0 | — | — |

NOTE: A zero indicates that although a few raters identified this problem in some tapes, not enough did so to allow a calculation of the intraclass correlation coefficients. A dash indicates that no raters identified this problem on any of the tapes. Since this research was completed, the problem types were changed in response to the difficulties users reported in differentiating between several of the types. The old types are listed here with their new types: control/power = power; conflict/ambivalence = ambivalence; responsibility/performance expectation = responsibility; dependence/reactive + independence/proactive = dependency; status/status change + separation/loss = loss; isolation/withdrawal = isolation; intimidation/victimization = victimization.

*Indicates categories for which the between-subjects variance is sufficient (.05 or higher) to reflect a stable estimate.

into account the conditionality of the problem types on the social roles. For example, agreement was calculated for the control/power type of problem separately for each social role (the control/power type is now the control type). Table 1 presents these data for family roles, nonfamilial roles (now changed to other interpersonal roles), and occupational roles.

In Tables 1 and 2, asterisks are used to indicate the few intraclass correlation coefficients for which between-subject variance is sufficient (.05 or higher) to have any degree of confidence in the stability of the estimate. Unfortunately, there were no tapes on which any rater identified a problem in any of the Special Life Situation Roles. For most of the social roles, only two of the problem types had sufficient between-subject variance to calculate an interrater correlation estimate that had any stability. Thus, it is impossible to conclude anything about agreement on most of the social role problem types for any of the social roles. Ideally, one would test enough stratified tapes so that all of the social roles and problem types were sufficiently represented to estimate their reliability. However, in this limited data set, certain of the problem types, such as the dependence/

reactive and independence/proactive types, were rarely recorded. (Since this study was completed, the dependence/reactive and independence/proactive types have been combined to form the new dependency type.)

Important steps in establishing the usefulness of a new classification system include the systematic assessment of its acceptability, feasibility, coverage, reliability, and correlates of category judgments. Acceptability concerns whether users agree that the categories and their definitions have face validity. Feasibility indicates whether the system is understandable and easily applied. Coverage is achieved to the extent that there is goodness-of-fit of the system in practice and that not many clients fall within residual (for example, unspecified or other) categories. The reliability of a system indicates how well clinicians using the system can agree with each other on the identification of the categories and is generally thought to impose an upper limit on its usefulness. Correlates of a judgment that a certain category is present or not are a measure of the categories' usefulness and reflect how well the system measures what it is supposed to measure.

The main purpose of this initial reliability study was to test the feasibility of the method of having groups of social workers apply the PIE system to videotapes. With limited resources, it was not possible to gather enough ratings across a range of PIE categories to make definitive statements about their reliabilities. However, this experience suggests that the PIE system has likely acceptability and feasibility in practice, and likely satisfactory reliability, at least for the major role categories, and thus is a reasonable system to use in social work research.

Still to be tested on a comprehensive large-scale basis are the PIE system's reliability and correlates of PIE judgments in real-life situations and in a variety of cases that represent the range of social work practice (medical social work, family services, corrections, and so on). This research will enable an evaluation of the degree to which there is a differential relationship between the PIE categories and various treatments, an indication of the validity of the system. For example, family therapy should be planned as an intervention much more frequently for familial role problems than for occupational role problems recorded on Factor I. Likewise, there should be distinct relationships between the specific types of Factor I role problems and specific interventions. In addition, the severity of the problem recorded should be related to the priority given to the intervention planned to address it. Finally, Factor II problems should be related to environmental interventions.

## Conclusion

Standardization of the variables of interest is essential for social work research to advance. The PIE system offers the first broadly applicable system of classifying social problems that appears to be useful to clinicians. The use of such a classification system is new to most social workers and will take time to become accepted and refined. However, its usefulness in research is already evident, as reflected in Irvin and Penk's chapter on their use of PIE in research with mentally ill persons in recovery from substance abuse (see chapter 8). The computerization of the system should further facilitate its usefulness in research (see chapter 16).

As the PIE system is used, considerable changes and refinements, will no doubt occur. However, at last the field of social work has begun to establish a common language and a standard classification system that can provide the groundwork for the growing focus on research. Researchers would do well to consider the use of the PIE system to standardize collection of data about social functioning and environmental problems.

## References

American Psychiatric Association. (1980). *Diagnostic and statistical manual of mental disorders* (3rd ed.). Washington, DC: American Psychiatric Press.

American Psychiatric Association. (1994). *Diagnostic and statistical manual of mental disorders* (4th ed.). Washington, DC: American Psychiatric Press.

Task Force on Social Work Research. (1991). *Building social work knowledge for effective services and policies: A plan for research development.* (Final report of the Task Force on Social Work Research supported by the National Institute of Mental Health). Austin, TX: Author.

U.S. Department of Health and Human Services. (1991). *International classification of diseases–9th revision–clinical modification* (4th ed.). Washington, DC: U.S. Government Printing Office.

Williams, J.B.W. (1981). DSM: A comprehensive approach to diagnosis. *Social Work, 26*, 101–106.

Williams, J.B.W. (1985a). The multiaxial system of DSM-III: Where did it come from and where should it go? I. Its origins and critiques. *Archives of General Psychiatry, 42,* 175–180.

Williams, J.B.W. (1985b). The multiaxial system of DSM-III: Where did it come from and where should it go? II. Empirical studies, innovations, recommendations. *Archives of General Psychiatry, 42,* 181–186.

# 16.

# Computerizing the PIE System

James M. Karls and Karin E. Wandrei

*This chapter describes the general problem of collecting and recording case
data, the current state of social work's adoption of computer technology, the
software currently in development for PIE, a case example using PIE
software, and the potential uses for a computerized PIE system.*

One of the most difficult and time-consuming tasks facing the social worker is recording the findings in a case and communicating the assessment of the client's problems and the interventions
needed. More staff time is probably spent on this task than on almost any other function in agency practice. Computers can help
streamline this task so the social worker can focus more on interventions with the client.

Mutschler (1987) and Ginsberg (1988) reviewed the history and
current use of computers in social work. They noted, to no one's sur-
prise, that social work lags far behind other professions in adapting
the computer to its use. Nurius and Cnaan (1991), in their very informative article on software for social work practice, pointed out
some of the difficulties of finding existing software that meets social
work needs. Despite the advances in computer technology, "because the bulk of software was developed to meet the needs of the
business sector, it is, not surprisingly, geared more to activities of
administrators and managers than to those of service providers,
counselors, and therapists" (p. 536).

Without a system that is client-oriented, meaning that its primary
focus is on the problems for which the client seeks help, or a system
that meets the needs of the practitioner to record the least amount
of information that can provide effective interventions, the effort to
bring social work into the electronic information era will be a difficult one at best.

A number of computerized systems in use (Nurius & Cnaan,
1991) are agency specific, meet the agency's needs to fit the client
into a problem, focus on the needs of the practitioner to fit a practice theory, or focus on the needs of a researcher to test a hy-
pothesis.

Schoech (1987) wrote that "information systems that support information needs at the service delivery level are less readily available than management applications. This is partly because social work practice varies by agency and type of client to such an extent that most information systems must be unique" (p. 923).

Mutschler described one reason why the application of computers in direct practice has lagged behind fiscal and administrative users: "the standardization of treatment processes necessary for computerization [is] hard to achieve because of the differences in the way different practitioners assess, treat, and evaluate clients with similar problems" (p. 318).

Mutschler described a successful integrated clinical and financial database management system developed by Newkham and Bawcom (1981) in a community mental health center in Texas. "One requirement of this computerized database management system was the conversion of the previously used nonstandardized recording system into a problem-oriented record system" (Mutschler, 1987, p. 317). Newkham and Bawcom would have saved themselves much effort if the person-in-environment (PIE) system had been in existence.

The PIE system, as construed, permits the practitioner to produce a clear, concise description of the client's problem complex in much less time than with any other system. Because the PIE system incorporates principles of social work practice taught in the current social work curriculum, the time needed for the individual practitioner to learn the system is in hours of study, not days or weeks.

## PIE Software

A computerized PIE system is currently being developed. This task has required adapting software not specific to social work practice. Because the PIE system is relatively simple and straightforward, the adaptation problem has been reduced.

The computerized PIE classification system will contain five related files:

1. Client File
2. Factor I
3. Factor II
4. Factor III
5. Factor IV.

The Client File will be the parent record, and each of the four factor files will be subordinately related files. This structure will allow each worksheet to contain as many or as few factors as one might need. Along with these factors, the client name, the case number, the practitioner name, and the date will be saved. The database will be set up so that after the assessment session, the data can be quickly and easily entered either by a series of choices or by typing corresponding codes. An assessment report can be immediately printed. The client data will be confidential and protected for privacy. The whole process should take only a few minutes.

The following is a case example of how computerizing PIE can streamline the process of recording the results of the assessment process.

## Case Study

In a psychiatric inpatient unit, the social worker is assigned to work with a 57-year-old woman, Alma Street, who has been in and out of the mental health system many times over the past 40 years. She has never been able to survive outside of an institutional setting for very long, but because of laws and cutbacks in state services, it has not been possible to keep Alma in the hospital for an extended stay. Alma constantly engages in behavior (in this case wandering in and out of traffic) that causes her to be rehospitalized. The social worker determines that this woman has an Inpatient/Client Role Problem of very high severity. The problem has been going on for 40 years so the duration is noted as more than 5 years, and Alma appears to have no coping skills for this problem.

This client's problem is increased by the lack of adequate mental health services in her community. This environmental problem is designated a Health, Safety, and Social Services System Problem of high severity and has been going on for many years, so the duration is more than 5 years.

As the result of a mental status examination, the social worker determines that Alma is suffering from chronic paranoid schizophrenia. She does not have a personality or developmental disorder.

A physical examination reveals that this client has scabies and diabetes.

After the intake assessment, the social worker sits at the computer and loads up the PIE software. The first screen might look like this:

Computer: What is the client's first name?
Social worker: Alma
Computer: What is the client's last name?
Social worker: Street
Computer: What is the rater's first name?
Social worker: Karin
Computer: What is the rater's last name?
Social worker: Wandrei
Computer: What is the date?
Social worker: 1/26/95

The next screen would contain a listing of the Factor I codes. The section of this screen pertaining to Special Life Situation Roles might look like Exhibit 1.

*Exhibit 1*

**Special Life Situation Roles**

---

| Consumer Role |
|---|

| Inpatient/Client Role |
|---|

| Outpatient/Client Role |
|---|

| Probationer/Parolee Role |
|---|

| Prisoner Role |
|---|

| Immigrant Role–Legal |
|---|

| Immigrant Role–Undocumented |
|---|

| Immigrant Role–Refugee |
|---|

| Other Special Life Situation Role (specify) |
|---|

---

The social worker would click on the "Inpatient/Client Role" problem. The second screen would display a listing of types; dependency type would be clicked on. The next screen would be the Severity Index and the social worker would click on the "very high" code (Exhibit 2).

Next, the social worker would see screens for the Duration and Coping Indexes, and he or she would click on the appropriate codes.

The social worker would go through a similar process for Factor II. The next screen might appear like this:

Computer: What is the DSM-IV coding for the client's first Axis I diagnosis?

Social worker: 295.32

*Exhibit 2*
**Severity Index**

| No problem |
|---|

| Low |
|---|

| Moderate |
|---|

| High |
|---|

| Very High |
|---|

| Catastrophic |
|---|

Computer: What is the client's first Axis I diagnosis?
Social worker: Schizophrenia, paranoid type, chronic
Computer: Are there any other Axis I diagnoses for this client?
Social worker: No
Computer: What is the DSM-IV coding for the client's first Axis II diagnosis?
Social worker: V71.09
Computer: What is the client's first Axis II diagnosis?
Social worker: No diagnosis
Computer: What is the ICD–9–CM code for the client's first physical health diagnosis?
Social worker: {blank}
Computer: What is the client's first physical health diagnosis?
Social worker: Diabetes
Computer: Who made this diagnosis?
Social worker: Dr. Z
Computer: Are there any other physical health diagnoses?
Social worker: Yes
Computer: Please list additional health problems.
Social worker: Scabies

After doing this, the software would generate the following printout:

Client Name: Alma Street
Rater: Karin Wandrei
Date: 1/26/95

| Factor I | 4240.516 | Inpatient/Client Role Problem, dependency type, very high severity, more than five years' duration, no coping skills |
|---|---|---|
| Factor II | 8105.41 | Health, Safety, and Social Services System Problem, absence of adequate mental health services, high severity, more than five years' duration |

Factor III
  Axis I    295.32    Schizophrenia, paranoid type, chronic
  Axis II   V71.09   No diagnosis on Axis II

Factor IV             Diabetes (by Dr. Z)

As the client progresses in treatment, the social worker could easily update the PIE listing by going into the saved PIE listing file and adding, deleting, or changing the relevant information without completely redoing the entire data entry.

## Applications of a Computerized PIE System

There is little doubt that a practitioner using a computerized PIE system would be able to quickly and efficiently produce a clear, concise statement of the client's problem complex. The statement thus produced will not provide a description of the causes of the problems but, like a genogram, will give a view of the problem complex that should lead to a better diagnostic assessment and to more effective relief for the client. A problem statement produced in this manner will enhance agency function and worker efficiency. The hours of agonizing and writing a diagnostic assessment that usually ends up in a seldom used file can be replaced with a descriptive, concise problem statement produced in minutes. The computerized PIE statement can serve as an ongoing intervention guide. Additions and changes to a client's PIE statement can be made in minutes as problems are resolved and new ones are identified.

The computerized PIE system can fit into existing management information systems and allow for data collection that can help with funding problems, personnel use, allocation of resources, and the myriad of management and planning issues that are the administrator's task. PIE will allow administrators to answer a number of important questions:

- What are the prominent environmental problems affecting the community in which our clients reside?
- What are the prominent social role problems experienced by our agency's clients?

- Do different staff members tend to deal more with certain kinds of social role and environmental problems than others?
- Does our agency clientele tend to have more acute or chronic problems?
- Does our agency clientele tend to have problems that are less serious or more serious?

Although PIE does not eliminate all of the potential barriers involved in the computerization of assessment information, it is a step in the direction of more efficiently collecting and recording client data. More important, it can lead as directly as possible to selecting and implementing interventions that are most likely to bring relief to the client. The eventual computerization of PIE will make the everyday lives of both practitioners and administrators who use it much easier.

## References

Ginsberg, L. H. (1988). Data processing and social work management. In P. R. Keys & L. H. Ginsberg (Eds.), *New management in human services* (pp. 70–80). Silver Spring, MD: National Association of Social Workers.

Mutschler, E. (1987). Computer utilization. In A. Minahan (Ed.-in-Chief), *Encyclopedia of social work* (18th ed., Vol. 1, pp. 316–326). Silver Spring, MD: National Association of Social Workers.

Newkham, J., & Bawcom, L. (1981). Computerizing an integrated clinical and financial record system in a CMHC: A pilot project. *Administration in Social Work, 5,* 97–111.

Nurius, P. S., & Cnaan, R. A. (1991). Classifying software to better support social work practice. *Social Work, 36,* 536–541.

Schoech, D. (1987). Information systems: Agency. In A. Minahan (Ed.-in-Chief), *Encyclopedia of social work* (18th ed., Vol. 1, pp. 920–931). Silver Spring, MD: National Association of Social Workers.

# Editors

**James M. Karls, PhD, LCSW, ACSW,** received a master's degree in social work from the University of Chicago and a doctorate from the University of Southern California. Dr. Karls has had an extensive career as a clinician, administrator, and teacher in social work. He has held numerous appointed and elected offices within NASW, including the presidency of the California chapter. Dr. Karls has served on the national NASW Health/Mental Health Commission, has been chair of the NASW Task Force on Standards for Case Management, and is the past chair of the NASW Certification and Accreditation Commission. Dr. Karls is the author of many journal articles, has been a contributing editor to *Hospital and Community Psychiatry,* and coauthored *Case Management in Human Service Practice* with Marie Weil.

**Karin E. Wandrei, DSW, LCSW, BCD,** has been associated with the PIE project since 1984 when she joined Dr. Karls to conduct the initial field-testing of the system. Dr. Wandrei received her MSW in 1977 and her DSW in 1983 from the University of California at Berkeley. She received a certificate in non-profit administration from San Francisco State University in 1994. She has experience as an administrator, clinician, supervisor, teacher, and researcher. Her specialty areas have included children and families, women's issues, and mental health. She has held a number of positions within the California Chapter of NASW. She has been the Executive Director of the Mendocino County Youth Project in Ukiah, California, since 1996.

# Contributors

**Elizabeth A. Adkins** received her MSW from San Diego State University in 1969 and her MS in education from the University of Southern California in 1990. She worked for 17 years as a clinical social work supervisor and clinical social work education coordinator at the Los Angeles County–University of Southern California Medical Center. She is currently semiretired and working as a senior grief counselor in the New Mexico Office of the Medical Investigator's Grief Intervention Program, which provides crisis intervention to families who have lost children to a sudden death, including suicide, homicide, accidents, and sudden infant death syndrome.

**Helen Cahalane, ACSW,** received her MSW from the University of Pittsburgh in 1979, and is currently completing doctoral studies at the University of Pittsburgh School of Social Work. Her research focuses on family satisfaction with psychiatric treatment and the effect of anxiety disorders on parenting behaviors. Currently the director of Family Studies and Social Work at Western Psychiatric Institute and Clinic, Ms. Cahalane has published in the area of psychiatric disorders and the family and psychoeducational treatment approaches in affective disorders. From 1980 to 1988 Ms. Cahalane worked in a community-based partial hospital and school program for emotionally disturbed children and adolescents.

**Cathie Hanes Delewski, DSW, LCSW,** received her MSW and DSW from the University of Washington. She currently is an assistant professor of social work at the University of Utah Graduate School of Social Work, Salt Lake City. She teaches in the clinical direct practice track. She specializes in crisis intervention, mental health practice, and working with individuals with serious and persistent mental illness. She is also a practicing licensed clinical social worker.

**Suzanne Dworak-Peck, MSW, LCSW, ACSW,** is president of the International Federation of Social Workers, which represents more than 350,000 social workers in 55 countries. She is also the founder and president of the NASW Communications Network, which provides the media with a centralized information and resource outlet

for social issues. Dworak-Peck served as president of NASW from
1987 to 1989. A social work practitioner for more than 25 years,
Dworak-Peck has spent much of her career working with vulnera-
ble and traditionally excluded populations, as well as in clinical supervision and treatment of families and individuals.

**Kathleen O'C. Hoekstra, MSW, DSW,** is coordinator of the Youth
at Risk program of the Lakeland School District in Westchester
County, New York. She maintains a private practice in family therapy and is a frequent lecturer and workshop presenter in family
and child welfare, mental health, and elementary and secondary education. Dr. Hoekstra holds social work faculty appointments at
Fordham University and Columbia University in New York City.
She is a consultant and trainer for the School of Social Work in Amsterdam, the Netherlands.

**Elizabeth A. Irvin, ACSW,** is the director of services integration for
the Massachusetts Department of Mental Health with responsibility
for statewide oversight of case management and dual-diagnosis services. She is a consultant to the Center for Psychiatric Rehabilitation at Boston University with research interests in social and
environmental factors influencing addiction among persons with serious mental illness. Ms. Irvin received her MSW from the Smith
College School for Social Work in 1973 and is a doctoral candidate
at Simmons College School of Social Work.

**Joseph D. Kestnbaum, AM,** received his master's degree from the
School of Social Service Administration at the University of Chicago. He is currently the director of the Adult and Child Guidance
Center at St. Francis Hospital in Evanston, Illinois, and previously
worked for United Charities in Chicago for 25 years. He is also on
the faculty of the school of social work at Loyola University.

**James M. Mandiberg, MSW, LCSW,** was associate professor of social welfare at Shikoku Gakuin University in Zentsuji, Japan, when
he cowrote his chapter. The former director of Community Support
and Community Mental Health Services in Santa Clara County, California, he is currently completing his PhD in social work and organizational psychology at the University of Michigan. His major
research is in human services organizations, mental health service
delivery systems, and cross-cultural/cross-national organizational
behavior.

**Kyoko Miyaoka, MSW,** is a consultant at the Kagawa Prefecture
Mental Health Center; she is also a lecturer in social work at Shikoku Gakuin University and at the Nurses Training School, National Children's Hospital in Zentsuji, Japan. Her principal research
interests are in social work methods and mental health.

**Walter E. Penk, PhD,** is chief of the psychology service at the Edith Nourse Rogers Veterans Memorial Hospital in Bedford, Massachusetts, and consultant to the Massachusetts Department of Mental Health on matters of mental health services delivery evaluation. He serves on the clinical faculties of the Department of Psychiatry at Harvard Medical School, Boston University, the University of Massachusetts, and Tufts University School of Medicine. He is a diplomate in clinical psychology, with clinical research interests in the treatment of addiction and stress disorders among persons with serious mental illness.

**Richard Ramsay, RSW,** received an MSW in social work from McGill University, Montreal, Canada, in 1965. He is an associate professor at the University of Calgary Faculty of Social Work and has worked as a social worker and administrator in correctional aftercare and youth residential services. Mr. Ramsay has a long history of volunteer involvement with the profession and has held elected officer positions in the Alberta Association of Social Workers, the Canadian Association of Social Workers, and the International Federation of Social Workers. He is a cofounder and developer of an internationally disseminated program for suicide prevention training.

**Paul M. Saxton, MA, PhD,** received his master's degree from the University of Chicago and his doctorate in social clinical psychology from the Wright Institute, Berkeley, California. He is a clinical social worker in the independent practice of psychotherapy and consultation in Oakland, California. He has worked as clinical director of an integrated employee assistance/managed care firm and as a clinical representative and consultant on policies and procedures for several companies. He was a certified employee assistance professional, is a member of the Employee Assistance Professionals Association, and has held state and national positions in NASW.

**Mehl L. Simmons, MSW, LCSW,** has 31 years of experience administering public welfare. He was the director of the Tulare County, California, Department of Public Social Services for eight years. He previously worked in Sacramento County for 22 years, rising to the position of deputy director. He has also been involved in university teaching and the private practice of clinical social work. He has been involved with NASW for many years and is the president of the California chapter. In 1989 he was the Koshland Award recipient as Administrator of the Year.

**Joanne E. Turnbull, PhD,** received an MSW, MA, and PhD from the University of Michigan. Dr. Turnbull was assistant professor of psychiatry at Duke University Medical Center from 1985 to 1990, and associate professor at Columbia University School of Social Work from 1990 to 1992. She is currently associate professor of psychiatry at Western Psychiatric Institute and Clinic, Department of Psychiatry, University of Pittsburgh, and associate administrator at the University of Pittsburgh Medical Center. She has published in the area of practice research and psychiatric disorders, particularly depression and substance abuse in women. Her current research is on depression in homeless women and acquired immune deficiency syndrome prevention for depressed adolescent girls. Dr. Turnbull is completing a book entitled *Empowerment of Depressed Clients: A Social Work Model for Depression.*

**Maureen K. Wahl, PhD,** is director of research for Family Service of America, Milwaukee, Wisconsin. She received her PhD in urban education from the University of Wisconsin in Milwaukee. Family Service of America is the world's largest support network for services, education, and advocacy on behalf of families in need. Dr. Wahl's current research includes a longitudinal study of a Milwaukee-based school choice program and the development of outcome measures for family services agency programs.

**Karen Walsh, RSW,** received an MSW from the University of Manitoba Winnepeg, Canada, in 1979. She is a senior social worker with Alberta Mental Health Services in Calgary, Alberta, and has worked as a clinician, administrator, health specialist, and medical social worker. She also is interested in research, policy, and social work standards of practice.

**Leila Whiting, ACSW, LCSW,** is recently retired from the position of acting director, Division of Professional Affairs, NASW. She received her MSW from the University of Pennsylvania. Since 1976 she has held a variety of senior professional positions at NASW. Prior experience includes 20 years in psychiatric clinics and family agencies as a clinical social worker, university teaching, community organization work, and social sciences research in the United States and Australia.

**Janet B. W. Williams** received her DSW from Columbia University in 1981. She is currently professor of clinical psychiatric social work (in psychiatry and neurology), Department of Psychiatry, Columbia University College of Physicians and Surgeons, and research scientist and deputy chief of the Biometrics Research Department, New York State Psychiatric Institute. She has been actively involved in the development of DSM-III, DSM-III-R, and DSM-IV.

# Index

*Person-in-Environment System*

Designed by Naylor Design, Inc.

Composed by Graphic Composition, Inc., in Palatino and Gill Sans

Printed by Boyd Printing Company, Inc., on 50# Windsor